1978

Central African Republic

PALL MALL LIBRARY OF AFRICAN AFFAIRS

The Pall Mall Library of African Affairs is intended to provide clear, authoritative, and objective information about the historical, political, cultural, and economic background of modern Africa. Individual countries and groupings of countries will be dealt with as will general themes affecting the whole continent and its relations with the rest of the world. The library appears under the general editorship of Colin Legum, with Philippe Decraene as consultant editor.

Also available

RICHARD GREENFIELD	Ethiopia: *A New Political History*
RENÉ LEMARCHAND	Rwanda and Burundi
GUY DE LUSIGNAN	French-Speaking Africa Since Independence
JOHN G. PIKE	Malawi: *A Political and Economic History*
WALTER SCHWARZ	Nigeria
DOUGLAS WHEELER and RENÉ PÉLISSIER	Angola

Central African Republic
A Failure in De-Colonisation

PIERRE KALCK
Translated by Barbara Thomson

PALL MALL PRESS · LONDON

Pall Mall Press Limited
5 Cromwell Place, London SW7

First published 1971
© 1971 by Pall Mall Press Ltd
Translation © 1971 by Pall Mall Press Ltd
ISBN 0 269 02801 3

Printed in Great Britain by
The Garden City Press Limited
Letchworth, Hertfordshire

Contents

	List of Abbreviations	vii
	Map: Administrative Districts	ix
1	The Country and the People	1
	The Country	1
	The People	9
2	The Colony of Oubangui Chari	32
	The Slave-Trade	32
	Coveted by European Powers	43
	The Concessionary Regime	50
	From Concession to Monopoly	58
	From Crisis to War	62
3	Emancipation of the Central African People	71
	Political Awakening	71
	Towards Autonomy	84
	Towards Independence	94
	Illusions and Realities	111
4	Building a Nation	118
	The Early Stages	118
	Personal Power, a United Party	132
5	Military Leadership	153
	A Soldier in Power	153
6	After Ten Years' Independence	175
	Bibliography	190
	Notes and References	184
	Index	199

List of Abbreviations

AEF	*Afrique Equatoriale Française*
ATEC	*Agence Transéquatoriale des Communications*
BDPA	*Bureau Français pour le Développement de la Production Agricole*
BIRD	*Banque Internationale pour la Reconstruction et le Développement*
CEA	*Commission Economique pour l'Afrique*
CEA	*Commissariat Française à l'Energie Atomique*
CEE	*Communauté Economique Européenne*
CFA	*Communauté Financière Africaine*
CFDT	*Compagnie Française pour le Développement des Fibres Textiles Tropicales*
CGTA	*Compagnie Générale de Transports en Afrique*
CIC	*Comptoir Israelo-Centrafricain*
CMOO	*Compagnie Minière de l'Oubangui Oriental*
CND	*Comptoir National du Diamant*
CODRO	*Commissariat pour le Développement Rural de l'Oubangui*
CTFT	*Centre Technique Forestier Tropical*
DDI	Diamond Distributors Inc.
EEC	European Economic Community
FAC	*Fonds d'Aide et de Coopération*
FIDES	*Fonds d'Investissement pour le Développement Economique et Social des Territoires d'Outre Mer*
ICAD	Israeli and Central African Diamond Company
ICOT	*Industrie Cotonnière de l'Oubangui et du Tchad*
ILO	*Intergroupe Libéral Oubanguien*
JPN	*Jeunesse Pionnière Nationale*
LICA	*Ligue Contre l'Antisémitisme et le Racisme*
MEDAC	*Mouvement pour l'Evolution Démocratique de l'Afrique Centrale*
MEOC	*Mission Evangelique de l'Oubangui-Chari*

MESAN	*Mouvement pour l'Evolution Sociale de l'Afrique Noire*
MRP	*Mouvement Républicain Populaire*
MSA	*Mouvement Socialiste Africain*
OAU	Organisation for African Unity
OCAM	*Organisation Commune Africaine et Malgache*
OND	*Office National du Diamant*
ORD	*Offices Régionaux de Développement*
PRA	*Parti du Regroupement Africain*
PRS	*Parti Radical Socialiste*
RDA	*Rassemblement Démocratique Africain*
RPF	*Rassemblement du Peuple Français*
SCADIA	*Société Centrafricaine du Diamant*
SEEE	*Société Equatoriale d'Energie Electrique*
SEITA	*Service d'Exploitation Industrielle des Tabacs et Allumettes*
SFCF	*Société Franco-Centrafricaine des Tabacs*
SIAN	*Société Industrielle et Agricole du Niari*
SNEA	*Société Nationale d'Exploitation Agricole*
SOCOULOLÉ	*Société Coopérative de la Lobaye-Lessé*
UCCA	*Union Cotonnière Centrafricaine*
UDE	*Union Douanière Equatoriale*
UDEAC	*Union Douanière et Economique de l'Afrique Centrale*
UDSR	*Union Démocratique et Socialiste de la Résistance*
UEAC	*Union des Etats de l'Afrique Centrale*
UGTC	*Union Générale des Travailleurs Centrafricains*
UNELCO	*Union Electrique Coloniale*
URAC	*Union des Républiques d'Afrique Centrale*

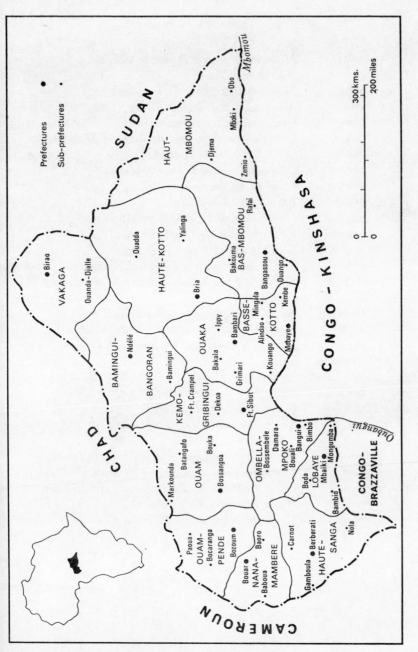

Administrative districts of the Central African Republic

1. The Country and the People

THE COUNTRY

Situation and Dimensions

Although the Central African Republic has been a member of the United Nations Organization since September 20, 1960, it remains the least known region in the world. In 1890, the future colony of Oubangui Chari was no more than a great white blank on the maps, and the Oubangui river itself had only just been discovered. This great tributary of the Congo marks the present frontier between the Central African Republic and Congo-Kinshasa.

The boundaries were the outcome of hazardous explorations, diplomatic agreements and the whims of colonial administrators, and emerged slowly during the period from 1890 to 1940. Today, the country covers a huge quadrilateral of savanna and forest, stretching mainly from latitudes 4° south to 11° north and from longitudes 14° and 28° east Greenwich. The extreme south-western and north-eastern points approach latitudes 2° south and 11° north respectively.

Originally the leaders had hoped that the Central African Republic would be a vast mid-African state, including Cameroun and the whole of former French Equatorial Africa. But on August 13, 1960, Oubangui Chari finally became independent alone. It had a population of about 1,200,000 scattered over some 206,000 square miles.

The Central African Republic is bordered by five sovereign states, all of which have emerged from half a century of French, Belgian, or British rule. A conventional frontier of 650 miles separates the territory from Chad in the north and joins the course of the river Aouk, a tributary of the Chari, at its eastern end. In the east, the Congo-Nile watershed divides it from the Sudan (Darfur, Bahr el Ghazal, and Equatoria) for about 620 miles, and the Mbomou and the Oubangui valleys mark the southern frontier of just over 660 miles with Congo-Kinshasa (eastern

1

province, Equateur). The Congo-Brazzaville boundary in the south-west, traced through 250 miles of sparsely inhabited rain forest put Bangui in control of the Lobaye and the Haute-Sanga basins, which previously had been administered from Brazzaville. The western frontier with Cameroun cuts across 435 miles of Baya country and dates back to the compromise made between the French and German administrations in 1894. The arrangement led to the foundation of French Equatorial Africa in 1910, allowing a single colony to stretch from the Atlantic to the Sahara.

Central African Republic is an eminently suitable name for this land in the very heart of Africa at the crossing of the Timbuktu-Zanzibar, Kinshasa-Cairo axis and the Abidjan-Addis Ababa, Tunis-Salisbury diagonals. Obo, the eastern point, is just over 1,060 miles as the crow flies from Mombasa on the Indian Ocean; in the west Berberati is only 375 miles or so from Douala in the Gulf of Guinea and Bangui is 650 miles from Pointe Noire, still as the crow flies, the present gateway to the Atlantic, while the sub-prefecture of Paoua in the north-west lies about 1,750 miles from Tripoli, the port which for centuries was Central Africa's outlet to the Mediterranean. At the north-eastern end of the territory, the administrative centre of Birao lies about 1,430 miles from Alexandria and approximately 1,120 miles from Port Sudan on the Red Sea. Such distances emphasise the extreme isolation of this country in an enormous continent, but they also evoke the former role it played as a meeting-place of routes. At present, its strategic position is likely to increase with the development of air, road and rail communications.

Relief and Waterways

The physical character of the Central African territory is a vast peneplain with an average altitude varying between 3,000 and 2,000 feet. Two mountainous areas in the north-west and the north-east mark the transition to the Adamawa highlands in Cameroun and the Darfur ranges in the Sudan. Mount Gaou in the Yadé massif on the Camerounian border has an altitude of 5,250 feet, and in the north-east, the Bongo and Dar Challa mountains close to the Sudanese frontier reach similar heights. North of a line connecting the two regions, the Central African territory becomes a mere prolongation of the Chad depression, a comparatively fertile zone with sandy alluvial tracts. To the south of the same line there are great expanses of sandstone of the Secondary era, like the Carnot region in the west and Mouka in the east, and both are rich in diamond deposits. The rest of the territory has a clay surface with occasional laterite formations.

Some rugged granite peaks tower up in the middle of the savanna, looking rather like feudal strongholds. In the past, these natural citadels, which the natives call *kaga*, often served as places of refuge during the slave-hunts or the colonial uprisings, and some of them have become important landmarks in Central African history. Mount Mela, in the south of the Dar Challa range, guards the ancient road to the copper mines. This is one of the oldest trans-African routes and is now widely recognised as a pilgrim way. Mount Kazangba witnessed the Mandjia victory of 1885, when Rabah's army was obliged to retreat on its way to join the Foulbe emirates of north Cameroun. The Yadé massif also has a number of mountains that are regarded as sacred by the Baya and the Mboum. There seems to be conclusive evidence that the area played a significant role in African settlement in prehistoric times. At Bouar, the French set up a base of operations enabling their garrison to intervene at a moment's notice in all territories of Cameroun, Chad and Oubangui Chari.

Perhaps the Central African Republic holds the world record for abundance of waterways. A third of the territory forms part of the Chad basin and a tenth belongs to the basin of the Sanga, the great north-south tributary of the Congo. The rest of the country, covering more than 135,000 square miles, lies in the basin of the Oubangui, which is a river of exceptional size, well deserving its attribute of 'great river'. The Oubangui and the town of Bangui both owe their names to a great trading people, the Boubangui, who commanded the entire north-south course of the river for several centuries. The Oubangui flows east-west from the Mbomou confluence for more than 310 miles, then changes direction abruptly at Bangui, and after about another 435 miles pours a huge quantity of its waters into the Congo. Altogether its basin is more than 230,000 square miles.

Previously, the term Oubangui was only used for the section of the river actually under the control of the Boubangui, its upper course being generally known as the Uele, while the myth of an

3

Oubangui rising at the Mbomou confluence originated in the ruse King Leopold employed in 1892. As a result of his cunning the boundary between French Haut Oubangui and the Congo Free State was fixed to the thalweg of the Mbomou in 1894. The Mbomou, rising about fifty miles from the source of a tributary of the Bahr el Ghazal, is 466 miles long, and the Uele, 714 miles long, rises quite close to the valley of the Upper Nile itself. This seems to explain why the map-makers of the ancient world charted the Oubangui as the upper lateral course of the sacred river. It must almost certainly have been the great western river, known as Baboura to the Arab caravaneers. During the rainy season it flows at a rate of more than 33,300 cubic feet per second at Bangui. It rushes into the Congo in the midst of an immense semi-lacustrine region of changing dimensions, also receiving the Sanga a few miles further downstream. For a very long time explorers were puzzled by the intricate maze of natural canals linking the three waterways, and it was 1884 before the Oubangui was finally navigated by the protestant minister, George Grenfell, aboard the *Peace*. The Congress of Berlin had established the frontiers of King Leopold's Congo, unaware that such a great river existed.

Most of the tributaries of the Mbomou basin flow from the Central African bank, and some, such as the Mbomou itself, the Ouarra, the Chinko, and the Mbari, are the size of the great European rivers. The valley of the Kotto, connecting the Dar Challa range with the Oubangui, is as long as the Mbomou and formerly served as the major highway between Darfur and the Congo. The other right-bank tributaries of the Oubangui between the Kotto and the Lobaye confluences, the Kouango-Ouaka, the Kemo, the Ombella and the Mpoko, had similar functions, linking Chad with the elbow of the Oubangui. The Oubangui is divided up into a number of navigable reaches between rapids, and the area from the Bangui rapids to Yakoma formed one of the most important trading thoroughfares in ancient Africa. It was by the river that the Anziques, or Boubangui, used to communicate with the Nubians, from the sixteenth century onwards.

The Lobaye, rising in the Yadé massif, drains into the Oubangui below Bangui and forms the principal artery in the west of the Central African territory, though in 1911 its entire basin was ceded to Germany along with the Sanga basin. The Germans had hoped to use the Lobaye to link Douala with Dar-es-Salaam as part of their Mittelafrika project.

The Sanga gets its name below Nola at the confluence of the Kadei and the Mbéré, which also rises in the Yadé massif. It continues its course to Ouesso in Congo-Brazzaville, one of the most important markets in pre-colonial Africa, and at that point receives the great south-Camerounian waterway, the Dja-Ngoko. The valley of the Sanga is more than 800 miles long and was used for exchanges between the Congo Basin and the Muslim kingdoms in the north. It also provided a trading route for kola and ivory. In the past, all the navigable bays of these great rivers were ploughed by immense canoes, some of which could hold up to 200 men.

The two great tributaries of Lake Chad, the Logone and the Chari, flow through the north of the Central African territory. In the north-east, the Mbéré marks the frontier with Cameroun and becomes the western Logone in Chad. Slightly further east, the Pende drains into the eastern Logone. On the Ngou, a tributary of the Mbéré, the Lancrenon falls, more than 490 feet high, remain one of the wonders of the world unknown to tourists.

The true upper course of the Chari is probably the Ouham, or Baya river, which becomes the Bahr Sara, the river of the Sara, further downstream in Chad. The other possibility is the Bamingui —still called Bahr el Abied, 'river of slaves'—which previously formed the frontier between the protectorate of Dar Kouti and the Central African territory under direct French administration. France used the Gribingui, the great tributary of the Bamingui, as a means of access to Chad in 1896. The Aouk, the right-bank tributary of the Chari and the north-east frontier of the Central African Republic, has an uneven flow because one of its tributaries rises in Darfur.

This profusion of rivers, great rivers and innumerable tributaries has endowed Central Africa with a greenness, which is in startling contrast to the desolate character of the northern countries. The abundance of fresh water at all seasons fired the imagination of the peoples who came from the north to seek their ivory and slaves in the Central African savanna. W. G. Browne, a Scotsman travelling in Darfur in 1795, learned of this land with the many rivers.[1] His Forian informer called it Dar Koulla, perhaps because of the Goula tribes established in the south-west of Chad and in the north-west of the Central African Republic.

Climate and Vegetation

Africa's different zones of climate and vegetation are known to be evenly distributed in broad horizontal belts north and south of the Equator. The capital of the Central African Republic, Bangui, is less than 310 miles from the Equator, but Birao, the main town in the north-east is only 310 miles from the desert. The expanse of country between the two forms a climatically intermediate zone with a correspondingly intermediate type of vegetation. The Central African quadrilateral is divided into three unequal climatic regions, the most northerly covering little more than the north-eastern extremity, Birao, and the southernmost reaching Nola, in the south-west.

Beyond latitude 9° north, the climate is the Sahelo-Sudanese type, with a dry season of six months from November to April, mean temperatures reaching 30° C in April and May. The annual rainfall remains around 30 inches on average. This attracts many herds from Chad and the Sudan, and the area has an extraordinary variety of wild animals.

Between latitudes 9° and 5° north, that is, over most of the Central African territory, the climate is much more humid. The number of dry months with less than two inches of rainfall, varies from three to five between November and March. The inhabitants choose this season for protracted hunting expeditions, often causing outbreaks of fire in the savanna. Much of the savanna is still forested and during the rains it takes on a park-like appearance, delighting the European traveller. Temperatures are mitigated by the altitude, except in the Oubangui valley, and the nights are sometimes cool in the dry season with frequent mists in the morning. In the centre of the country at Bambari, the extreme temperatures recorded for December are 10° C and 33° C. The annual rainfall increases from north to south, varying from almost 54 to 62 inches, with violent precipitation in the space of a few hours. Luckily, the stability of the soil makes the numerous roads and tracks always passable, though they are not asphalted and their upkeep poses many problems. The climate in this zone is usually known as the Sudanese-Guinea type, but some authors call it Oubanguian.

Finally, south of latitude 5° north, the climate becomes more or less equatorial. The number of dry months is reduced to three or below in the thickly forested areas, where rain falls abundantly almost all the year round. This zone has a very high degree of humidity and the annual rainfall is generally about 66 inches at Bangui and at Berberati near latitude 4° north. The rainy season brings milder temperatures with an annual mean of 25° C at Bangui, and with maximum temperatures of around 33° C in February and March.

The amount of rainfall can vary in the three zones depending on the year and micro-climates are also found in different parts of the country. In fact, the heaviest annual rainfall has been recorded to the north of the zone which is reputedly the wettest. In 1940, Bangassou had 82 inches and Bouar marked 74 inches in 1955. Sunshine is plentiful throughout the year. Bangui attains an average of 2,100 hours annually and the figures for the north are even higher.

Three principal zones of vegetation correspond to the climatic zones. In the south there is the great primeval forest, dense, humid, and tropical. It covers more than one-fifth of the surface area and creeps up to the outskirts of Berberati and Bangui. In the east, it fringes the right bank of the Mbomou between Bangassou and Zemio, forming bands of trees along the river. The northern regions of the great rain forest have remained almost entirely unexploited because of their great distance from the ports of embarkation. For the Central African authorities, they represent considerable wealth: a systematic inventory has estimated that about 4,700 square miles could profitably be exploited. There is a high concentration of very rare species and experts regard it as one of the most valuable forests in the world.[2] This zone and its immediate surroundings especially favour the growth of coffee, hevea, cacao, and kola-nut trees, pepper-plants, palm-trees, and all kinds of subsistence crops. The region round Nola possesses the most fertile soils in the whole of former French Equatorial Africa.

The Sudanese-Guinea zone is typical of the savanna. It covers an area of more than 150,000 square miles, with vegetation differing according to the region. Between the Camerounian frontier and a line linking Bocaranga, Baboua and Berberati in the west there is a stretch of upland savanna called Adamawa savanna providing excellent pastures, where Bororo shepherds brought their herds after the First World War. The animals are little trouble to planters because very few people have lived in the region since the entire area was devastated by the long hostilities between the Fulani slave-trader, the Sultan of Ngaoundéré, and the Baya peasants at the end of the nineteenth century. A little farther east, a not particularly fertile stretch of savanna called Burkea covers the sandstone region bounded by Bozoum, Bossembele, Boda and Carnot.

The rest of this zone can be divided into a northern part, the Sudanese savanna north of a line through Paoua, Bossangoa, Crampel, Bria and Obo, and a southern section called Guinea savanna to the south of the same line.[3] Some vestiges of a desiccated forest are still visible in the southern part of the Sudanese savanna area, where the valleys are bordered with bands of trees, often quite considerable in size. In the centre between Ippy and Alindao there is excellent pasture-land for the Bororo.

René Dumont thought the grasslands of these two savanna zones were the best humid prairies in Africa.[4] For the last forty years however, about 432,000 acres of cotton have been cultivated annually with very little regard for the condition of the soil and without the use of fertilizers. This extensive cultivation, which for a long time was made compulsory, is responsible for the deterioration of the soil and, unfortunately, for 300,000 Central Africans it also remains associated with the payment of tax. A few tentative efforts have been made to encourage afforestation, but these have been limited by financial aid and shortage of labour.

The excelsa coffee-tree, which thrives in this climate and on the savanna type of soil, originated in the Central African territory. It gives a more abundant crop than any other of the known types, but its taste is not popular with the consumer. The saturation of the world market has discouraged its cultivation on a large scale.

Finally, the Sahelo-Sudanese climate favours a totally different type of vegetation from that in the rest of the territory. The wealth of the region lies in its karite and gum arabic, which so far have hardly been exploited. It is sparsely inhabited, as it too suffered from slave-raids for half a century from 1860 to 1910.

THE PEOPLE

The colonial administrators took several surveys of the population of Oubangui Chari, but their estimates were anything but exact. The villagers inevitably associated the census with the payment of the so-called numerical tax and with the compulsory cultivation of cotton, and a minority consistently managed to evade it.

The last census based on the administration's village monographs dates from 1962, but in 1965 another more exhaustive survey was carried out. On December 31, 1962, the population was given as 1,279,642 persons, an increase of about 200,000 on the figures published ten years earlier in 1952 showing 1,088,000.[5] President Dacko's 1965 census practically doubled the 1962 results and produced a total of 2,088,000 persons, exactly one million more than in 1952. On the whole, experts are reluctant to accept the government's official estimate and, without vouching for accuracy, usually opt for a figure somewhere in the region of 1,400,000.

The population of Bangui has always proved particularly hard to calculate. In 1962 it was estimated at 86,000, although the true figure was thought to be nearer 100,000 at the time. The 1965 census brought this number to 237,971. In the secondary towns, the population in 1962 was assessed as follows: Bouar 24,000 inhabitants, Bambari 20,500, Bossangoa 17,000, Berberati 14,300, Batangafo 10,400, Mbaiki 9,700. These figures were considerably revised in 1965. Official documents give: Berberati 40,000 inhabitants, Bossangoa 35,000, Bambari 32,000, Bangassou 29,000, Bouar 28,000, Bria 25,000, Mbaiki 17,000. The number of European inhabitants, which had stayed at about 5,000 (1962 estimate) since 1950, was suddenly raised to 11,000 in 1965. Probably the Central African President wished to augment the density of the population in his country, so that it would not lag too far behind that of Cameroun with 4,500,000 and above all Chad with 2,750,000 inhabitants.

The demographic surveys carried out before the government's readjustments showed an annual birth-rate averaging 48 per thousand and a mortality rate of 26 per thousand, although for children under one year the number reached 190 per thousand. These figures were little different from the estimates in other parts

9

of tropical Africa. Young people of under twenty constituted about 45 per cent of the population and people of over fifty a mere 6·5 per cent. Only a faint proportion of births and deaths were recorded at the registry office and the administration issued any certificates that happened to be needed, rather as the fancy took them.

Since the number of voters, tax-payers and cotton planters has not changed to any great extent despite the 1965 reassessment, the 1962 figures should be regarded as valid. The birth- and death-rates, however, show that the population increases appreciably each year. Unfortunately it is hard to arrive at the exact figures because of the people's basic distrust of the census. Nor is there much point in trying to reach an estimate for the average density in the territory as a whole. Since 1925 almost all the villages have been established besides roads and tracks suitable for cars. Elsewhere several thousands of square miles are totally uninhabited. There is so much depopulation going on in the east and north-east that not more than 71,000 persons can be counted for 87,200 square miles. The sub-prefecture of Ouadda in Haute Kotto has only 3,761 inhabitants for 12,000 square miles and Yalinga has 5,114 for 16,000 square miles. The prefecture of Vakaga (Birao) fares little better with 9,701 inhabitants for 17,000 square miles; or Obo—an area which in 1860 constituted the powerful Zande kingdom of Mofio—with 10,671 for just over 17,000 square miles. If the 82,000 square miles of semi-desert in the east are discounted, that is about a third of the total surface area, the density of population becomes approximately three persons for about a third of a square mile.

Obviously the Central African Republic is a long way from having to wrestle with problems of overcrowding, and although there is a considerable rural exodus towards Bangui, as well as to Bambari, Berberati and Bossangoa, which begin to look more and more like the chief towns of the east, west and north, the urban population is still smaller than that in many other African countries. At the most it accounts for 15 per cent of the total number of inhabitants and even then many town-dwellers in the populous secondary centres are still cultivators and could just as easily be classed among the rural population.

The active members of the population number about 600,000,

that is 50 per cent of the whole. This includes 300,000 or more cotton planters and 55,000 salaried workers, about 4,000 of whom are civil servants paid by the month. Part of the population is Christian (240,000 Catholics, 190,000 Protestants) and a minority are Muslim (about 20,000).

Distribution by Ethnic Groups

The Central African authorities are obsessed with tribal problems, and censuses are no longer based on ethnic distinctions. The name of the original tribe is gradually disappearing from official documents, and in 1959 a law prohibited the use of ethnic terms even to denote rural communities.

During the colonial period however, it was usual to separate the natives into easily recognisable racial groups, occupying specific geographical areas. In the Central African territory, this procedure was particularly reprehensible because the supposed groups overlapped to a high degree in each district. Consequently, when the ethnic map of the whole country had to be filled in, only the dominant group in each constituency appeared. Some administrators merely covered the ordinary map with a jumble of names of groups and sub-groups.

Nevertheless, the ethnographic map of Oubangui Chari charted at Bangui in 1952 has provided some sort of foundation for later documents. In an attempt to simplify the mass of information the administrators had collected, and avoid the extraordinary puzzle of applying it geographically, the 'ethnic groups' were limited to eight, and these were subdivided into fifty-four 'races'.

The following eight ethnic groups were apparently determined according to the linguistic characteristics they had in common: Baya-Mandjia, Banda, Oubanguians, Sara, Zande, Nzakara, Muslims, Camerounians. The peoples the ethnologists called broker tribes, who had settled exclusively in the Oubangui valley between the Mbomou and the Kemo, were regarded as the Oubanguians, but the administration also included the Bantu tribes in the forests of Haute-Sanga, the Mbimou, the Kaka, and the Pande, and Basse Lobaye, the Mbaka and the Lissongo. By Muslims they meant the floating population of Muslim traders established in the vicinities of the administrative posts, and also the former subjects of the Sultan of Dar Kouti. These peoples had been converted to Islam several generations earlier and were mainly Rounga, of Banda origin. Although 'Muslim' corresponds to no ethnic concept, it is definitely an improvement on 'Arabised', which was the term employed by the Europeans in Bangui. The label 'Camerounians' referred to the remote mountain communities in the north-west belonging to the Camerounian population of the Mboum, who had been the masters of Adamawa before the Fulani invasion.

The groups were localised as follows:

1. *Baya*: almost the whole of the west of the Central African territory within the quadrilateral of Bouar-Bossangoa-Boda-Berberati; *Mandjia:* in the Bouca-Crampel-Sibut area.
2. *Banda*: the region attributed to these people included the whole of Haute Kotto, the south of the Ndélé district, almost all Basse Kotto and Ouaka, the south of Kemo-Gribingui and the east of Ombella-Mpoko. Isolated Banda communities were indicated within the districts of Paoua, Bouca, Carnot and Boda in the north-west and south-west.
3. The *Oubanguian* group was marked by a thin strip along the Oubangui and, for the forest Bantu in the districts of Boali, Mbaiki and Mongoumba, by a zone of about sixty miles around Bangui.
4. The *Sara* area from the Pende to the Bamingui covered the north of the Paoua, Bossangoa, Batangafo and Crampel districts.
5. The *Zande* area corresponded mainly to the districts of Zemio and Obo.
6. The region occupied by the *Nzakara* slightly overlapped the Bakouma and Bangassou districts.
7. A line from Bamingui to Ndélé, Ouanda-Djallé and Djebel Mela formed the southern boundary of the *Muslim* region.
8. Two small patches west of Bocaranga and Baboua marked the home of the *Mboum*, or *Camerounians*.

Such a breakdown could obviously give only a very rough idea of the ethnic composition of the people in Oubangui Chari, particularly as the list of fifty-four races, usually tribes, bristled with error and confusion. However it was from within this framework that a tentative classification of the ethnic distribution of the population in the Central African territory was eventually made: Banda 436,000, Baya 420,000, Mandjia 90,000, Sara 85,000,

Mboum, 73,000, south-western Bantu 50,000, Muslims 40,000, Nzakara 30,000, Zande 20,000, Oubanguians of the valley 20,000, Bororo (Fulani nomads) 15,000, aliens 10,000, Pygmies 10,000 (not included in the census).

The peoples classed in the Sudanese group were the savanna tribes, the Banda, Baya, Mandjia, Sara, Mboum, Nzakara, and Zande, also found in the neighbouring territories of Cameroun, Chad, the Sudan and Congo-Kinshasa. They represent 1,154,000 inhabitants, that is to say more than 90 per cent of the total population. The ethnic groups of the valley of the Oubangui and the forest Bantu supply more than 60 per cent of the country's civil servants and an even greater proportion of the senior officials, although numerically they are less than 5 per cent of the total inhabitants. The Bororo provide more than 90 per cent of the cattle-herders and the Muslims more than 75 per cent of the small traders.

Central Africans in Prehistoric Times

During the years of colonisation much credit was given to the theory of a fairly recent settlement in Oubangui Chari. A few missionaries and administrators had made investigations—which aroused great suspicion on the part of the natives—and managed to assemble a number of traditions. These all supported the view that the arrival of the great mass of the present inhabitants, the Baya, Mandjia, Banda and Zande, could be dated between approximately 1780 and 1850. Some people rather hastily concluded that the country up till then was only sparsely populated, if at all, as it was almost entirely covered by the Great Forest.[6]

Soon, a succession of prehistoric discoveries in the regions of the Great Lakes, the Nile Valley, Chad (tchadantropus uxoris, found by Yves Coppens in 1961) and Lake Toumba in the Congo basin not far from the Oubangui, put the whole subject of human settlement in Central Africa into question once more. Félix Eboué[7] and a number of geologists had in fact been collecting flint implements since 1930, but at a time when the aborigines of Australia and the inhabitants of Oubangui Chari were being placed on the same level of cultural development, these thunder-stones, as they were called by the natives, were not thought very ancient. In the centre of the territory some polishers found to have been in recent use

13

were popularly compared to those the river-bank dwellers of the Dordogne had used in the late stone age. But a new light was cast on the matter when the finds of some research carried out near the Great Lakes, less than 700 miles from the eastern part of the Central African Republic, were made known. They prompted Teilhard de Chardin to affirm in 1955 that 'man must have emerged for the first time in the heart of Africa'.[8] Almost two thousand years ago Diodorus of Sicily had said the same.

From 1966 to 1968, the Muséum d'Histoire Naturelle de Paris and the Centre National de la Recherche Scientifique organised several expeditions in the west, centre and north-east, which revealed an amazing quantity of objects belonging to various neolithic and paleolithic civilisations. The mine workings in the valleys greatly facilitated this research and the mining companies themselves assisted in the excavations. As a result, it is safe to claim a totally unexpected density of population for these areas, even at the very earliest times.[9] The Sanga and the Mbéré-Lobaye-Oubangui axis, Kouango-Ouaka and the whole of Bongou-Kotto all appear to have been important paths of communication during the prehistoric period.

Some more quite recent discoveries are likely to contribute to our knowledge of the spread of the use of iron from Haute Benoué (Nok) to the Congo basin. At Bouar, not far from the source of the Lobaye, P. Vidal, a French ethnologist, examined some megaliths, known in Baya as *tadjounou*, the 'standing stones',[10] and found at the foot of one of them a stone chest containing a number of iron votive objects, which are now being dated.

Historians such as R. Cornevin, who subscribe to the hypothesis of a Proto-Bangui migration from Haute Benoué after 2500 BC, believe that the Central African region of Haute-Sanga and also the area round the elbow of the Oubangui played definite roles in the movement and distribution of these numerous tribes.[11] The west and later the east, near Kouch territory, consequently take on a hitherto unsuspected importance in the early history of mankind. There are large quantities of remains in the grottoes in Central Africa too, presumably left by the successive races that sheltered there. This part of the world affords an extremely vast field of study for the archaeologist, as well as the historian, and so far has been completely overlooked.

The First Inhabitants of the Forest

Although the equatorial forest is supposedly very hostile to human life, it is the home of the last survivors of a very ancient people, the Pygmies. Several thousand Bantu-speaking tribes also live in the rain forest, and this seems to point to a more extensive Bantu settlement before the great Central African migrations of the nineteenth century. Toponymy shows how widespread the settlement must have been, and there are numerous traces in the basin of the Mbomou, although many Bantu groups in fact merged with the former Zande nation in this particular area.

The Pygmies of the rain forest, called Babinga by other Central Africans (and Tvides according to contemporary African scholars), congregate in the forests of Haute-Sanga and Lobaye. They are exclusively hunters and harvesters and live in symbiosis with the farmers who have settled in the valleys and the clearings. They also inhabit the Uele forests at the eastern end of the Oubangui basin only a short distance from the Central African frontier, where they are known as Aka. This was where Georg Schweinfurth visited them for the first time. In Ancient Egyptian inscriptions dating back more than 4,000 years, there are also references to the Aka, the 'dwarfs, the dancers of God', who lived 'in the land of palms and spirits', or the 'land of Yam' (tomb of Harkuf, Governor of the southern territories, Assiut, 2400 BC). Several authors of antiquity seem to have had access to rather vague information about the countries close to the great black kingdom of Kouch (Napata-Meroë) and both Homer and Aristotle mention dwarfs.

The Pygmies are all that remain of a race of men who apparently occupied a geographical area stretching considerably beyond the bounds of Africa. Today, they number about 10,000 in the Central African Republic alone. They are undoubtedly the oldest settlement and are widely dispersed over the southern parts of the prefectures of Haute-Sanga and Lobaye bordering on Cameroun and Congo-Brazzaville. They are perfectly adapted to the forest, migrating with the wild animals, and preserve their ancestral customs. It seems very unlikely that the race is dying out, as is sometimes alleged.

Portuguese documents of the seventeenth century[12] state that Stanley Pool, called Mpoumbou by the Congolese, was a trading centre for slaves, who were bought or captured in the more

15

northerly regions. The great Western slave-trade reached its peak
in the second half of the eighteenth century and masses of slaves
were deported. Many of them were conducted to the Atlantic
by the network of the Pombeiros, the people of Mpoumbou, and
sold under the name of 'Congo'. Numerous broker tribes, also
dealing in slaves, dwelt in the valleys of the Sanga and the Oubangui basins. They are classified under the generic terms of Bakota
for the Sanga and Boubangui for the Oubangui.

The great invasions at the end of the eighteenth century
gradually overwhelmed the Bakota who had earlier established
commercial communications with the Muslims in the north and
also with the Congolese, the allies of the Portuguese, in the south.
First they were dispersed by the Fang, who marched southwards,
and then, in the nineteenth century, the Baya and the Yanguéré
Banda forced them back towards the islands (which is why some
are called Pande) and into the forest. The ravages of sleeping-
sickness from 1905 to 1930 finally exterminated the Haute-Sanga
Bantu, and today only a few miserable villages subsist, belonging
to the Mbimou and the Kaka tribes.

According to seventeenth- and eighteenth-century sources,[13]
the Boubangui were very probably the Anziques (or Anguicos)
who communicated with the Nubians along the river. They harried
and invaded the kingdom of the Congo repeatedly, and when
Brazza arrived in 1880, were already in touch with the Bateke, or
Tyo, sometimes mistakenly assimilated to the former Anziques.
The Boubangui had taken possession of a great part of the west and
centre of the Central African territory by the time the Baya drove
them from the Oubangui elbow in about 1825, and they have left
abundant toponymical traces. For centuries they navigated the
Lobaye and all the tributaries of the Oubangui as far as Kouango-
Ouaka to trade and to purchase slaves.

As the slave-trade intensified, large numbers of tribes in the west
fled towards the south-east and the east. Some of those who had
settled near the Congo, like a section of the Mbaka, or Ngbaka,
returned to their nineteenth-century homes. Their rivals, the
Lissongo, went back to the Lobaye forests. Other tribes in the
Mbomou and the Uele basins stayed to defend their soil against
the Sudanese attacks from the north-east.

The eastern Bantu were assimilated by the Zande conquerors

during the nineteenth century, any who resisted being overcome by force and handed over to the slavers. A few groups nevertheless preserved their individuality for a number of years, such as the Karre—the word Mbomou means water in their language—and the Vodo group, whose name is perpetuated in the great left-bank tributary of the Chinko, though the tribe itself has completely disappeared. The significance of the Bantu settlement before the nineteenth-century migrations is evoked in the opening words of the Central African national anthem, 'The Renaissance', composed by President Boganda.

'O Centre Afrique, ô berceau des Bantous.'*

The Peoples of the Savanna before the Great Migrations

Before the arrival of the Baya, the Banda and the Zande conquerors, the greater part of the unforested land was inhabited by a variety of tribes said to be of Sudanese origin. Some, such as the Sara groups and the Nzakara, still survive, but others like the Sabanga, the Kreich and the Sudanese tribes in Mbomou and Vakaga were surrounded and either assimilated or annihilated.

The name Sara, or Nsara, from Nassara meaning Christians, points to a Nilotic origin, and embraces a vast collection of tribes who settled in the basin of the Chari[14] after the disintegration of the mountain kingdom of Gaoga, or Kouka, which the Moroccan diplomat, Leon the African, visited in 1514. The Muslims of the north had given them this nickname to distinguish them from other tribes of similar origin who helped to found the Muslim kingdom of Baguirmi. The Sara managed to remain in the same area, mainly the Central African region called Ouam-Pende, from the sixteenth to the nineteenth century, when they were joined by the Baya, the Mandjia and the Banda. A small group of Sara people, the Baguiri, still survive on the edge of Mobaye along the Oubangui, where they probably settled before the Baya-Banda invasions.

The Sabanga, Nzakara and Kreich had a different fate. Sabanga, meaning 'the ones who tear out the jaw', was the name the Banda gave to the tribes they found firmly established in the Ouaka basin at the upper course of the Kouango, the great cross-roads of the Oubanguian savanna. Today, only a few isolated groups are

* 'O Centre of Africa, cradle of the Bantu.'

still alive and they have even lost their original language. Some authors regard the Sabanga as completely assimilated and class them among the Banda and other related groups of uncertain ethnic origin, like the Dokoa, the Patri and the Pata. A few Banda tribes, such as the Ouadda, are probably Sabanga and Nzakara in origin, but they have long since given up their name, their individual customs and their language. One very independent Sabanga group, the Nzakara who adopted the name Boro, managed to avoid complete assimilation by the Zande conquerors because they had a strong military and political organisation.[15] Later they checked the advance of the Banda on both the Mbari and the Kotto until the early years of the colonial occupation.

The Kreich, from the Arab dialect word *Kirdi* meaning 'unfaithful', who called themselves Gbaya or Kpalla, wielded tremendous power at the end of the eighteenth century. They were the masters of the copper mines from Hofrat en Nahas to Bahr el Ghazal, and also commanded the Bongou, the upper Kotto, the upper Mbari and the upper Chinko basins. The Banda concentrated west of the Bongo highlands were unable either to conquer or to assimilate these people and in many areas chose to become their allies. Zubeir (1850–75) and Rabah (1880–90) obtained thousands of slaves from the Kreich and marshalled thousands of their mercenaries into fighting squads under their own war-chiefs. The last survivors of this disrupted nation were systematically annihilated by Senoussi, the Sultan of Dar Kouti from 1890 to 1911. The colonial authorities generally regarded them as rebels and harried them in Haute Kotto on the grounds that they had broken hunting regulations. Their name has no more than a historical significance among the ethnic components of the Central African Republic, and only a few isolated hamlets and families appear on the census. At Bangui and Fort Lamy a small minority still call themselves Kreich, but the administration insists on classing them as Banda.

The savanna peoples who arrived on Central African soil before the nineteenth century have either completely disappeared or been reduced to a few clans of interest to no one but the ethnologist. In Haut Mbomou, these older inhabitants, whom the Zande called Diga, or 'the vanquished', were annihilated, taken into servitude, assimilated by the conquerors, or handed over to the

18

slavers in return for fire-arms. Only a toponymic study of the now waste lands in the upper basins of the great right-bank tributaries of the Mbomou could establish the site of their former home. Even their name has become unimportant although it is occasionally used by geographers for an area of about 38,000 to 60,000 square miles, where there is no trace of human life.

A similar situation has occurred in the mountain ranges in the north-east, where the place-names evoke peoples who have entirely vanished, like the Bongo, the Challa, the Binga and the Mela. However, Father Santandrea, an Italian missionary from the Sudan, mentions the existence of a few clans belonging to these former tribes, who took refuge close to Darfur and Bahr el Ghazal.[16] Only the Youlou of Ouanda-Djalle, who put up a heroic resistance to Senoussi until 1911, and the Kara of Birao have managed to preserve their individuality. The Kara call themselves Yama and have recently become Muslims. They occupy a few scattered villages.

The 'Water-People' of the North-East and the Oubangui Valley

In the Chari basin, the Goula, who are subdivided into red and black Goula like the ancient Meroë peoples, almost entirely disappeared from the valleys in south Chad and the north-east of the Central African Republic during the wars waged by Rabah and the sultans of Dar Kouti and Ouadaï. Some tiny groups in the autonomous Central African sub-prefectures of Vakaga (Birao) and Bamingui-Bangoran (Ndélé) still call themselves Goula. According to the folklore traditions of south-east Chad, Goula was used before Arabic as the language for trade. These people are the sole survivors of Dar Koulla, the powerful negro state the Forians described to Browne in 1795.

The 'water-people', or people of the river, inhabiting the Oubangui valley between Bangui and Yakoma belong to related ethnic groups. They settled in this area in the sixteenth century, probably immediately after the kingdom of Alwa was sacked by the Fung, the 'victors', who came from the south. Although they number little more than 20,000 persons, the water-people have always been in the forefront of history and at present they play an important role on the political stage. General Mobutu comes from the Mobaye region and Goumba, the first head of the Oubanguian government, is from Kouango; several other Central African politicians are also from this region.

These people escaped from the invasions by hiding in the great islands in the Oubangui, particularly the large island of Ya. The first years of the colonial period however proved their downfall. Canoers were requisitioned in large numbers and sleeping-sickness eventually devastated the villages which had extended for miles along the river banks. They were canoers, fishermen, traders and craftsmen, and were the first natives to assist in colonisation. Sango, the 'water-language', a tongue spoken by one of the groups, prevailed as the vehicular language of the country and in 1964 was adopted as the official language of the Central African Republic.

The Oubanguian group is divided into several tribes whose previous and present homes correspond to the reaches of the river valley bounded by the rapids of the Oubangui or by its confluences. East can thus meet west. The Banziri occupy the area from the Mokouangué rapids to the Kouango confluence, the Bouraka from the Kouango confluence to the Mio confluence, the Sango from the Mio confluence to the Setema rapids, and finally the Yakoma dwell in the region from Setema to the Hanssens falls beyond the Uele-Mbomou confluence. Higher up the river from the Mbomou, the Dendi, belonging to a group the Belgians called Gbandi, played a part in the history of the Nzakara. Some of the Banziri became scattered in small groups in Bahr el Ghazal in the course of their migration from the Nile to the Oubangui basin. The Ndogo and the Bolo still survive in that area today.

The Great Central African Migrations of the Nineteenth Century

The present physiognomy of the Central African population was largely wrought by a succession of events taking place in the nineteenth century. The major periods of settlement were the Zande conquest, the Baya migrations, and the Banda exodus. There is a great deal of controversy over the origin of the Zande. The word seems to be a variant of 'zand', or 'zandj', used in the Sudan and in east Africa as a term of admiration for the negro race. Many of their features suggest a north-eastern origin such as Kordofan or the Nile, although most of the Zande traditions give the west of Chad as their home before the migrations. In fact, the

warrior caste nowadays called Zande, or Azande, migrated in
several waves, sweeping across the map of Africa in a large curve.

At the end of the eighteenth century, Ngoura led his fighters
into the Mbomou and Uele territories and his descendants pressed
victoriously as far as the Nile. Ngoura established the first Zande
principalities in the Central African territory and in 1800 founded
his own empire, calling it and all its inhabitants Zande.[17] His
companions had been known as Kobobili when they left the Chad
basin. West of Mbari, the Zande met with an organised community, the Nzakara, with a similar language to their own. They became
the allies of an important family, the Bandia, and helped to overcome
their adversaries, the Voukpata; thus by 1890, Bangassou, the
Bandia king, had reasserted his rule in spite of internal feuds. A
branch of the Bandia family between the Mbari and the Ouarra
joined the cause of the new arrivals and rose to become the rulers
of a vast Zande principality, the future sultanate of Rafai. East
of the Ouarra, the Zande encountered no centralised political
authorities and easily exerted their command over the Diga
tribes. Ngoura's descendants, Mabengue and later Tikima, were
the most outstanding of the great Zande feudatories established
in the area. Ngoura's family is called Voungoura, that is, Ngoura's
vassals, not descendants.

After 1850, the advent of the merchant princes from the Upper
Nile in search of ivory and slaves strengthened the authority of
the Zande sultans and they soon overran the entire region north
of the Mbomou. Zubeir,[18] the most famous of the princes, became
Tikima's son-in-law and set up a vast empire of his own in between
the Kotto, the Uele and the approaches of the Nile. He conquered
Darfur in the name of Egypt in 1872, after which he was taken
prisoner in Cairo. The sultans of Haut Oubangui, notably Rafai
and Zemio, made contact with the European governors of Bahr el
Ghazal, Gessi and Lupton, to protect themselves from Zubeir's
son, Suleiman, and his lieutenant Rabah, and later from the
Mahdist forces, who were supported by several Zande chiefs.
Five years after Lupton's defeat, they thankfully welcomed the
Belgians and subsequently the French. Zemio's Zande warriors
allowed King Leopold's troops to break through to the Nile in
1892.

As the Zande nation had split up into rival sultanates, it was unable to survive the colonial partitions. The treaties between France and King Leopold in 1894 and between France and England in 1899 established frontiers which divided the country into three unequal parts. The area north of the Mbomou, which had suffered most from the deportations caused by the sultans themselves, passed under French control along with the capitals of the two most important principalities, Rafai and Zemio.

The Baya, or Gbaya, migrations, which followed the Zande expeditions at the beginning of the nineteenth century were of a different nature. The Baya were extremely numerous, with traditions still reminiscent of their long contact with the Hausa of Nigeria.[19] Older people in their tribes talk of a war-chief of that period, Gazargamou, who led his people beyond the country of the Mboum as far as the regions of Haut Sanaga and Haute-Sanga.[20] The upheaval caused by the conquest of Hausa territory by the Fulani emir, Usuman Dan Fodio, and the war he waged with varying success on the Bornu from 1810–17 was really responsible for the migration. The Fulani Modibo, Adama, settled in the area which bears his name today, and drove the Baya towards the Lobaye and the Oubangui. There they either assimilated the peoples they met—the Fang of Haute-Sanga and Haute Sanaga, the Bakota of Sanga and the Boubangui of the Oubangui basin—or forced them to fly to the south. During these migrations, the Baya formed new, sometimes mixed, groups, who either preserved the name Baya, like the Baya-Kara, the Baya-Bouli, the Baya-Bokoto, and the Baya-Kaka, or adopted other names after much intermingling with the defeated tribes. The main group was the Bouaka in the Oubangui elbow, who assimilated the Bantu, by then the vassals of the Boubangui. Folklore traditions of the southern peoples and especially the Boubangui, recall the Baya invasion, led by 'savages'.

An important section of the Baya crossed the Oubangui and clashed with the Banda-Banza tribes. Then, in about 1850, they suddenly withdrew to the north to settle in the Chari and the Oubangui basins. Their largest group, known as Mandjia, had to face renewed attacks from the west. Other groups such as the Ali, the Banou and finally the Boffi, arrived gradually during the following decades, and also gave up their original Baya name. The Baya firmly established in the west of the Central African territory often managed to put up a victorious resistance to the Foulbe Lamibe of north Cameroun who came regularly each year to hunt for slaves among the Mboum and the Laka in the north-west, and the Baya in Haute-Sanga and Lobaye. In 1896 the Baya persuaded a French administrator, Alphonse Goujon, to help them in a fierce offensive against their inveterate enemy, the Lamido of Ngaoundéré.

At the end of the eighteenth century the Banda settled in a territory which the sultans of the north had called Dar Fertit, from Ferra, the old name for Darfur. At the time, they represented a very large number of tribes and part of them had already occupied the mountains in south Chad. Others in Goula country had formed a separate group and had become Muslims under the influence of the Ouadaians, taking the name Rounga, or Rougna. Many Banda, called Marba, of the Ngokolo highlands in Ndélé, were joined by armies from Ouadaï and in 1830 their leader Omar, or Djougoultoum, an exiled Baguirmian prince, founded Dar Kouti, south of the Aouk. This region henceforth became the military highway from Ouadaï to the heart of the Central African territory.

From 1830 until the Europeans arrived the Banda found they had to face the combined enterprises of the Ouadaians—with their satellite Dar Kouti—Darfur, and then of Zubeir;[21] conse-quently there was a series of exoduses. The groups in the west became separated from the others when the Mandjia arrived, and penetrated into the forests in the south-west beyond Carnot and Bambio, where they are now known as the Yanguéré, the 'separ-ated'. Other nuclei remained isolated right in the heart of Baya country in the north-west. Relatively few Banda still inhabit the vast area of Haute Kotto, as it was first overrun by Rabah and afterwards by Senoussi, whom Rabah named Sultan of Dar Kouti and Rounga in defiance of the Ouadaï. The great majority of the Banda settled in what was formerly Sabanga country, mainly in the basin of the Ouaka. A particularly dynamic group, the Ngao, reached the edge of the Gribingui and bitterly disputed the land with the Mandjia. Some groups, who had crossed the Oubangui into the ex-Belgian Congo before 1850, were known as Banza. Finally, other groups fled to Bahr el Ghazal to escape the deportations and massacres of the slavers from Dar Kouti. The

Oubanguian tribes forbade them access to the valley of the Ouban-gui itself and the Nzakara halted them on the right bank of the Kotto.

During these migrations, which sometimes forced the Banda to undertake very long treks of over 500 miles, they would split up into a number of minor groups. The colonists discovered such an extraordinary number of Banda groups and sub-groups that some authors, including Eboué, despaired of ever finding a satisfactory means of classifying them, and suggested placing them in alpha-betical order.

Some Banda leagues under the command of famous war-chiefs played a determining role in the pre-colonial and colonial history of the Central African territory. These were the Ngao, finally annihilated after putting up fierce resistance to Rabah, Senoussi and the French; the Vidri, the most independent and most famous of all the Banda tribes; the Bougbou, the sworn enemies of the Nzakara; the Togbo of Haute Kotto and Kemo; and the Ndi of the Damara region. Ndi or Ndre was a nickname meaning 'savages' which the canoers gave the Banda who reached Bangui. At the start of the colonial era the Langba, Yacpa and the Lang-bassi were still trying to force the dam which the river-people of the Oubangui had erected, while the Yanguéré Banda, whom the mass of the Baya had isolated in the west and the south-west, finally united with the latter to defend themselves against the Foulbe of Ngaoundéré.

Building the Central African Nation

This brief outline of the past history of Central African tribes is ample evidence that a sense of nationality was not solely the product of France's administrative efforts to unify the country. The great nineteenth-century migrations had brought groups together in areas where a certain uniformity of language and customs had been achieved, although constructive political organisation was still lacking. Without the colonial intervention, large communities of Baya-Mandjia, Banda and Zande-speaking peoples would have soon flourished, despite repeated aggression from Ouadaï, Darfur, the Foulbe and the Bahara.

In 1870, a coalition of Zande chiefs under the command of Ndorouma, the Mbia—which means chief or sultan in Zande—

annihilated an army formed by the leading merchant princes of
the Upper Nile and this victory quite close to the source of the
Soueh incited Zubeir to come to terms with the chiefs of the Zande
nation. His ambition was in fact to establish an immense political
and commercial territory stretching from Darfur to the Uele and
from the Kotto to the Nile, but in 1876 the Khedive of Egypt
set a trap for him, which put an end to these plans. Rabah, his
lieutenant, was unable to carry them any further.

A Kreich-Ngao coalition overran Dar Kouti in 1874 and succeeded in imprisoning the Sultan, Kober, in Cha. Had it not been
for Rabah's activities from 1880–90, the Banda might consequently
have managed to recapture Ndélé, while Ouadaï was absorbed by
its quarrels with Darfur, the neighbouring territory. In the west,
the coalition of all the Baya tribes had spread to the Yanguéré
Banda, thus providing a consolidated front against the Foulbe
invaders, which seemed likely to unify the whole area between
the Mambéré (Sanga) and the Lobaye sources, and the elbow of the
Oubangui. In 1885, the Mandjia, who had made peace with the
Sara, forced Rabah to retreat. Under the leadership of Bangassou,
the kingdom of Nzakara had resisted Rabah's army in 1884 and
continued to maintain its independence from its Zande neighbours.

Although some localised conflicts persisted between certain
tribes, the peoples who settled on Central African soil during the
nineteenth century generally withstood or avoided the Muslim
attacks from the west, north-east and east. This was largely
because the Muslims were reluctant to press any further into
Madjou, or pagan, territories, and the Madjou survived most of
the massacres.

The Baya-Mandjia, the Banda, the Sara and the Zande (or
rather Zandeised) all attracted the ethnologists' attention because
of the number of common characteristics they shared. Obviously
some form of prolonged contact must have taken place in the past
in a similar geographical area. A few scholars, mainly the Belgians
de Calonne-Beaufaict, Leyder and Tanghe,[22] have elaborated on
the hypothesis of a common region of dispersion perhaps in
Darfur, the former Gaoga of Leon the African. The Darfur
specialist, MacMichael,[23] on the other hand, supports the theory
that the country was populated by the Fertit race. There would
thus also have been close ties with the tribes who moved towards

25

the ocean, the Fang or Pahouines, whom several authors have linked with the Central African peoples, and also with the great Central African tribes who finally settled round the Oubangui and the Chari in the nineteenth century, after the mass movement across the savanna. The late President Leon Mba, who resided in Centre and Haut Oubangui for many years, subscribed to this theory. It is interesting that Schweinfurth's observation of the Uele tribes, who are very different from the Chillouk of the Upper Nile, should have led him to believe in the hypothesis of an Uele as an upper branch of the Chari. Others, who noted the similarities between the Zande and the Fang went so far as to suppose a connection between the Uele and the Ogoué. Despite the apparent diversity of Central Africa, a number of important unifying factors were in evidence even before the colonial period.

These affinities stood out even more plainly under the impact of colonisation. Although the police forces, consisting of about a thousand men for Oubangui Chari, were totally ineffective, the tribal wars, or feuds, between the Nzakara and the Bougbou, the Mandjia and the Banda, and the Baya and the Mboum ceased. The French managed to create a new framework for social life by extending communications and setting up administrative posts at strategic points, by laying down a tax—only too obviously a tribute—and above all by reducing the danger of attacks from the Foulbe, the Ouadaians, and the Bahara. In this way, the colonial administration favoured the growth of a new nation. The regime's excessive abuse later on only contributed to reinforcing the general feeling of solidarity. This became evident in 1930, when the Baya war, called 'the war of the hoe-handle', or the Kongo Ouarra, spread to a great proportion of the tribes living in the savanna and in the forest between the Chari and the Ogoué.

Traditional Social Structures

The social structures of the various Central African peoples are remarkably similar. They did not disappear in the regions subjected to Zande political and military regimes and they even survive among the tribes in the extreme north-west, who usually only pay lip service to Islam, and whose conversion did not protect them from the slave-raids.

Central African society rests partly on the close family connections underlying all the dynasties and the clans—an association of several dynasties—and partly on the feeling of solidaιity among members of a similar age group over a particular geographical area. The power of these deep-rooted social structures made it pointless to establish an organised political authority, a legislative system, or the machinery of a police force. The rule of the Zande princes in Haut Oubangui and of the Muslim chiefs in the northern territories had been superimposed on the traditional structures in the manner of a colonial administration. An absolute trading monopoly, the assertion of the rights of ownership over all the tribal lands, and the availability of an army, trained first on Turkish, then on European lines, had constituted the strength of these few organised regimes. When the colonists removed the military and commercial privileges of the sovereigns, they automatically lost all authority over their peoples. The deposed kings Rafai, Bangassou and Zemio became pensioners of the French government. Their deaths in 1900, 1909 and 1912 respectively, left their subjects totally indifferent. When Senoussi died in 1911, the French military authorities proclaimed the *hurria*, or general emancipation, of all the inhabitants. In the Zande territories and Dar Kouti, the sultans' descendants never achieved the same ascendancy over the tribes.

The traditional basis of society had in fact remained as undisturbed as that of the Baya, Banda and Sara communities, who were all opposed to the very notion of state and had been living in 'ordered anarchy' for centuries. In the case of a common danger, the clans would select war-chiefs with very wide powers, but strictly limited to the duration of the hostilities. Those who infringed this rule were generally executed by their peoples. All the Banda traditions mention a great chief, Ngakola,[24] who was put to death by his subjects and whose spirit is worshipped according to a common cult by all the tribes of the group, and even by neighbouring groups like the Mandjia. Banda traditions also tell of mountain kings belonging to their race—possibly the former Dadjo sovereigns of Darfur—from whom Zubeir claimed to descend on his mother's side. The traditions of the Baya refer to sovereigns called *konga*, who reigned over all the tribes. But every tradition specifies that the kings were temporary rulers, with a limited period of office.

The killing of the king seems to be a very ancient tradition common to the whole of the peoples of Central Africa and found from the Benoué as far as the Blue Nile. The custom springs from a profoundly democratic conception of society, the chiefs of villages or the heads of wider geographical areas being considered as mere mediators among the dynasties. The arbitration is the expression of popular consent and their apparent superiority no more than the symbol of the vitality of a particular group. Even recently, it was not unusual to meet true cases of suicide among old Mandjia arbiter chiefs. If they felt their strength declining, they would leave the village to die in the bush far out of the sight of their fellow people, for fear of contaminating the group. There was no better example of the colonist's misunderstanding of Central African customs than the attempt to replace these chiefs by administrative magistrates. The idea of a chief whose competence was restricted to a given geographical area, was so alien to traditional Central African conceptions that the people invented a new term, of foreign origin, to refer to these official chiefs, the Congolese word, *makoundji*.

The only organised social unit was the clan, or group of dynasties. Its role was so important that in 1957 Boganda described it as corresponding to the European concept of nation.[25] In no event could the land belong to one individual. It was always regarded as being the property of the clan. Nor could foreign goods brought from the north by Arab caravaneers or from the south by the broker tribes be owned by individuals. They were kept by the head of the clan in a secret place and distributed according to the needs of each member. In order to purchase goods, the head of the clan asked for the necessary articles of exchange, such as ivory or slaves, depending on demand. Individual trading of products was only permitted with other clans, but it had to be carried out publicly in isolated places and according to well-defined rules which permitted the immediate public sacrifice of any disputants or speculators. The head of the clan settled marriages and successions and the rights of individuals, and organised hunting, fishing and planting. As a priest he was responsible for the fertility of the soil which was closely linked with the fertility of the women in the clan.

The dynasty corresponded to a joint-family claiming a common ancestor. It allowed each individual a place in society and the enumeration of ancestors enabled each man to recognise his 'blood brothers'. Between men of very different dynasties, the exchange of blood was the traditional form of naturalisation or alliance and this was practised particularly with the first Europeans.

Age groups were also fundamental to the structure of ancient society. In 1949 Boganda based his first political party on this custom, but the organisation he set up could never replace the traditional initiation societies. The rites differed according to each ethnic group although they were in fact very similar, and served to constitute the 'generations' formed by the age groups. In the so-called secret societies—Semali for the Banda, Yondo for the Sara, and Labi for the Baya—young people received an agricultural, social and religious training which lasted several years and produced an accomplished member of society.[26] During the period of initiation a secret language was used, which was generally an ancient language the tribe had abandoned in the course of migration. Even today, and in spite of colonisation, the initiation societies are very much alive among the rural population. Not to have been initiated is regarded as a form of illegitimacy which can place a person outside of society.

European schools and religious instruction, together with the attraction of the towns dealt all these traditions a severe blow which has caused the ever-widening rift between the rural population and the de-tribalised masses in the towns. It also accounts for the general instability of present-day Central African society.

As in most other countries in the continent, the traditional social organisation has a religious basis. European authors stress the totem and taboo systems and attribute them to a primitive type of society; but a careful examination of the ritual of the Central African initiation societies allows us to believe that the religious traditions have grown out of the fusion of several lost religions, including Nubian Christianity, which has left very marked traces. All the tribes believe in the existence of a supreme being—the Ele of the Banda, Ngale of the Baya, Nzapa of the Sango, and the Nouba of the Sara—but this god is worshipped from afar and his name is not pronounced. Religious life is still dominated by a number of genies, needing to be placated. The water genie—the Badagui of the Banda, Ndiba of the Mandjia, and the Sangou of the Banziri and the Yakoma—occupies a privileged position in the life of Central Africans. The dead are not only the object of a general cult, but they are regarded as still belonging to the clan of the living. The fear of death is fairly rare because, in a sense, it forms part of the preoccupations of life, and the Central African is not haunted by the knowledge of the number of years he can still expect to live.

Twenty-five centuries ago, Herodotus remarked that the negroes of Africa were the most religious people on earth. On the whole the Central Africans remain so. Their sense of religion explains the sudden appearance of prophets in the tribes when events seem likely to upset traditional social concepts. By announcing the existence of a white God, the missionaries filled these people with anxious expectation of the coming of a Black Christ, who would restore the Golden Age of the past. Since then, the modern political leader, unable to find any basis for his authority in traditional anarchic society, has sought to identify himself with the figure of the saviour-prophet.

Ways of Life

Although colonisation did not succeed in destroying the fundamental structures, it considerably modified the outward ways of life. Rubber gathering and the compulsory cultivation of cotton, the introduction of European articles for trade, and above all, the diffusion of money in coins, greatly affected the traditional activities of the Central African peoples. Formerly they grew subsistence crops, hunted and fished, and worked at their local crafts. The accounts of the early explorers between 1880 and 1900 all concur in their observations of enormous remarkably well-kept plantations full of all kinds of crops. But these gradually declined, and in the savanna, cassava—used for ballast—has almost entirely replaced millet, now cultivated only in the north. The daily life of Central Africans also suffered much upheaval from the sleeping-sickness epidemic, which raged in the porterage and harvesting zones, and in the canoers' villages along the river, for several decades.

Today, there are hardly more than 600,000 Central African adult peasants left, and they work the whole year to provide for the capitation tax and all its attendant ills. The so-called subsistence activities can scarcely guarantee the livelihood of the village populations from one season to the next. In the suburbs of Bangui, alcoholism, prostitution and juvenile delinquency have produced a totally unscrupulous 'lumpenproletariat' called the *Godobe*.

The persistence of the ancient social structures in the interior of the country has preserved a comparative stability among the rural people. The workers have not yet realised to what extent they are exploited, and strive to recover the ancestral rhythm of their traditional activities. In spite of the 'work campaigns' launched first by the colonial and then by the national authorities to augment the country's exports by expanding industrial cultivation, the villagers still have no alternative but passive resistance, often mistaken for indolence. The Baya and the Banda have an agri-cultural tradition and devote themselves to hunting big game, but this is becoming less profitable as the animals are no longer so numerous in the inhabited areas. The river-peoples continue to rely on fishing, but canoes are also becoming scarcer. The forest Bantu are largely employed and housed on the afforestation sites and on the coffee plantations. They have abandoned their original villages to the old people, who find it hard to obtain a reliable source of food.

The greatest disrupting element in the traditional way of life in the west was brought by the diamond rush. The natives accumu-lated large sums of money after months of work spent far from their villages, and then dissipated them in a few days on alcohol and all kinds of consumer goods. Their villages look utterly wretched, but all the money received in remuneration is regarded as 'money from the devil' and has to be squandered. The educa-tion of the masses, which might temper these disastrous conse-quences, has not got beyond the stage of good intentions.

The Central African Republic thus presents the picture of a country that has been profoundly shaken by the introduction of an economic regime ill adapted to its social structures. In order to hasten development, many advocate suppressing all the old cus-toms—such as the solidarity of family and clan—although they offer a kind of protection to many Central Africans, because they do not foster the desire to prosper in the European sense.

2. The Colony of Oubangui Chari

The slave-trade flourished to such an extent in the seventeenth, eighteenth and nineteenth centuries that few people bothered to find out where the slaves actually came from. They merely knew that the caravans reached the coast from distant parts of the interior and that the natives were terror-stricken when they saw the sea for the first time, a fact which many traders recorded in their log-books. Others, however, believed that the trade only affected the thin fringe of tribes scattered along the Atlantic coast.

This misapprehension was largely due to the way the slaves were classified on their arrival in America. Very often, when they were asked their 'nation', they gave the name of the tribe that had delivered them to the trader or had bought or captured them. And the coastal peoples themselves did not know what the remote 'ebony' countries were called.

The natives from all over Haut Congo were labelled 'Congo' and the inhabitants of the populous Sanga and Oubangui basins often reached America under this name too. The sale of slaves from these areas was widespread in the former kingdom of the Congo during the sixteenth and seventeenth centuries. In the account dictated to Pigafetta in 1591, Lopez mentions the information he obtained from the Pombeiros, the brokers based at Mpoumbou (Stanley Pool), and also notes that the Anziques (Anguicos or Boubangui) exchanged slaves 'from their own nation and from Nubia, their neighbour' in return for salt, n'zimbou—the cowry shells they used for money—and ornaments. The missionaries have left eloquent descriptions of the great canoes employed in the traffic.

Some military and trading principalities sprang up in the sixteenth century to the north of Anzique country, between Haut Chari and Darfur. Their monarchs had become Muslims and had dealings with the slave purchasers from the East. The Baguirmi, Darfur and Ouadaï soon spread their quest for ivory and slaves to the southern countries, which till then had been the preserve of the old Bornu empire, and the veritable hunts they organised grew more and more frequent as their need for Turkish fire-arms increased. The upper basins of the Chari, the Sanga and the Oubangui, which were regarded as being especially 'rich in men', constituted a kind of reserve for both the Eastern and the Western slave-trades.

Slavers from the North

The recurring wars among the rival northern states between 1750 and 1800 were responsible for the intensification of the *ghazua*, the slave-hunts, in the south. After Ouadaï defeated the Forians in 1752, the Kalak obtained the greater part of the king of Darfur's slaving monopoly in Dar Fertit, the area north-east of the Central African territory, while the whole of the north was split up into three zones reserved for each slaver sultan respectively.

The region from the Ouham to the Gribingui was regarded as belonging to the Mbang of Baguirmi and his great feudatories, who concentrated their attention on the Kirdi, or Kirdi Nsara. Ouadaï tried to establish bases of operation from the Gribingui to the Bongou so that it could carry its enterprises even further south. The name the Ouadaians gave the various victims of these expeditions was Djenakheraï meaning savages. The eastern part of the territory from the Bongou to Djebel Mela remained nominally dependent on the Forian kings, who continued to refer to all the southern tribes as Fertit, generally in the provinces of Dar Raunah, Fangarau, Dar Byna and Dar Challa.

Mohammed el Tounsy, a Tunisian sheikh, [1] who later became ulema in Cairo, resided in Darfur and Ouadaï from 1803 to 1813. He left a description of the great difference between these hunts and the traditional holy war of Islam. Every freeman in Darfur could obtain a special permit to hunt slaves in the area now the Central African territory. The king would grant him a firman and also a heavy lance, called *salatyeh*, as proof of his authority. It was stipulated that the booty had to be shared out in accordance with minutely-detailed regulations. In Ouadaï, slaving remained the monopoly of the state, and military expeditions frequently left for the south to harry the region of Dar Koulla, or Goula, described to Browne in 1795.

Omar, a Baguirmian prince and brother of the Mbang, known as Djougoultoum, had fled to Ouadaï and become a war-chief, or aguid. He led a force across the Aouk and up the Diangara, and in about 1830 succeeded in establishing a base of operations at Cha at the foot of the Ndélé plateau, then occupied by the Banda. There, he made himself the ally of a local Muslim family belonging to the Rounga group and eventually founded an Ouadaian principality, calling it Dar Kouti, 'strong land'.[2]

In Baguirmi, where the traders were renowned for their eunuchs as far as Constantinople, various nobles competed for Sara slaves. To be sure of making a profit their usual practice was to kill all the adult prisoners and keep only the young. Gassargamo, Kouka in Bornou, Massenya in Baguirmi, Kouka in Dar Rounga, Ouarra in Ouadaï, Kabkabieh and Fasher in Darfur, and En Nahoud in Kordofan were all great dispatching centres, sending slaves to Tunis, Tripoli, Cairo and the Red Sea ports. The earliest information we possess about the Sara and their neighbours is the report from Fresnel, the French Consul at Jedda in 1845, who had questioned the slaves brought from Central Africa.[3]

The Bahara in the Central African Territory

Mehemet Ali's dream was to carry his conquests as far as the Niger and, after much difficulty, he succeeded in annexing what is now part of the Sudan. In Khartoum in about 1840, a number of European commercial establishments were set up and their agents were anxious to make contact with the regions in the interior outside Egyptian control. They first associated with the Muslim traders to purchase ivory from Bahr el Ghazal and the Upper Nile, and very soon the commerce spread to include human beings. Eventually, they formed a semi-clandestine confraternity, calling themselves 'the merchant princes of the Upper Nile'.[4] After about ten years some courageous explorers finally revealed what was happening and the general outcry caused the Europeans to withdraw in the 1860s. As a result, Zubeir Pasha made a fortune and was able to ruin the whole of eastern Oubangui.

Zubeir established his *zeriba*, fortified trading stations, and *dem*, depots, quite near to the Oubangui-Nile ridge. First of all, he attacked the Golo, the enemies of the Zande, and killed their high chief. Then he became the ally of the Zande king, Tikima, the father of Zemio, and occupied the states of Mofio in Haute Ouarra. Zubeir's Zande associates supplied him with thousands of slaves. He found the Kreich proved outstanding fighters, but this did not prevent him from plundering their lands and their cattle-markets. His expeditions led him as far as the river Kotto and into the land of the Tiki or Pygmies on the Uele. Finally, in 1867, Zubeir assumed the title of sheikh and declared that he no longer recognised the authority of the Khedive.

In 1869, Sir Samuel White Baker was appointed Governor of the southern territories with express instructions to put an end to all slave-trading activities. But Zubeir, who was well-armed, reigned supreme in Bahr el Ghazal and in the area to the west of the Oubangui-Nile ridge. In 1874, the Egyptian authorities suggested he march on Darfur and during this campaign, Rabah, his first lieutenant, distinguished himself. However, when the all too powerful Zubeir was lured to Cairo, he was put in gaol.

Zubeir's son, Suleiman, took over the great slaving domain. His lieutenants, Ma Ati and Kheir Alla, pressed further into Banda country to hunt the Mbagga of Bamingui, the Ngao of Bangoran and the Tambago of Kotto and Bamingui. They also attacked Kober, the sultan of Dar Kouti, in Cha, and sacked the small Ouadaian principality. In 1876, Rabah established himself a few days march from the Chinko. He made war on the neighbouring chiefs and the king of the Nzakara, Bari, the father of Bangassou.

The twenty years of Bahara raids in the eastern half of the Central African territory had caused more damage than all the operations of the northern sultans put together. Zande resistance was now concentrated in the mountains where the Mbomou and the Uele rise and where the loyal supporters of King Mofio were in hiding.

A Land Closed to Europeans

Heinrich Barth, who reached Baguirmi in 1850, obtained some information about the Sara and also learned of a great river called the Koubanda, in fact the Oubangui. Barth had intended to cross the Central African territory and make for Zanzibar, but he finally resolved to travel through west Africa without leaving the Muslim zone. He made note, however, of a route which led from Massenya to the Rounga and continued into Central African territory in the direction of Dar Challa and Dar Dinga. In point of fact, a journey into 'Pagan country' entailed very grave risks for a white man, as the terrorised tribes were convinced that the black slave-hunters were in the pay of white cannibals. This belief persisted for a long time in the Central African bush.

When Eduard Vogel, one of Barth's companions, disappeared in the Oudaian capital several European expeditions started out for this area. Gustav Nachtigal came quite close to the frontiers of the Central African territory and in 1872 visited the Somraï in south Chad at Goundi and Palem. He also witnessed Baguirmian slave-hunters massacring entire villages of Sara tribes. In 1873 he reached Abéché, the capital of Ouadaï, and then began to explore Dar Kouti and Banda country, after making very careful enquiries about an itinerary through the region south of the Aouk, leading to the Bamingui and the Gribingui, the north-east and centre of the Central African territory. Unfortunately he had to turn back when he reached the edge of Rounga country, as he had left Abéché at the height of the rainy season.

Meanwhile Georg Schweinfurth, who set out from Khartoum on January 5, 1869, exactly two weeks after Nachtigal left Tripoli, had already discovered the far eastern part of the Central African territory. The slave caravans helped him to get as far as the valley of the Uele by March 19, 1870. His very detailed comments on the Zande tribes and the area of Haut-Mbomou and Uele are really the first serious documents about Haut Oubangui. If the notes made by Barth, Nachtigal and Schweinfurth are put together, it is possible to form some idea of the mysterious country, which the Muslims of the north called the land of fear, or more prosaically, the land of the small traders. But the enigma of the great western river remained unsolved, although Schweinfurth in fact reached it in 1870 without knowing.

The first European actually to set foot on Central African soil was a Greek 'globe-trotter' called Panoyotis Potagos.[5] He left Hofrat en Nahas on June 30, 1876 and reached the Zande states along the Mbomou by following the Chinko. There he found Egyptian officials and slavers of all nationalities—including an Albanian he had known in Greece—still harrying the last survivors of Mofio's former kingdom. Rafai, the sultan of Mbomou, told him of a Sabanga river, the Kotto, in the west, but as Potagos unfortunately lacked the scientific background of his illustrious German rivals, his geographical observations were not accurate enough to be illuminating.

Frederick Bohndorff's expedition a little later was a similar case.[6] Bohndorff was a jeweller from Mecklenburg, whom Gordon had engaged as an interpreter in 1874. In 1876, he left Zubeir and set out for Mofio's former capital in Haut Chinko, where, like Potagos, he was received by the Egyptian administrator, Ofterrah. Further down the river on the right bank, he visited the post held by Rabah with a garrison of 2,000 men. Bohndorff was obliged to make a halt during the rains and in November 1878, he returned to the south of Kordofan, then in a state of upheaval because of Suleiman's rebellion. He was arrested as a spy, but managed to escape and finally reach the territory controlled by Gessi Pasha, a remarkable Italian officer, who had been appointed Governor of the whole of south Sudan. The attempts to subdue Suleiman brought a third European on the scene, the English colonel, Djesser Pasha, who arrived as far as Am-Dafog near Birao.

A Russian on the Mbomou, an Englishman on the Kotto

The Russian doctor, Wilhelm Junker,[7] was the first European explorer to spend any length of time on Central African soil and to leave a description of the country and its inhabitants. In 1876 Schweinfurth had advised him to choose Darfur as a base, but since he was forestalled in that area by two American officers in the service of the Khedive, he decided to join Dr Schnitzer, Emin Pasha, on the Upper Nile. Emin directed him towards the east of Zande country, but it was not until a second journey, from 1880 to 1883, that Junker managed to reach the Uere and visit the Zande king, Ndorouma, who had fought brilliantly against the merchant princes.

Junker later made friends with the young Zemio, the son of Tikima, who had refused to join in the revolt of Zubeir and Rabah against the Egyptian government. With Zemio as a base, Junker was able to persevere with his expeditions. He pushed almost as far west as the Mbomou-Uele confluence, visited the *zeriba* of Alikobo, who ruled over the southern Bandia, and also sent several presents to Bangassou, the young heir apparent to the kingdom of the Nzakara. Junker remained in Mbomou until 1883, before finally joining Emin Pasha in Equatoria. By this time, all the routes to the Sudan had fallen to the Mahdists.

In 1879, Suleiman ouled Zubeir submitted to Gessi Pasha. He had retreated with his last faithful supporters to within a few miles of the Central African territory south of Darfur and his surrender obliged Rabah to move his forces to Banda country, from where he could still put up a resistance to the Egyptians. Rabah soon appropriated a vast domain in the region he knew well from the slave-hunts. Gessi meanwhile had undertaken to raise Bahr el Ghazal from its ruins and he started rubber trading and the cultivation of coffee as ways of fighting the slave-trade. The Zande kings spontaneously offered their help, and Gessi began to hope that the land would prosper.

When Frank Lupton succeeded Gessi in 1880, he inherited a province with a surplus balance, but his arrival coincided with the year of the Mahdist revolt which seemed to be a consequence of all the social upheavals caused by the long period of slavery and its ultimate suppression. Lupton was only too aware that in such unstable circumstances, he could count on little support from Bahr el Ghazal, which had long served as a battlefield for Zubeir, Suleiman and their adversaries.

By 1881, Rafai, the king of the Bandia, had become one of the Governor's most respected counsellors and Lupton did not hesitate to fulfil Gessi's promise by recognising his rule over all the Banda and Kreich territories. The fact that Rabah was active north of the Kotto was, however, worrying, as Rabah had previously been Rafai's companion in arms.

Lupton pushed into Central African territory in 1882 and reached the great market of Foro north of what is now Bria on the Kotto. He noted that this great river, Zubeir's Sabanga river, drained into another 'great river' further downstream, which was in fact the Oubangui, called the Kota.[8] Once again, two Europeans, on the Mbomou and on the Kotto, were very close to penetrating the mystery of the great western river.

When Lupton returned to Bahr el Ghazal, he found it in the hands of the Madhists. In January 1883, he summoned Rafai and the two Egyptian administrators of Haut Chinko and Haute Ouarra, Katambur and Kordofali, to meet him in the capital. Zemio wrote offering him shelter for all his garrison, but Lupton in the end decided to defend the moudiriah of Dem Zubeir with the help of the Zande sultans, Rafai and Sasa, and heavy contingents of Zemio's men. Before he surrendered, he handed over all his arms to the Zande chiefs, who were afterwards able to ward off the attacks on their country in 1884, when the Mahdist Karamallah marched on the Mbomou.

Banda chiefs in the north, like Yango Mbili, who had been struggling against the Zande, went over to the Madhi, but Rabah kept his distance from the Danagla in the Mahdist camp. Kober, the sultan of Dar Kouti became uneasy at Rabah's presence so near his domain and was unwilling to show too much sympathy for the Mahdist cause.

Apart from a few years under the Sudanese administration in the extreme east, almost the whole of the Central African territory remained unaffected by the great Mahdist movement. And another seven years were to pass before the Europeans reappeared on the Mbomou and the Kotto; this time they were to come from the Atlantic.

Baya Resistance to the Foulbe Slavers

The Baya had been driven from their original home by Dan Fodio's military undertakings in the early nineteenth century and were firmly established in the west of the Central African territory. The Lamibe of Ngaoundéré succeeded in annihilating the Mboum, the Panha and the Laka Karre from 1840 to 1850 and had begun to attack the Sara Kaba. But the second Lamido, Issa, also embarked on a war with the Baya which dragged on for more than forty years. All these operations were destined to re-populate the region of Ngaoundéré, where there were very few inhabitants and famine was a constant threat, and to exchange slaves for fire-arms, which were very expensive in Adamawa.

Issa set up a base at Koundé (a word meaning fortress in Hausa), which today marks the western extremity of the Central African frontier. However, frequent disagreement among the Foulbe Lamibe of Adamawa acted in the Baya's favour and they had time to organise their country for long resistance. The raids of

Bello, Issa's leading war-chief, from 1875 to 1880 nevertheless inflicted much hardship on the country and Bello's horsemen are said to have thrust as far as the Oubangui. But in 1880 Bello was suddenly called to Yola to attend to family affairs and the Baya and the Yanguéré Banda were able to join forces against the slavers.

No European explorer had as yet penetrated the regions of Haute-Sanga and Lobaye; in 1884, a Russian, Eduard Flegel, crossed into Ngaoundéré, although he did not continue eastwards as he had intended, and the French did not navigate the Sanga until after 1890. On the whole, however, the Foulbe incursions year after year had far less disastrous effects than Zubeir's activities in the east.

King Leopold's Interest in Central Africa

European administration in the Upper Nile over an area reaching as far as the edge of the Central African territory had been limited to organising the public services and attempting to relieve the long-suffering populations of the scourge of slavery. Conversion to Islam in the centre of the continent was in no way regarded as harmful at the time, rather the reverse. However, only four years before the Mahdist insurrection, King Leopold II of the Belgians took steps to modify this traditional attitude.

During an important geographical conference in 1876 the King disclosed his ambition to co-ordinate all the efforts made by European explorers in Central Africa and his wish to found an international association to set up 'scientific and medical posts' at strategic points. These would serve as relay stations for the explorers and consequently make it unnecessary for them to rely on help from the Muslim slave-traders to reconnoitre the country. His aim was to conduct a 'war on slavery', although he did not define what form this would take; the 'crusade' would be led on behalf of Christianity, Civilization and Commerce, the three ideals the king fervently cherished. The French rather irreverently referred to them as the three C's.

In 1876 Stones, an American officer on the Khedive's General Staff, condemned the dangerous character of this 'organisation for the exploration and colonisation of Central African countries under the auspices of the King of the Belgians'. After Stanley had completed his fantastic expedition of 999 days and penetrated the mysterious Congo, King Leopold decided he was his man and contacted him in Marseilles on October 17, 1877. *The Association internationale du Congo* was founded in 1878 and the *Comité d'Etudes du Haut Congo* on November 25, 1878, but these were merely formulae used to disguise the project the Belgian King was hatching. His ultimate purpose was to set up a vast Central African negro state which would be governed from Brussels.

The King sacrificed his personal fortune, scorned the sarcastic comments of the rest of Europe, who thought his crusade was folly, and set the pace for fresh exploration, though this time the goal was no longer purely scientific. The King also tried to enlist the services of Gordon after he resigned in 1880. The Mahdist uprising, far from warning him to be more prudent, merely whetted his appetite to become the great Christian sovereign of the Congo and the Upper Nile. He had a passion for geography, devouring every explorer's report avidly; the accounts by Barth, Nachtigal and Schweinfurth were his favourite reading. The white blank that still subsisted between the Congo and the Nile obsessed him more and more.

For almost twenty years, he strove to arouse the opinion of Catholic circles against the slave-trade, which he identified with Islam. King Leopold II was really the force behind the colonial occupation of these remote regions and more especially of the Oubangui basin. Like Brazza, he remains inseparably linked with the history of Central Africa.

The Boubangui and Access to the Oubangui

Contrary to all expectations, the first white men to reach Central Africa came from the Indian Ocean and not from the Atlantic. Stanley sailed his way through the successive trading reaches of the Congo with five steamers and a lot of gun-fire; his most violent encounter was with the Boubangui tribes. He recorded his admiration for these fearless adversaries, who were quite prepared to leave their villages and to travel 500 miles further down the river, where they would await the caravans from the coast for months on end. The Boubangui also had all kinds of European fire-arms. On April 20, 1877, he noticed a broad tributary on his right flowing from the country of the Boubangui.

Little more than a year after Stanley's engagement with the Boubangui, Brazza and his small escort reached the western point of the vast trading area where they were obliged to halt in the basin of the Alima, a right-bank tributary of the Congo, and to search for a way to the east through the valleys further north. Close to Equateur, Brazza discovered a series of small watercourses which often bore similar names, such as Lebaï, meaning river, and Ngouko, great river. Brazza was convinced that all these rivers drained into one immense river, the Congo, and that the trading rights lay with the Boubangui tribes, with whom he would have to negotiate his passage. It was by promising to compensate the families who had been victimised in the combat of April 1878 that the French explorer obtained access to Bateke country in 1880 and made the acquaintance of the high chief, a descendant of the sixteenth-century Makoko.

The ceremony of the treaty celebrated on September 19, 1880, forms part of colonial iconography, as in fact Brazza had overstepped his instructions by acquiring the rights over Stanley Pool in the name of France. Considerable bargaining with the Bateke and also with Boubangui chiefs was necessary before the Makoko finally consented. The Boubangui (Brazza wrote Oubandji or Oubangui) controlled the trade higher up the Congo and also a large tributary which the explorer did not even suspect was there. Michel Dolisie also mentions a commercial treaty dating from about 1840, after the Boubangui had evacuated the area round the Oubangui elbow and pushed up towards the Bateke trading domain after the Baya-Bouaka invasion. This agreement allowed the Boubangui to take their products and their slaves downstream as far as Mpoumbou (Stanley Pool) but they could only trade there through the Bateke. When Brazza finally hoisted the French flag at Okila on the pool on October 3, 1880, the Boubangui chiefs insisted on being present.

The European settlement on the pool thus broke a centuries-old system of commercial transactions based on slavery. The fact that the Europeans of 1880 were no longer slavers must in itself have been a disturbing factor. Brazza found large numbers of slaves from the north, whom he brought back and freed, and then sent to their homes as an example. Father Augouard, the first French missionary on the Congo, reported that the river was still littered with canoes heavily loaded with slaves, but the demand had sub-sided since secret traders had stopped coming to the coast for their supplies. This decline was probably responsible for the spread of cannibalism round the elbow of the Oubangui.

As the explorers made more progress, the traffic fell off rapidly, but in 1880 no Boubangui canoer would agree to guide the Euro-peans from the pool to the Congo's greatest tributary, then still uncharted. The Sanga, leading to a region close to the Muslim states in the north, which was probably a meeting-place for both Eastern and Western slave-traders, was also kept secret.

COVETED BY EUROPEAN POWERS

The quarrel over the Oubangui[9] is an excellent illustration of the bitterness with which the European powers competed for the unexplored territories between the Congo and the Nile during the last two decades of the nineteenth century. After Brazza had made the treaty with the Makoko of the Bateke, his report was passed on to the President of the Council by the Minister for the Admir-alty with the comment: 'This traveller was never officially spon-sored by the Admiralty and Colonial Department.' However, public demonstrations on November 23, 1882, forced parliament to ratify the humble Makoko treaty, France's first stake in the Congo.

After this, Brazza's main concern was to attempt to gain at least the right bank of the Congo for France, and thereby win access to the unknown lands in the north. But he had very limited re-sources at his disposal, and meanwhile, between November 1882 and December 1883, King Leopold, by a remarkable piece of diplomatic mystification, succeeded in obtaining recognition for a state which up to then had existed only in his imagination. He had offered France the right of pre-emption over this future domain, and on April 24 received a letter from Jules Ferry amounting to a *de facto* recognition of the Congolese state. The next scene in the King's diplomatic manoeuvres went off perfectly on November 15, when the great powers gathered round a conference table in Berlin to work out a new international colonial law. At the end of the talks King Leopold's Congolese kingdom was recognised, and by the judicious manipulation of different maps he obtained very advantageous frontiers for it.

But while Stanley had explored the course of the Congo itself, the entire region north of the river was still unknown. During the frontier discussions with France which took place on February 5, Leopold's delegation took care not to mention the Oubangui, which Stanley had discovered in 1877. The map annexed to the treaty showed a curious right-bank tributary of the Congo called the Licona-Kundja. The upper part of this stream corresponded to one of the minor tributaries of the Likouala-Mossaka, which Brazza had explored in 1878, and its lower part more or less coincided with the last stretch of the Oubangui before it flows into the Congo. The rest of this imaginary river was marked by a dotted line running almost straight from east to west. According to the agreement between France and Leopold, the whole of this basin was allotted to France, with longitude 17° east denoting the boundary between French and Belgian territory as far as latitude 4° north.

The Discovery of the Oubangui

While the delegations bargained over faked or incorrect maps, an English protestant minister, George Grenfell, started out on February 20, 1884, up the waters of the Oubangui. He noted its north-south direction, and the rate of flow which made it the Congo's most important tributary. In the same area, on April 21, 1884, a Belgian, Captain Hanssens, signed a protectorate treaty with a Boubangui chief, Mokako. In July Grenfell came back with a new boat, the *Peace*, donated by a Leeds industrialist, and by October 13 had sailed some 150 miles up the Oubangui.[10] Great care was taken to keep all these attempts at exploration secret. But on March 6, 1885, as he was going through Brazzaville, a Belgian captain called Vangèle was foolish enough to show his maps to the French administrator, Albert Dolisie. Dolisie immediately took off for the north in a canoe, and at the beginning of May founded Nkoundjia, the first European post on the Oubangui.

When the text of the agreement arrived at in February first reached Kinshasa, the Belgians were mystified by what King Leopold had done. On May 31, 1885, Wauters, the King's geographer, published an article describing the Oubangui as the lower course of the Uele. Grenfell had reconnoitred the well-known elbow of the Oubangui, but had been forced back by the hostility of the people. On January 26, 1886, a boundary commission met at the French post of Nkoundjia and proposed that the frontier should begin from the confluence of the Oubangui and the Congo. Back in France, Brazza maintained that the whole of the Oubangui basin belonged to France and should have been mentioned in the agreement of February 25, 1885. But King Leopold did not want to relinquish what he knew to be the road to the Sudan. He formed a plan to launch an expedition up the Oubangui in the direction of the Sudan which he hoped one day to annex to his Congolese kingdom.

Acting on his instructions, Leopold's agents had in 1885 diverted the German explorer who, with his compatriot Friedrich Bohndorff, Wilhelm Junker's former companion, was planning to go up the Oubangui as far as the Zande sultanates. When the results of the Nkoundjia conference were announced in March 1886, the King disowned his representatives, accusing them of having been too hasty in correcting the geographical error of the convention of February 5, 1885. He then informed the French government that he would be willing to cede a part of the Oubangui basin against the authorisation to float a loan. Thus, at the very moment when Leopold was obliged to confess to financial difficulties in his new state, the Oubangui and its inhabitants became the object of a haggle.

During his visit to Paris in April, Brazza again alerted public opinion on the wily manoeuvres of the King of the Belgians. The French Foreign Office stood firm.

On April 27, 1887, France and Leopold agreed to recognise the Oubangui as the frontier as far as latitude 4° north, beyond which the French and Belgian zones of influence were to lie on either side of this parallel. Leopold had to be content with the promise of a loan, but feeling that he had been tricked, he reserved the right to re-open the 'quarrel over the Oubangui'.

The Fight for the Upper Oubangui

Captain Vangèle had been ordered to reach the Uele as quickly as possible and on October 20, 1886 he arrived at the Bangui rapids. He turned back at this point, but in November of the

45

following year advanced some distance further, until on January 5, 1888, at Yakoma, not far from the confluence with the Mbomou, a native army forced him to retreat. The French had very few canoes and had not yet reached the elbow of the Oubangui. Competition began in earnest in 1889. Bangui on the right bank and Zongo on the left were founded simultaneously, the first by the Frenchman, Michel Dolisie, on June 25, and the second by the Belgians on the following day. In January 1890, while Vangèle was sailing up the lower reaches of the Kotto, the young head of the French post at Bangui, Albert Musy, was murdered by the Bondjo of the Bouaka tribe.

Between 1890 and 1892, Belgian officers treated with Bangassou, Rafai and Zemio in turn, and they all placed their territories under the protectorate of the Congo Free State. At the same time, French agents such as Ponel, Crampel, Gaillard, de Poumayrac and Liotard, reconnoitred and took possession of areas on the right bank. In July 1892 Zande troops led by Zemio allowed the Belgians to break through in the direction of the Nile, and Major Milz reached Wadelaï, Emin Pasha's former capital, on October 4. On March 16, 1892, Liotard arrived at Bangassou, where he was threatened by the Belgian lieutenants, Mathieu and Stroobant. Fighting was only just avoided, and France used diplomatic channels to demand that her 'rights' be respected in the area north of latitude 4° north. Once King Leopold had obtained recognition of the claim that the Oubangui ended at the confluence of the Mbomou and the Uele, he sent missions right to the borders of Ouadaï, Darfur and Bahr el Ghazal, and established posts in Banda country.

In France, on May 4, 1892, Delcassé made Monteil go with him to see President Sadi Carnot, who wanted a French post to be set up at Fashoda, on the Upper Nile. Liotard was sent reinforcements.

While frontier talks between Leopold and France were dragging on, an agreement was signed on May 12, 1894, between Leopold's representatives and those of the British government. This agreement leased Bahr el Ghazal to the Belgian King, but Germany protested and the arrangement was dropped. On July 10, 1894, Monteil's force left Marseilles for the upper Oubangui and three days later the French territory of Haut Oubangui was created, extending from Bangui to El Fasher. On August 23, 1894, France and Belgium agreed to fix the frontier at the Mbomou—the dismembered Zande kingdoms were ignored—and this boundary still constitutes the frontier between Congo-Kinshasa and the Central African Republic. At the beginning of 1895 the Belgians evacuated their posts north of the Mbomou.

Brazza in the Upper Sanga

In 1892 Lieutenant Mizon, a Frenchman, sailed up the Benoué and concluded a treaty with Zubeir, Sultan of Zola, though this agreement was later challenged by the British and the Germans. Meanwhile Brazza had reached the Haute-Sanga area and made contact with the Lamido of Ngaoundéré, and set up posts throughout the region to prevent the Germans from advancing eastward from Cameroun. This annexation had its diplomatic epilogue in Berlin in February 1894 when, according to the French delegate Monteil, Wilhelm II himself connived at it.[11] The Kaiser considered that at all costs England must be prevented from establishing a link between the Niger and the Nile, and he went so far as to propose an offensive and defensive alliance between Germany and France. By the agreement of February 4, 1894, the frontier between Cameroun and the French colony was temporarily fixed at longitude 15° east as far as latitude 10° north, and thence in a parrot's beak along a line running as far as the Chari. Koundé was also left to France. This agreement was kept secret until the Reichstag met, in order not to upset the German colonial party, who were unlikely to forgive their government for signing away areas connected with the explorations of Barth and Nachtigal.

Thus in one year, 1894, French diplomacy won access both to Chad and to the Nile. In spite of the meagreness of her resources in Africa, France had managed to secure a huge stretch of territory in the centre of the continent.

After Brazza had left the upper Sanga, the Baya recognised Goujon, his successor, as a true warrior-chief. Thousands of Baya and Yanguéré Banda tribesmen were under arms as a result of repeated incursions by the Lamido of Ngaoundéré, and after having asked his superiors in vain for arms to prevent more slave-raids, Goujon agreed to lead the popular militia himself. On June 30, 1896, near Chakoni, Goujon's Baya and Yanguéré troops destroyed

47

a column sent by the Lamido. Koundé was razed to the ground, French posts destroyed by the Lamido's vassals were re-established, and the Foulbe permanently banished from what is now Central African territory. The 'military exploits' of the 'king of the Sanga' were not much to the taste of the Ministry for the Colonies, but Goujon's efforts, which were carried out without any financial support from the French government, nevertheless assured France's presence in the area.

An Operational Base for Chad and the Nile

The idea of linking the Congo with the Mediterranean and establishing a vast French empire in West Africa dated from 1889. It originated with Brazza's young secretary, Paul Crampel, who with the help of Eugène Etienne, the Secretary of State, and of a journalist, had managed to assemble some funds from private sources. In October 1890 Crampel, without bloodshed, ensured the future safety of the little post of Bangui, the wretched straw hut in a clearing where Musy had died; treated with the Banziri; and set off due north into the heart of unknown territory. He got as far as Dar Kouti, which Rabah had separated from Ouadaï by means of a *coup d'état* and placed under the command of Senoussi, nephew of the deposed Sultan Kober.

Rabah, with all his men, had been heading for Baguirmi, and in attempting to join him, Crampel was killed by Senoussi's forces in April 1891, not far from the Aouk. The following year two French explorers, first Dybkowski and then Maistre, traversed central Oubangui. Maistre was unable to reach Baguirmi, and returned to the Atlantic through Sara country, Adamawa and Benoué.

The project of marching to Chad was finally revived in 1895 by Emile Gentil, and the Mandjia and the Banda, who had previously been so hostile, helped him to transfer his steamer from the Oubangui basin to the Chari. He reached the shores of Lake Chad on November 1, 1897, after signing protectorate treaties with Senoussi and with Gaourang, the Mbang of Baguirmi. Rabah, who had destroyed the thousand-year-old empire of Bornu and set up a capital at Dikoa, did not interfere.

By a decree of June 19, 1896, Captain Marchand was placed under the orders of Liotard, the Governor of Haut Oubangui.

Marchand aimed to plant the French flag in the Mahdist Nile and join up with the Ethiopians who at the time were the allies of France. His small force arrived at Bangui in April 1897 after having re-established the passage along the caravan track from Loango to Brazzaville; meanwhile Liotard had already occupied Dem Zubeir, the capital of Bahr el Ghazal. The entire population of Oubangui and Mbomou were enlisted to ensure Marchand's safe arrival in the Nile basin and despite many difficulties the expedition finally reached the old Egyptian fort of Fashoda on the Nile on July 10, 1898.

The expedition provoked considerable tension between France and England and on November 4 Marchand was eventually asked to retreat. But on March 20, 1899, another column under the command of Captain Roulet reached Gara-Chambé, higher up the river. Bahr el Ghazal was dotted with small posts, manned by forces from the tiny garrisons in Oubangui. The last diplomatic intervention in the European partition of Central Africa followed: on March 21, a convention between France and Britain granted the whole of the basin of the Bahr el Ghazal to the Sudan—which was more British than Egyptian—while in the north, Ouadaï was placed in the French zone and Darfur left to the British. Deprived of its outlet to the Nile, Haut Oubangui was to become a real cul-de-sac.

On July 17, 1899, at Togbao in the north, Rabah's army massacred a small force of French troops and Baguirmian tribesmen commanded by Bretonnet. A confrontation between France and the conqueror became inevitable. France in fact achieved one of the most daring exploits in European colonial history by thrusting three columns from Algiers, the Niger and the Oubangui into the heart of Africa. The god of war frowned on Rabah, and he was killed in combat at Kousseri on April 22, 1900.

It was due to the occupation of Oubangui that these various expeditions had been successful. The straw huts forming the administrative post of Bangui became one of the most important strategic bases of the French African Empire. But in 1900 the Central African territory was still practically unknown except for a few itineraries traced by the explorers, which the military columns had used. It was evident that a colony needed to be created urgently.

Second Thoughts on the Partition of Central Africa

The whole of the present Central African territory had been assigned to France under the 1894 and the 1899 conventions, but between 1900 and 1920 this ownership was again challenged. In 1910, the pan-Germanists evolved a plan to establish a German bloc in Central Africa, which would comprise most of the interior between Douala and Dar-es-Salaam. In May 1911, the Kaiser's government suggested co-operating with France in the construction of a railway from Douala to Oubangui, and when the gunboat, *Panther,* arrived off Agadir on July 1, 1911, France had no alternative but to negotiate. Since Wilhelm II was willing to remain impartial over Morocco, France agreed to grant a large portion of the Congolese domain to Germany. The Germans in fact demanded the whole of the forested zone, Gabon and Congo-Brazzaville, but in the agreement signed on November 4, 1911, they accepted the richest portion of the Central African territory: all the Sanga and the Lobaye basins, the upper basins of the Pende-Logone and the Ouham, and part of the Mpoko basin became German, and were called Neu-Kamerun. French Equatorial Africa, constituted by decree on January 15, 1910, was now split into three.

French colonial troops recuperated the lost territories during the years 1914–16, and after some hard fighting alongside the British army, succeeded in occupying the whole of German Cameroun. After the war a French mandate was set up, and with the collapse of the German dream of Mittelafrika, France now had possession of French Equatorial Africa and Cameroun. In 1917, it proposed ceding Haut Oubangui east of the Kotto to England as part of a series of exchanges affecting many of the African possessions. The colonial partition of Central Africa ceased to be challenged officially after 1920, though the Nazi regime laid claim to the former German colonies classing Neu-Kamerun among them and Hitler took up the question of Mittelafrika once again.

THE CONCESSIONARY REGIME

Twenty-Seven Concessionary Companies

After 1890, the *Comité de l'Afrique Française* encouraged a number of prominent figures from the French business world to take an interest in the regions of the Chari and the Oubangui.

King Leopold's counsellors were also busy trying to found a large Franco-Belgian company to exploit Haut Oubangui, despite the diplomatic difficulties involved.

In 1897, the news of the brilliant results the Belgian companies were obtaining in the Congo started a kind of Congo fever in France, and applications for concessions flooded in. Two years later, a *grande commission* divided up the territory attributed to France and granted concessions to various private individuals, who for the most part were full of illusions about the natural resources of the country, but had no practical experience of Africa. The French government hoped to compensate itself for all the public charges in the colony by manipulating the dues imposed on the shareholders. On August 13, 1900, a finance law suspended all future subsidies to the colonies.

The land allocated was regarded as unoccupied, or free state property, as opposed to what was sometimes considered inalienable native territory, and the concessionary company was given the rights over all the natural resources, on the sole condition that inhabitants were remunerated for time spent gathering crops, usually rubber.

Political motives largely dictated the government's choice of thirty-nine companies.[13] Twenty-seven of them shared the Oubangui and the Ouham basins, with the biggest domains going to the *Compagnie des Sultanats du Haut Oubangui* (the whole of the east beyond the Kotto) and to the *Compagnie des Produits de la Lobaye* (the entire Lobaye basin). The only areas not actually conceded were the Kemo and the Gribingui basins, which were zones reserved for the recruitment of porters for the traffic to Chad, and Dar Kouti, a French protectorate called the States of Senoussi. The economist, Paul Leroy-Beaulieu, described the whole affair as an 'orgy of concessions'.

In almost every area the concessionary system produced disastrous results. The companies saw their capital dwindle away in a few months and the European agents, who, for economic reasons, had been engaged from among the misfits of society, were guilty of shameful methods of exacting taxes and service from the natives. It was clearly folly to wish to develop the country at a profit, when there were no roads to speak of and human porterage was the only

3—CAR * *

means of transporting commodities and goods; but it was too late to give up.

After a visit to Bangui to review the troops, the future General Mangin did not hesitate to express his alarm at the atrocities the company agents indulged in.[14] 'As a sample of our race,' he wrote, 'the choice of agents could hardly have been worse. Unless the regime is radically changed, all kinds of abuse and vengeance will irremediably stain the history of this unfortunate colony.'

But the French government, swayed by base political considerations at home, refused to reform the system established in 1900. However, when the 'red rubber" scandal broke out in King Leopold's Congo, raising an outcry all over the world, France turned once more to Brazza, who had been recalled from Africa in 1897. He was asked to undertake a mission for the express purpose of confirming that the French concessionary system was run along different lines from the one in the Belgian state.

Brazza concentrated his inspection chiefly on the area which stretched from the Lobaye to the Gribingui.[15] On July 16, 1905, he inquired into the deaths of forty-five women and children, who had been imprisoned in Bangui as hostages. Finally, he sent a telegram to the President of the Council to the effect that the general state of affairs revealed during his inspection 'made it difficult and dangerous' to compare the French procedure with the system in the Belgian Congo according to his instructions. Brazza, the founder of the French Congo, died in Dakar, but his report provided the basis for an impassioned anti-colonial campaign in France.

Many of the companies had been unable to take advantage of their concessions because of the geographical errors contained in the decrees, and they brought an action against the government, demanding substantial damages. Some of them, like the directors of the *Compagnie Ngoko-Sangha*, defended by André Tardieu, speculated on the growing tension between France and Germany.[16] 'This system is unworthy of France,' cried Gustave Rouanet, the Deputy for the Seine, addressing the Assembly on June 20, 1906, 'and unworthy of a democracy. First of all, it harms public morality because of the intrigues carried on in a number of political and administrative circles to protect the interests of the concessionary companies, but it is also dangerous, because these companies, as we know, are counting on ulterior international decisions to be able to claim compensation for capital, which very often has not been paid out, and what is more, to demand the refund of capital, which not only has not gone to Africa, but is in the hands of Africans from the streets of Paris and elsewhere.'

Abuse of Porterage and Taxation

The consequences of the porterage service demanded of the Mandjia and the neighbouring tribes for military manoeuvres in Chad and for the general requirements of the new colony, provide a classic example of the harm caused by excessive exploitation in the early part of the century.[17] The geographer, Pierre Gourou, saw this as one of the most blatant causes of de-population under the colonial system.

When the small number of administrators in the Gribingui region were ordered to proceed with the recruitment of porters, they soon expressed their dismay as they knew this meant the destruction of a whole region. In 1902, the administrator of Fort Crampel wrote:

Manu militari [by hand to hand fighting] our small posts have pushed them back on all sides, to the north, east, west and south in an attempt to halt this wholesale flight across the Fafa and the Ouham. The Mandjia hides like a lone fighter, trapped in a corner of the bush, or he shelters in the caverns of some inaccessible kaga, and becomes a troglodyte, subsisting wretchedly on roots until he starves to death, rather than accept these terrible burdens. We have tried everything . . . we had to. Provisions have to come first. Arms, ammunition and goods for exchange have to be passed. We tried gentleness and persuasion, threats, violence, oppression, presents and wages, but everything fails before the sheer terror of the Mandjia race, who only a few years ago, or even a few months, was rich, populous and firmly established in large villages. Soon, the whole of the eastern Gribingui up to the Fafa in the west, Ungourras in the south and Crampel in the north will have become waste-land, sown with dilapidated villages and deserted plantations. There will be no more crops and no more labour. The region is finished.

Central African Republic

The despair, isolation and disease which killed five out of six of the officials, who sacrificed themselves to work in the area, drove some of them to take advantage of their position. On July 14, 1903, Georges Toqué at Fort Crampel allowed one of his subalterns to execute a prisoner with dynamite. This affair was exploited in France in the daily paper *Le Matin* and also by the Deputy for the colonial group, Le Hérissé, in an attempt to distract attention from the company agents' behaviour.

The collection in kind of the capitation tax tied to the harvesting of rubber and started in 1903 gave rise to veritable man hunts. The dealers would buy back the rubber paid over to the administration in lieu of tax at a cheap rate. Apart from this tax, the villages had to supply dues for the building of tracks and posts. The so-called *indigénat* system—that is to say the institution of multiple administrative police sanctions—provided an abundant penal work force.

Monetary circulation was practically non-existent and those groups which made handsome profits on barter opposed its penetration into the interior.

The intense exploitation or 'pillage' economy (German *Raubwirtschaft*) to which this system of administrative obligations was added led to the ruin of a country which was already suffering from the slave trade.

Sleeping-Sickness and Smallpox

When sleeping-sickness broke out, the Central African population, already physically exhausted from rubber gathering and the burdens of porterage, succumbed rapidly. The disease spread in the camps in the west where the rubber gatherers had been grouped, in the porters' villages, and also along the Oubangui, where the abusive recruitment of canoers had reduced the population by about three-quarters. In 1907, the Martin-Leboeuf mission exposed the ravages caused by the epidemic, while the companies themselves were highly alarmed at the almost total disappearance of their workers over large areas. One company even financed a chair of tropical medicine in Paris. Of the six military doctors resident in the colony four were posted to Haut Oubangui in 1912, but only two were able to attend to the population. Medication in any case, was entirely lacking in the colony.

The First World War prevented any spectacular improvement, but Colonel Jamot, who was also a doctor, was sent out to Cameroun and French Equatorial Africa and remained on after the war to devote the rest of his life to fighting the epidemic; sanitary campaigns were also conducted. But in Haute-Sanga hundreds of villages were struck from the map and the banks of the Oubangui became deserted for many miles. When Ernest Psichari took part in a French military expedition into Baya country in 1908, he entitled his journal, *Land of sun and sleep*.

Outbreaks of smallpox were less notorious than sleeping-sickness, but they also contributed to wiping out many villages in the west, centre and east. In Mandjia country during the grimmest years of porterage, the administration was obliged to erect pyres in all the villages to burn the corpses of the people who had died of smallpox. At the time they had no other means of extirminating the disease.

The Establishment of a Direct Administration

While Senoussi had been left to look after Dar Kouti and could peacefully proceed with his extermination of the Kreich and most of the Banda in Haute Kotto, the rest of the Central African territory was split up into four administrative sectors. The country still depended on the authorities in Brazzaville west of a line from Bangui to Logone, and east of a line from Bangui to Darfur there was the expanse of Haut Oubangui, which had been created in 1894 to reach to the Nile. Between these two lay the area called Chari, which was linked with the military zone of Chad founded in 1900. The region around Bangui was separate.

The territory christened Oubangui Chari and divided from the French Congo emerged from the decrees of December 29, 1903, and February 11, 1904. The second decree established Bangui as the residence of a delegate of the General Commissioner of the French Congo. For a long time the administrative centre had been alternately Abiras, Zemio and Mobaye in Haut Oubangui, but the plan to transfer it back to Fort de Possel was swiftly abandoned, and on December 11, 1906, another decree designated Bangui as permanent capital.

The first Governor of Oubangui Chari, Emile Merwart, arrived at Bangui on December 25, 1906. As the colony legally included the military zone of Chad, it was known as Oubangui-Chari-Chad and was divided into administrative regions and *cercles*, provincial divisions. But in actual fact, it consisted of eighteen poorly equipped posts, nine of which were almost permanently unoccupied due to shortage of staff. Haute-Sanga, called Sanga country, and the Lobaye basin were part of the Middle Congo, though the Lobaye area was not far from Bangui. A plan to give up the Chad area north of latitude 10° north in 1906 met with the opposition of the officers who were stationed there.

In 1909, when the tribes began to revolt, the Governor-General, Martial Merlin, set up constituencies for occupation and for administrative purposes, and entrusted them indiscriminately to officers or to administrators. The officers had the help of a small military detachment, and the administrators recruited a people's militia from their particular region. The administrative division of the country today reflects this period, and the sub-prefectures correspond exactly to the former colonial constituency bases.

The French Congo was decreed French Equatorial Africa in 1910 and organised into three not very autonomous colonies, Oubangui-Chari-Chad, Gabon and the Middle Congo. Although Oubangui received about forty administrators and officers, they were far from sufficient to control the population throughout the country.

General Insurrection and Conquest

In May 1908, a French magistrate examining the case of the Mpoko concessionary company, charged seventeen European agents with the murder of large numbers of natives. This affair frightened the government, especially when the acting General Commissioner, Alfred Martineau, wrote to the Minister for the Colonies stating: 'In our modern societies, the fortunate capitalists all too often forget the price that is paid for their well-being. I demand justice in the name of the thousand natives who have died and I am confident that you, as Minister, will know how to reconcile the principle of justice with the necessities of colonisation.' The head of the judiciary added: 'If only a hundredth part of the atrocities in Mpoko had been committed in France, the people's anger would have wiped out all trace of pity for the guilty men.' [18]

The necessities of colonisation prevailed, but within a few months the desperate population had raised the standard of revolt over the whole of the territory. The Mandjia and the tribes in Lobaye and the forest regions had already been forcibly subdued during the years 1905–7, and in many areas the concessionary companies themselves had sold large consignments of rifles to the natives. For three years, 1909–12, the colonial troops had to fight to win back the country valley by valley and village by village. 'It was a question,' explained the Chief of Staff at Brazzaville,[19] 'of achieving not a passive but an active occupation. In addition to manning the posts to keep order, this involved waging a real war of conquest.' In the west, the operations in the heart of the forest vanquished the religious chief, Beran-Djoko, but in Banda country, all the tribes between the Ouaka and the Kotto rose against the French, behind the Vidri chief, Baram Bakié.

In Dar Kouti, Senoussi had strengthened his army and had spread his slave-hunts as far as Anglo-Egyptian Sudan. In 1910 he seized the rock of Ouanda-Djalle, where the Youlou were in hiding. But on January 12, 1911, the French resident, Captain Modat, laid an ambush at the entry to Ndélé and the sultan and his son, Adem, were killed. The struggle continued into December 1912 on the river Kji and at Ouanda-Djalle despite the defeat of Senoussi's army, until, after being a protectorate for seventeen years, Dar Kouti finally passed under direct French control. The entire north-east of the present Central African territory had been ravaged by Senoussi's campaigns.

The concessionary company that took over the sultanates of Haut Oubangui progressively ruled what remained of the former Zande and Nzakara lands. In 1909, however, Governor Merwart treated with Labassou, the son of Bangassou, with Hetman, the son of Rafai, and with Zemio, and restored part of their former prestige.[20] The Governor-General and the Minister for the Colonies refused to ratify those conventions on the grounds that treaties with native chiefs 'no longer presented the same advantages as they had during the period of penetration into the country'.

Zemio died on October 12, 1912, but the news awoke little response from Europe. Yet this man had been Lupton's friend, had defeated the Mahdists, and later proved an invaluable ally to the Belgians during the Arab war. He had also been instrumental in the achievements of Marchand's force. When the last insurrections were put down, Oubangui Chari was a colony from which all traces of traditional authority had been removed. The direct administration steadily consolidated its hold in the course of the next forty-five years, until it turned into the 'militarism' operating on the eve of independence.

FROM CONCESSION TO MONOPOLY

After the Scandals

Although there had been serious charges levelled at the concessionary companies, their downfall was still not proclaimed, and in France, the right wing accused 'the Liverpool group' of financing the anti-colonial campaigns. The Minister for the Colonies, Etienne Clémentel, declared that the colonisation of Central Africa should be continued for the benefit of the inhabitants who, before the white men arrived, had had 'no sense of family, no sense of property and fled their own kind'.

Between 1908 and 1910 the government encouraged the association of several companies. This led to the creation of a *Compagnie Forestière de la Sangha-Oubangui* in the west; covering more than thirty thousand acres. The companies in this part of the territory were smoothly transferred to German control after the 1911 agreements. In the same year, a case between the *Compagnie des Sultanats du Haut Oubangui* and a licensed private trader, who had bought goods from the natives inhabiting the concession, went against the company. The principle of free trade was invoked and the court did not hesitate to qualify as a *de facto* monopoly, what the company hitherto had considered as a right. Fresh revelations about company agents' excesses incited Maurice Violette to launch another offensive in the Assembly: 'The era of the great concessions is past,' he declared, 'we will have no more of it under any pretext.'

The government, however, had to pursue patient negotiations with each individual company to transform the concessionary contracts into leases over more restricted areas. In addition, the companies had agreed to entrust all their transport to one single company, which would thus enjoy a powerful monopoly and be able to fix its own tariffs for exporting and conveying goods. The scandals during the early part of the century had made many companies feel that some kind of coalition was necessary. This had turned into a professional body called the *Union Congolaise*, which soon became an important pressure group in France.

The new conventions passed between 1910 and 1920 granted the former concessionary companies a commercial monopoly, which mainly affected the exploitation and export of rubber essences. In return for the thousands of square miles that had been theirs in 1900, the surviving companies were allowed to choose smaller freehold concessions. Thus, although the system was legally suppressed, the same companies retained their privileged position, often without even having to alter their names.

All this was still a far cry from the free trade regime envisaged in 1885, and which the various European nations involved in Central Africa still pretended to respect. Once the newly associated companies saw that they were not going to lose their privileges, they began to call upon loans from private sources and a number of important trading concerns were formed. The practice of exclusive representation prevented speculation among the importers.

The Rubber Crisis and the Easing of Political Tension

The steep fall in prices on the rubber market between 1920 and 1922 had the ironical consequence of alleviating the inhuman system in force in Oubangui. Abuse had in fact reached its peak in 1920 when the creeper rubber failed and grass rubber had to be exploited. A French missionary, Father Daigre, drew a sombre picture of Banda country during this period:[21]

Auxiliaries behave like police and hunt out all the gatherers who try to escape the ordeal. It is common to meet long files of prisoners, naked and in a pitiful state, being dragged along by a rope round their necks. Countless poor wretches are taken along the remoter tracks, completely stupefied by the harsh treatment. They are famished, sick, and fall down like flies. The really ill and the little children are left in the villages to die of starvation. Several times I found regions where the people least affected killed the ones who were dying, for food.

59

On the administrative side, Auguste Lamblin, the Governor, can be regarded as having saved what still remained of the Central African population. He reduced the rate of taxation in some areas, and had the villages rebuilt along recognised tracks. He set up collective plantations to fight the famine and prohibited rubber gathering during the months when subsistence crops could be picked Once the first cars began to appear, he organised a vast network of roads to link up the posts. The miracle of it all was that the people continued to accept the burden of extra unremunerated work, which was also closely supervised by guards and sharp-shooters. But, after enduring the famine of 1918 and the intensi-fication of rubber gathering, they were at last being employed in tasks that concerned them directly, and which were to put an end to the horrors of porterage.

On October 1, Victor Augagneur, the Governor-General, made a statement[22] condemning the 'police manoeuvres' practised during the war and which had been particularly effective in dis-persing the Banda of the Bangana in Haute Kotto in 1915. 'You must absolutely forbid,' he wrote, 'the violent methods that have been employed to subject refractory natives, who flee from our con-tact. Such measures can never be excused, but, at the start of the occupation, when the country was still new, and the numbers, weapons and customs of the tribes unknown, perhaps they could be understood. Now, they are to be severely condemned. Sharp-shooters and militia guards are all too often left to their own devices on their rounds and they are no more civilised than the people they pursue; their excesses have brought evil consequences, and the proof of their failure lies in the need to repeat their round of visits each year.' The Governor added: 'It is not hard to imagine the hatred and the terror aroused by the white man and his native agents after a few operations of this kind . . . The people must be taught to be accustomed to our presence and gradually to associate with us.'

By the end of 1925, the administration was more concerned about subsistence crops than rubber. 'Your divisional chiefs must be aware,' wrote Raphaël Antonetti, the Governor-General at the time, to the Governor of Oubangui, 'that they are responsible above all else, for the nourishment of the peoples under their care.

This is more important than revenue from taxes, and any food shortage will be regarded as criminal.'

Belated Decisions

The fifteen years following the parliamentary debate that almost excluded the concessionary companies from Oubangui and the Congo were scarcely propitious for equipping and developing the colony. The war was largely responsible, but some authors, such as Georges Bruel, laid the blame for the delay on Brazza's inspection. 'In 1905,' he wrote, 'there were impassioned attacks on the colonists after news of the scandals broke, and campaigns, which were not always disinterested, were waged against the very principle of concessionary companies. All that was really needed was to try to suppress abuse, and for both parties to apply the terms of their contract as loyally as possible and work towards free colonisation. The most obvious result of all the campaigns and of Brazza's mission was merely to heap disgrace on the French Congo, and to retard the effort France would have to make sooner or later to ensure the integral occupation of the country, as well as the launching of public works on a large scale.' [23]

A loan was voted by Parliament a few weeks before the First World War to finance the construction of a railway from Pointe Noire to Brazzaville, and possibly another one from Bangui to Fort Crampel. The arrangements finally drawn up in 1922 included only the first of the two projects. In fact Brazza had wanted to build a railway from the Congo to the sea as early as 1887, but his plan was postponed to avoid interfering with the profits of the Belgian railway running from Matadi to Kinshasa. No sum was set aside to develop the colony itself.

All the achievements in Oubangui Chari depended on that peculiar form of investment which consisted of hard labour in various guises, including payment of tax, prestation and penal servitude. The plants owned by the companies could scarcely have been more poorly equipped. In 1924 there had been fresh harvesting, especially in the forest regions, due to the favourable rates of exchange, but this also revived the old methods of exactions. The *Compagnie Forestière Sangha-Oubangui* was among the worst offenders in this respect.

61

Central African Republic

In 1925 André Gide witnessed the appalling conditions during a visit to Haut Oubangui and the centre of the territory. He crossed the south of the present prefectures of Lobaye and Haute-Sanga on foot. The journal of these experiences was published under the title *Voyage au Congo*.[24] It contained a long series of indictments of a regime that most people in France thought had disappeared at the beginning of the century and, on October 20, 1927, the book was even distributed to the members of the International Labour Office as a document on the system of hard labour still obtaining in the colonies.

'It is not enough to tell me,' wrote Gide, 'as I have so often been told, that the natives were even more wretched before the French occupation. We have accepted responsibilities toward these people and we have no right to shirk them. I cannot express the sorrow and impotence I feel. What demon urged me to go to Africa. What did I ever seek there? I was at peace, but now I must speak.' In Sara territory, Gide noted the alarming consequences of the conscription of labour and the requisitioning of foodstuffs for Congo-Ocean. The *Société des Batignolles* had taken over the construction of the railway, but work had been started with practically no equipment. Enormous numbers of men were 'consumed' by the sites, and natives from Chad and Oubangui had to be called in after the Congolese.

The workers were so totally exhausted after years of the concessionary system and the ravages of the epidemics that they were incapable of carrying out the tasks demanded of them and died by the thousand. Albert Londres described the unbelievable misery of these labourers: 'Their utter desolation,' he noted, 'seemed to have no name. They dragged along the railway-line like nostalgic phantoms. Cries and beatings could not bring them back to this world. As they dreamed of their distant Oubangui, they tried to grope their way to the grave.' [25]

FROM CRISIS TO WAR

The Least Endowed of All the Colonies

From 1926–31, French representatives did what they could to rescue the remaining populations and provide them with work, which would at the same time help straighten the budget. This turned out to be the exploitation of cotton, coffee and diamonds, and today, these products bring in 90 per cent of the revenue from exports. Great hopes were also placed on other resources, such as gold, but they had to be abandoned.

Metropolitan France, however, continued virtually to ignore the efforts of Lamblin and his administrators. The situation throughout French Equatorial Africa, the most neglected of all the colonies, was described by Albert Londres in *Terre d'Ebène, la traite des Noirs*: 'The colony lives in total isolation,' he remarked, 'it trails as best it can along the river beds, and France is never ready to congratulate its administrators when they do well, or to encourage them if they are waiting for the wind. The colonial official is a neglected child, remembered only if he is the cause of scandal, or if a protest in the Assembly shoots his name into all the headlines. Some Governors have been directing our colonies for ten years and the Ministers still do not know their names.' André Gide had written in *Voyage au Congo*: 'All over French Equatorial Africa, the two most worrying factors are shortage of staff and shortage of money.'

The new undertakings also met with an unfortunate concatenation of events. First of all, in July 1928,[26] Karinou, a Baya war-chief, provoked a rising in the west, which quickly spread to the tribes in the area from the Chari to the Ogoué (the Kongo Ouarra war, or 'the war of the hoe-handle'). Then two years later the great slump of October 1929 hit France heavily and proved another setback for the African colonies. To remedy these disasters the administration introduced a system of subsidies on a large scale, which inevitably reinforced the *de facto* monopolies of the local trading companies. The colonial authorities were unable to put down the Baya rising for some time, and the extent of the operations was carefully hidden from public opinion in France. In fact, it was not until the Second World War that the development of the most backward region in tropical Africa really got under way.

The Introduction of Cotton

Before the colonial era, cotton had been cultivated mainly by the Banda and the Zande, but local textiles died out when cloth was imported from Europe. After the First World War, the administration started to plant cotton in the region of Basse Kotto, using seed imported from the Belgian Congo, but agriculture was far from organised and by 1924 there was still only one foreman for the whole of Oubangui Chari. In spite of protests from the *Compagnie des Sultanats*, Félix Eboué succeeded in spreading the planting to the Bangassou region.

The first crop recorded in official statistics was 585 tons for about 2,073 hectares in 1925–6. In 1929–30, the output of 1,915 tons for 9,456 hectares was regarded as satisfactory. Agreements were made with Belgian and Dutch companies as well as with the concessionary companies in the process of liquidation; these granted the new cotton companies a purchasing monopoly over a very vast area and fixed the price paid to the producer, so that the shareholders would be guaranteed a steady profit. The markets were supervised by the administration, and taxes were collected at source. This was facilitated by the custom of paying a collective amount to the village chief, instead of dealing with each producer individually. Notes were only issued for large sums. It was not until 1936 that the principle of individual fields and payment based on the market price were admitted.

In 1934–5 production was more than 10,000 tons and in 1935–7 it rose to almost 16,000 tons, but in spite of an increased number of planters—more than 100,000 at that time—it then remained more or less stationary until the Second World War.

The need for a war effort favoured the introduction of coercive measures. Rubber gathering was revived and the cultivation of cotton made compulsory. The output consequently rose from 23,929 tons in 1939–40 to 39,311 tons in 1940–1, with 389,225 planters. Henceforth, the primary concern of the colonial administrators was to maintain production at this level, which meant continuing widespread compulsory cultivation. The social and political shortcomings of the policy and the drastic deterioration of the soil were totally disregarded.

The Cultivation of Coffee

The Central African Republic produces several local varieties of coffee-trees. The most famous are the dybowski type, discovered by Dybkowski on the banks of the Oubangui in 1892, and the excelsa, which Auguste Chevalier found in Dar Kouti in 1902.

Nana coffee is another variety found in the forested regions of Haute-Sanga.

Up to 1924 coffee was picked by hand and was limited to a crop of a few tons, but in 1924 and 1927 Lamblin set up the first plantations, mainly in Banou country at Yaloké and Bossembele. He even organised an agricultural college for young Central Africans. The first output of plantation coffee in 1927 was just over a ton. A number of Europeans were interested in coffee-growing and in several villages the administrators arranged for trees to be planted. In 1930 the crop was still very small, about 16 tons, but almost 900 hectares had been planted. By 1938 the output reached 1,475 tons and the total surface of European plantation 4,509 hectares. The villagers themselves prepared more than 11,000 hectares for cultivation and the Governor-General took an interest and helped to keep selling prices steady. The results obtained were very encouraging, as the Oubanguian soil seemed particularly suited to producing coffee of a very high quality.

'The future of French Equatorial Africa depends on coffee,' François-Joseph Reste, the Governor-General, went so far as to declare in 1938 in his annual speech. But the authorities were caught completely unawares by the disease of tracheomycosis and were powerless to prevent the destruction of most of the plantations which took place inside a few months. In the forested zones and close to the forest, it was decided to replace them by plantations of the robusta type which had more resistance. Output continued to rise during the war years, bringing in a considerable income. But the blight had interrupted the planting and cultivation subsequently remained in the hands of the Europeans, so as not to interfere with the cotton growing, to which priority would in future be given. Cotton fields were sown as far as the clearings in the forest in the south-west near Bambio and Mbaiki, under incredible economic and agronomic conditions. The villagers confused cotton cultivation and fiscal duties, for the administration had begun to believe that exemption from cotton cultivation was a form of tax relief.

The Rush for Mining Permits. Gold and Diamonds

In 1912 some gold deposits were found in the beds of the water-courses north of Bambari, and in 1913 Brustier, an agent of one of the concessionary companies and an amateur geologist, discovered near Ippy the first Central African diamond, a small stone of half a carat. After the war, prospectors from the Belgian Congo formed a mining syndicate in Oubangui Chari and applied for a number of permits, as the concessionary companies' contracts bore no references to the sub-soil. These ventures produced a wave of prospectors and during the years 1928–30 almost 1,500 mining permits were granted.[28] In 1927 and 1928, two companies were formed, the *Compagnie Equatoriale des Mines*, and the *Compagnie Minière de l'Oubangui Chari*. The first of these exploited the gold deposits at Roandji between Bambari and Ippy, and in 1929 brought Oubangui its first annual output of four and a half pounds. In 1930, this rose to nearly 200 lbs and by 1931 it was almost 550 lbs. The record was reached in 1934 with more than 1,950 lbs. During the war, production remained at around 1,500 lbs.

Diamonds were mined in the Mouka sandstone region north of Bria. In 1930 and 1931 more than 3,000 carats were extracted, but in 1934 production fell to zero. It picked up again only very slowly; in 1937 the discovery of new deposits in Haute-Sanga brought more than 6,000 carats, rising to 14,491 in 1939. The war stimulated production and the figures rose again, from 31,927 carats in 1940, to 82,891 in 1945. In July 1944 the largest diamond ever extracted in a French possession was found at Carnot, 391 carats.

Oubangui Chari joins Free France

On July 21, 1940, a group of French reservists seized an ammunition depot at Bangui and were arrested by the officers. The garrison had not yet contemplated going over to General de Gaulle's movement, but on August 28, General Husson, the acting Governor-General of French Equatorial Africa, was taken prisoner at Brazzaville by a group of Gaullist insurgents and exiled to the Belgian Congo. On August 29, Colonel de Larminat's 'organic act no. 1', constituting a government of Free French Africa, appeared in the official gazette. The same day, at Bangui, the commanding officer, Cammas, proclaimed his loyalty to Marshal Pétain. Fighting between the military commander in chief and the supporters of the Governor, de Saint Mart, seemed inevitable. Finally Cammas surrendered on September 3 in order to avoid a fratricidal conflict—as civil war had already broken out among the French in Gabon—and on October 21, Bangui welcomed General de Gaulle.

The colony played an important part in the war and the sharp-shooters recruited by Cammas throughout the territory distinguished themselves in the field, mainly in Syria and at the battle of Bir Hacheim, where Lieutenant Koudoukou, the first Ouban-guian officer, was severely wounded. He died later in hospital at Alexandria.

Other consequences of the war were that French Equatorial Africa and Cameroun became integrated in the sterling zone for a few years. In May 1941, a memorandum of agreement was signed for one year and made renewable annually until the end of the hostilities. It guaranteed the sale of local products in Great Britain. French Equatorial Africa, and above all Oubangui Chari, were thus spared the economic stagnation that affected the colonies which had stayed faithful to the Vichy government. The need for provisions on the Middle Eastern front led the Allies to improve the ports, roads and aerodromes. At Bangui the aerodrome and the port were properly equipped and the road from Bangui to Batangafo and Fort Archambault became an important strategic highway. Concrete bridges were constructed to allow the convoys to pass and about a dozen centres were fitted up with radio stations. The Free French regime also introduced a uniform customs arrangement for the whole of French Equatorial Africa and Cameroun. The system of the conventional basin of the Congo before 1940 had in fact only concerned part of the federation. Oubangui Chari was therefore included in an economic entity prefiguring the present Customs Union. An agreement signed on February 8, 1944, finally brought French Equatorial Africa back into the franc zone.

A New Policy

When French Equatorial Africa changed sides during the war, Félix Eboué, who had served for more than twenty-five years in the Oubanguian bush, was made Governor-General. His appointment meant that for the first time France's policy in Oubangui would no longer be conducted from Parisian offices, but by a man who knew better than any other the sufferings and the aspirations of

67

the people. He reasoned that as the people were going to be asked to make a special effort for France, they could no longer be regarded as primitive or immature.

'The colony is in danger, it is threatened from within, like a granary being emptied,' he wrote in his famous circular of November 8, 1941, to all the divisional chiefs. He laid the blame for this situation on 'the great concessions, the disorganised exploitation of the economy, the often unfeeling proselytism, the neglect of education and above all the indifference and even contempt with which the political and social officials were treated'. He invited all the administrators to break with the assimilationist policy, for 'to make or recreate a society, if not in our image, at least according to our mental habits, is to head for disaster. The native has customs, laws and a fatherland, which are not ours'. He lamented the excesses of the direct administration, the disappearance of the traditional districts and the growth of officialdom. 'In general we shall remain extremely discreet legislators,' he asserted, thereby breaking with a colonial policy, which had stubbornly persisted in wishing to settle every detail of the villagers' life.

On February 27, 1941, a Council of Local Interests was set up by decree in each territory and consisted of senior officials, who were appointed, and delegates elected by the administrative Council. Eboué's new policy was confirmed at the Brazzaville conference on January 30, 1944, when the question of the 'political personality' of the territories was raised. But this assembly of Governors and colonists was apprehensive at the idea that these countries might one day break away from France. 'The targets of the civilising mission we have undertaken go beyond the notion of autonomy and eventual evolution away from the French empire. The idea of "self-government", even at a very remote date, is to be discarded.'

Although the Brazzaville recommendations were limited, everything pointed to the fact that the end of the war would mark the end of the colonial period as such, in Oubangui Chari as elsewhere. And so, only fifty-five years after the first Frenchman had set foot on the banks of the Oubangui, it was time to think of entrusting the destiny of the country to its inhabitants. In the opinion of the French colonists and government officials who had settled in Oubangui, this stage would not be reached for a few

68

more decades. The area had in fact been considerably retarded by its tragic history in comparison with the other African colonies, and although production had attained a fairly respectable rate by 1945, the educational level of the population still left much to be desired.

In February 1935, Edouard Renard, the Governor-General, set up a 'school' in Brazzaville to train local officials. This establishment accepted pupils holding a primary certificate of education and took them as far as the fifth form of secondary schools. In the whole of French Equatorial Africa in 1939, there were only 106 pupils at secondary school, 80 boys and 26 girls, mainly from Gabon and the Congo. At the end of the war, there were still less than 500 Oubanguian auxiliaries in the French administration, and all were interpreters, clerks, assistant teachers and nurses, confined to secondary tasks. The overseers and foremen engaged in public and private works were all European. However, in 1938, a peasant's son from Lobaye, Barthélémy Boganda, who had studied in Cameroun, the Belgian Congo and at Brazzaville, was ordained priest.

The Religious Missions

The first Catholic missionaries arrived in Oubangui in 1894, and in 1909 an apostolic prefecture was created at Bangui. As the missionaries had very limited recources at their disposal, their initial activities were confined to the river-bank zones of the Oubangui. They only very slowly penetrated into the interior although they frequently came into conflict with the administrators. Before 1930, there were comparatively few missionary posts in the interior, limited to Mbaiki, Bambari, Bangassou and Berberati.

The conversion of Banda and Baya country was the next step, and in 1937 Bangui was made an apostolic curacy. In 1940, an apostolic prefecture was established at Berberati, where missionaries had been coming from Ethiopia. By this time Catholics numbered about 45,000. The missionaries were the Fathers of the Holy Ghost and the Capuchin Fathers.

Protestant missions reached Oubangui after the Second World War, and soon there were almost as many Protestants as Cath~~~ in the country. The Mid Africa Mission, a branch ~~ ~~

Society missionaries, concentrated their efforts on the Mandjia, and the Ouaka-Kotto and Mbomou areas. In the west at about the same period, the Foreign Missionary Society of the Brethren Church founded the Evangelical Mission of Oubangui Chari (MEOC). From 1924–9, the Africa Inland Mission was established at Obo and Zemio, the Home Office Mid Missions - Mishiwara at Ndélé, the Lutheran Sudan Mission at Baboua, the Central Africa Pioneer Mission at Carnot, the Swedish Baptist Mission in Haute-Sanga and Ouam-Pende, and the Swiss mission at Alindao.

The memory of the slave wars checked the progress of Islam, and there has been no notable movement of conversion to this religion since the arrival of the French. The Muslim tribes in the north-east were satisfied with a summary form of worship, and in the Zande country, the Europeans' presence incited the sultans to give up their religious practices very quickly. More often than not, they had let themselves be converted for reasons of trade, and their families were among the first to adopt Christianity. The teaching of a few sects, who announced the coming of a Black Christ, has thrived in the areas along the river, but their influence is limited. In the savanna zones, tribes like the Labi, the Yondo and the Semali are still attached to their ancient traditional rites.

3. Emancipation of the Central African People

POLITICAL AWAKENING

At the end of the Second World War the movement in the colony, which more than any other African territory had suffered from the vicissitudes of history and the excesses of colonisation, could not really be termed nationalism. A rather special situation had arisen out of three converging factors. The colonial regime was in any case being relaxed all over French Black Africa at the time, though in Oubangui Chari it had little effect on the total apathy prevailing among the peasants after years of intensive exploitation. And the appearance of a remarkable leader, Barthélémy Boganda, brought the country a veritable prophet capable of incarnating all the aspirations of a humiliated people.

From 1945–51, Boganda, basing his arguments on the reforms that had been decided in Paris, virulently attacked the practices of the local administration and the colonists and succeeded in infusing the entire population with the will to throw off the colonial yoke. It was due to his strong personality that the Oubanguian political movement held together and developed independently of the great African parties, unaffected by the manoeuvres of the major political parties in France.

Political Reforms

Before the war was actually over, the *Comité Français de Libération Nationale* had elaborated a programme of reforms for all the colonies, including abandoning assimilation in Indo-China and North Africa, though not as it happened in Black Africa. After the liberation, it was soon made clear that the arrangements for Africa would depend on compromises reached between the representatives of the capitalists committed overseas and the members of the various French political parties eager to attract customers from among the educated classes in the former colonies.

Consequently, the destiny of the inhabitants of these territories was played out on the banks of the Seine, and not along the Senegal, the Niger or the Oubangui.

Although the government had advocated assimilation for Black Africa, it regarded universal suffrage as too premature a measure for an area like French Equatorial Africa. The decree of August 14, 1945, drew up electoral rolls by college, but the second 'non-citizens' college was restricted to the auxiliaries of the administration and to a few of the more educated of the population. The whole of Oubangui and Chad formed a single electoral constituency. The non-citizens eventually elected Guy de Boissoudy, a French officer who had played an important part in the Brazzaville putsch in August 1940, while the citizens—that is, the small group of government officials and European colonists—chose a veterinary surgeon, René Malbrant, notorious for his unwavering hostility to reform in French Equatorial Africa on the grounds that the territories were too backward. The elections to the Constituent Assembly on October 21, 1945, thus had no meaning for the majority of the Oubanguian people.

The African deputies immediately began to press for urgent reforms, and more especially for the extension of the rights of citizenship to all natives, the abolition of hard labour, and the establishment of local assemblies. Senghor recalled that in the year III (1795) the colonies had been declared 'an integral part of the mother country'. But Malbrant, speaking on behalf of the Chambers of Commerce of French Equatorial Africa, resolutely opposed any extension of the rights of citizenship within the federation and declared that elected local assemblies were quite out of the question. 'To take a concrete example,' he stated on April 25, 1946, 'I have no hesitation whatsoever in affirming that among the natives of Oubangui Chari it is impossible to find thirty-six general councillors capable of assuming these functions.' He added that he wished 'to prevent the local assemblies lapsing into impotence or anarchy, or becoming playthings in the hands of the governors, which would be equally disastrous'.

The same month however, a law permanently suppressing all forms of hard labour was proposed by Marius Moutet, the Minister for the Colonies. This was adopted by the National Assembly, although in theory coercion had already been abolished by various other laws in 1922 and 1945. The Minister particularly criticised 'recruitment by administrative means', which he clarified as 'recruitment of labour leading to intolerable abuse and permitting practices so appalling that we wonder if we should not pray to be forgiven for having understood liberty in such a fashion'.

The colonial party rejected the draft Constitution at the referendum of May 5, 1946, and in July, Malbrant and his friends convened a States General of Colonisation in Paris. The aim of this gathering was to check the wave of reforms by brandishing the threat of communism and by appealing to the nationalist sentiments that four years of German occupation had aroused in France. They proposed a federal structure for the Union designed to replace the empire, on the condition that each region retained its political supremacy. Next, they declared that 'the granting of French citizenship could not be a collective measure extended obligatorily to all the inhabitants of the legal empire, when the majority of the people concerned neither understood what it entailed nor were aware of its greatness, and when some would even deliberately refuse to take the step. It should therefore remain an individual act, open to all those in a position to appreciate its moral, social and political significance'. They raised a solemn protest against 'all legislation' designed 'to reshape all that the Third Republic had accomplished in the overseas territories, or to surrender an authority which was still necessary even for the population itself, who relied on France for the law and order without which their evolution towards freedom and independence would be impossible'. They deplored the 'tyrannies of tomorrow' and called upon the government 'over and above all parties, all local and temporary contingencies, to safeguard the sacred principle of French sovereignty'.

Anxiety among the Colonists

The protests from the States General of Colonisation were moderate compared with the reactions from the Consular Assembly in Bangui. This body went so far as to contemplate maintaining hard labour to avoid an economic setback in the colony. 'The new measures,' indicated a motion voted on June 7, 1946, 'seem suited only to peoples more advanced than the inhabitants of French Equatorial Africa. The natives evidently interpret the suppression of hard labour as the legal consecration of the right to do nothing . . . We can anticipate an abrupt drop in the cotton output . . . No one who knows this country will expect the mentality of the black to change overnight because of a text.' The Bangui Chamber of Commerce was genuinely afraid that the economy, based entirely on the compulsory cultivation of cotton and the administrative recruitment of labour, to the benefit of the cotton producers and the owners of the mines, was in danger of collapse.

The position in 1945 was fairly satisfactory. The cotton crop had risen to almost 34,850 tons, 14,500 of which were produced in Ouaka-Kotto alone. After a drought, coffee production had fallen from 4,759 tons in 1944 to 2,150 tons, but the 1946 crop looked promising. The diamond output had increased from 57,585 carats in 1944 to 80,700 in 1945. The secondary crops were improving. Also, in order to protect their interests and prevent an influx of newcomers, a few traders and colonists had formed partnerships or syndicates. On August 16, 1945, the Governor-General issued a decree authorising exporter groups and making illegal all future exportation not effected through their services.

The suppression of coercion and the organisation of political parties and workers' unions led many people in private circles to fear for their privileges, and in the second Constituent Assembly the conservative elements secured a small majority. This time the arrangements for the overseas territories were made with greater heed being paid to the observations of the States General of Colonisation than to the claims of the African deputies. The draft Constitution finally adopted on October 13, 1946, however, was so full of contradictions that it proved a constant source of misunderstanding for the next twelve years. Moreover, the Fourth Republic was soon involved in disastrous colonial wars in Indo-China, Madagascar and North Africa, quite apart from having to cope with periodic unrest in Black Africa.

Although the preamble to the text of the Constitution rejected 'any colonial system based on arbitrary rule', no degree of autonomy was actually granted to the African territories. They remained administrative sections of the French Republic, one and indivisible, and any nationalist or even autonomist standpoint on the part of one of these countries risked being legally interpreted as an attack on the inner security of the French State. Prospects of political evolution consequently remained very slight, while assimilation began to look impossible.

The First Oubanguian Deputy: Abbé Barthélémy Boganda

Barthélémy Boganda was born in the village of Boubangui in Lobaye on April 4, 1910. After much hardship as a child and the death of his mother, who was murdered by the guards in charge of the rubber gathering for the *Compagnie Forestière Sangha-Oubangui,* he was adopted by Catholic missionaries and baptised on December 24, 1922. At the time, the priesthood was the only means of promotion open to an Oubanguian and the missionaries used part of their small funds, donated largely by a few French families, to enable the precocious boy to study, first at St Paul des Rapides at Bangui, and then at the seminaries of Kisantu in the Belgian Congo, Brazzaville and Yaoundé. He was ordained on March 17, 1938. Next he went to various missions, including Grimari and Bakala and in 1946 Bishop Grandin of Bangui urged him to stand as a candidate for the National Assembly. On November 10 he was elected and set off for France which he was to see for the first time.

Apart from a few soldiers, no Oubanguian had as yet had any contact with the metropolis and Boganda was surprised at his respectful and even friendly reception. The difference in mentality between the Frenchmen of France and the colonists in Oubangui Chari was only too obvious. In his new capacity, Boganda directed his entire political action towards demanding equal rights for black and white and the effective application of Christian and Republican principles in his over-exploited country. He intended to make a public denunciation of the wretched state to which colonisation had reduced the Oubanguian people. He began by introducing himself as the son of a polygamous cannibal. Most of his French audience had never even heard of Oubangui Chari.

'The Africans,' he declared to the Assembly on August 4, 1947, 'must certainly seem very strange, because they will not be satisfied with speeches alone. They judge only the facts.' 'We are the citizens of one nation and we all share equal duties,' he continued. 'We must also share equal rights.' Although Boganda was a member of the *Mouvement Républicain Populaire* (MRP), the colonial party immediately accused him of being a communist. At the end of the year he wrote to the Minister for Overseas France, Paul Coste Floret, protesting once again about the many injustices still obtaining in the colony, and in his opinion, hiding 'the true face of France' from the Oubanguian people. He listed: 'Conscription of labour, arbitrary violence and arrest, unremunerated work and insufficient wages (a good worker in the towns sometimes earned a maximum of 45 francs a day, when he needed 150 francs in order to support himself and his family decently), the prohibition of public places (negroes were not normally admitted to public establishments, such as cafés, restaurants and cinemas) the abuse of authority in teaching, the compulsory cultivation of cotton and its exploitation, and the unfair distribution of the capitation tax.' He ended with the accusation: 'All these factors are causing a steady decrease in the population of Oubangui Chari.'

Boganda had been far too idealistic and soon began to realise that in spite of countless laws, speeches and circulars, nothing was actually done to alter the regime of subjection and exploitation. The administration merely viewed the deputy as an agitator and for the next ten years used its influence to the full to try to get rid of him. Boganda's disappointment with parliamentary circles and his refusal to have anything to do with their intrigues in Black Africa converted him to the idea of direct political action among the peasants themselves. It was not long before he began to be regarded more as a popular leader or tribune of the people, than as a politician in the classical sense.

Establishment of a Conseil Représentatif

The law of October 7, 1946, had placed the onus of organising the territorial assemblies on the French government. In Oubangui Chari, the *Conseil Représentatif* consisted of only 25 seats, 10 of which were reserved for European candidates from the first electoral college. The colony was divided up into four huge constituencies based on ethnic and historical considerations. The west was predominantly Baya, the south-west composed mainly of the cosmopolitan centre of Bangui, the eastern area largely Banda, while the remaining section covered the former sultanates of Haut Oubangui. The 'independent' candidates, who were chosen for their connections with the administration and the colonists, were backed by the Europeans against the supporters of Boganda.

On May 6, 1947, the *Conseil Représentatif* held its first meeting to choose the representatives for the *Conseil de la République*. Guiriec was elected, and was later replaced by Robert Aubé and Jane Viale. In October Antoine Darlan and Jean Lhuillier from the respective colleges were elected as councillors to represent Oubangui Chari in the *Union Française,* and another five representatives took part in a federal assembly called the *Grand Conseil de l'Afrique Equatoriale Française.* The *Grand Conseil* elected Paul Flandre, a French industrialist from Gabon, as President, and the Oubanguian, Antoine Darlan, a militant trade unionist known for his integrity, as Vice-President.

Both the *Conseil Représentatif* and the *Grand Conseil* had limited powers, mainly confined to financial matters. Boganda's supporters were not in a majority, as the independents had voted unconditionally with the representatives of the European college on all occasions and Boganda himself had not wished to stand for election to a local assembly that had no real political influence. At the time, he could conceive only of popular mass resistance to reinforce the action of the educated classes, as an effective means of combating the colonial regime.

Persecuted by the Administration

Boganda wished to create some form of political organisation that would not have to depend upon external subsidies or contributions from his poverty-stricken supporters, who very often were completely destitute once they had paid the capitation tax. The best method seemed to be a system of consumer and producer co-operative societies, which would also improve the income of all those who belonged. Unfortunately, Boganda had only the vaguest notions of political economy and he also tended to overestimate the capacities of his supporters: even the more educated had rarely got beyond the level of the primary school certificate because of the lack of facilities in the territory.

But Boganda forged ahead undeterred, refusing to bother about the qualifications of his staff or the basic requirements for packing the goods, or even about the special system of exportation. In 1948, he founded the *Socoulolé (Société Coopérative de la Lobaye-Lessé).* Meanwhile, Antoine Darlan, with the help of some friends

77

and a few lorries, started another experiment in the cotton zones, calling it the *Cotoncoop*. More Bogandists used their infinitesimal resources to found transport and consumer co-operative societies.

The big commercial companies holding the monopoly for the distribution of consumer goods and equipment, including the importation of the jute sacks for packing and the exclusive sale of vehicles and fuel, refused to negotiate with the new societies. However, René Malbrant approached the Minister for the Colonies, Jacques Soustelle, and asked him to place some money at the disposal of the *Conseil Représentatif*. On December 1, 1947, a loan of 42,500,000 fr. CFA was granted to finance the establishment and the running of the co-operatives.

This subsidy turned out to be a trap. It certainly enabled the apprentice co-operators to meet their working expenses, but it also helped out with a number of other expenses, which had little or no connection with trade. In 1949, when legal action was brought against those responsible for the organisation, they were found to be leading political activists and in 1951, Georges Darlan, the first Oubanguian President of the *Conseil*, was charged. Only a few months before the elections, the *Etincelle de l'*AEF, and the local organ of General de Gaulle's movement, the *Rassemblement du Peuple Français* (RPF), published the amount of money the co-operatives were said to have 'misappropriated'. Boganda was obliged to give up the whole scheme in the same year. His staff had reached the point where they could only obtain their products in exchange for hand-written 'coupons', bearing promises to pay later.

Boganda was also beset with all kinds of administrative annoyances such as the supervision of roads, the enforcing of hunting regulations, control of plant disease, and so on. Those of his supporters who held official functions were moved from one end of the country to the other, and political meetings, though not illegal, had to be held in secret.

When Boganda married a European parliamentary secretary, Malbrant and his electors launched a violent and undignified campaign, which contributed to intensifying racial feeling between blacks and whites. In Berberati the people formed a huge procession and marched through the streets bearing the corpse of a Camerounian clerk who had died in prison, and the frightened

Governor agreed to arrest the administrator. Urged on by the colonists, the administration sought more and more pretexts to arrest Boganda, but this merely augmented his prestige in the eyes of the population.

Creation of MESAN

On September 28, 1949, Boganda assembled a small group of his followers at Bangui, and decided, with their agreement, to found a popular mass movement called the *Mouvement d'Evolution Sociale d'Afrique Noire* (MESAN). The abbreviation had the exact messianic ring the Oubanguian deputy needed. 'MESAN', specified the regulations Boganda had drawn up, 'aims to develop and liberate the black race by progressive and pacific evolution, achieved by the combined efforts of all negroes throughout the world. Each ethnic or administrative group, each family, clan or tribe, each district, region, division, province or department, each territory, each federation, will organise its own branches, federations and committees.'

The statutes laid down in April 1950 stated that the movement must 'progressively encourage the full development of African society in harmony with the spirit and conditions of Black Africa'. The political programme was succint: 'To defend the liberty of the African people, to ensure equality among all men, respect of each African's human dignity and the individuality of each community or tribe.' '*Zo kwe zo*, a man is a man,' repeated Boganda. These elementary facts were still far from being recognised in Oubangui Chari, where the Africans had not even obtained so much as the right to freedom and dignity. The economic and social programme of MESAN underlined the need to generalise the co-operative action, which was then in serious difficulties.

This organisation produced a very hostile reaction on the part of the administration and the colonists, who grew more determined then ever to depose Boganda. This time they set about it by enlisting the help of a large number of government officials and ex-servicemen, over whom they still exerted considerable pressure, and the direct consequence of the creation of MESAN was the appearance of Gaullist RPF branches in Bangui and in some centres in the interior.[1] Malbrant, aided by the colonists and the administrators, and more particularly by those who had fought with

79

Free France, was chiefly responsible. It was hoped that these branches would directly undermine Boganda's activities. They were mostly composed of a few administrative chiefs, dignitaries, officials and clerks employed by private companies, as well as ex-servicemen.

The new measures introduced by the administration, such as a very moderate increase in the price of cotton after devaluation, the establishment of a few schools in the bush, some minor readjustments of the salaries of government officials together with provision of additional accommodation, were all described as the 'victories of the RPF'. But there was a rather dangerous ambiguity about the whole situation because their action tended to be confused with the colonists' movement of resistance to governmental reforms.

Boganda reacted sharply to the propaganda from the RPF, which was already spreading to the bush. But the methods they employed were generally so clumsy that even in the humblest Oubanguian village, the term RPF became synonymous with coercion and military rule.

The role of General de Gaulle at the time of the Brazzaville conference in 1944 was entirely unknown to the illiterate masses, who lacked the most rudimentary means of information. Boganda's little Roneo-produced bulletin *Pour sauver un peuple* circulated clandestinely in the interior and the young people who could read translated it for their elders.

Boganda Stresses his Status as a French Citizen

On December 19, 1947, at Boganda's suggestion, Antoine Darlan, the Vice-President of the *Grand Conseil*, moved a resolution to substitute the term 'Equatorial France' for French Equatorial Africa. Boganda's wife was French and he himself frequently declared his wish to remain a French citizen, insisting that it was in this capacity that he conducted his political campaign in Oubangui Chari. This also enabled him to be firmer and more exigent over the principle of equal rights.

'Justice comes before charity,' he stated to a Catholic audience in France, 'before you can help us, you have to grant us what is strictly ours, what constitutes our inalienable property, that is, our right to exist, our right to the respect and dignity of our persons and of our communities.' In June and November 1949, and again in September 1951, he laid a series of proposals before the Assembly, some of which dealt with 'family, clan, or tribal' ownership of the land, and not private property, which had never formed part of Central African common law. Other proposals tackled the problem of the prohibition of all the coercive measures still practised in the colony.

None of these suggestions spared invective against the colonists' spoliation of the land, the administration's laxity, the compulsory markets, administrative cultivation, the arbitrary recruitment of workers, female and child labour . . . It was unthinkable that such revelations could be made in a house where everyone was accustomed to hearing the highest praise of France's civilising mission overseas; Boganda's proposals were consequently never put on the agenda.

'The whole of Africa,' wrote the exasperated deputy in his bulletin,[2] 'demands the end of the slave-trade in all its myriad forms. Colonisation is slavery's eldest daughter. It has proved inhuman and must be outlawed forever from the vocabulary of the new society.' He described the dilemma confronting Oubangui Chari in 1951, when the rulers of the colony still refused to apply the new laws. It was a question of either 'hard labour for immediate results, or free persuasive labour. The first is the easy way out, the way to safeguard private interest. The second is the fruit of education and patience, because the people must first learn how to live, how to develop both in quantity and in quality, how to work for themselves, and then for society'.

The Incident of January 10, 1951

Boganda's co-operative in Lobaye had come to a standstill because his parliamentary indemnity proved insufficent to cover the rapidly increasing deficit. On January 10, 1951, a dispute flared up in the village of Bokanga over some transactions between a number of Portuguese traders and the *Socoulolé*. The Portuguese always formed a coalition and this time the agents of the co-operative society protested. They demanded that the market should be postponed so that Boganda could be fetched and by the time he reached the village, there was great excitement everywhere. Trees were being cut down and laid across the road to prevent the

European lorries from leaving. Believing that he would have to restore order, though in fact it had not yet been disturbed, the head of the district of Mbaiki hurriedly apprehended Boganda, who was accompanied by his wife and six-months' old daughter. They were taken to the post of Mbaiki and kept under close watch for forty-eight hours.

On March 29, the local court sentenced Boganda to two months imprisonment and his wife to two weeks imprisonment for aiding and abetting. Being caught in the act meant that Boganda's parliamentary immunity was not valid. The Governor of Oubangui Chari approved these rash decisions, thinking that at last he had got the deputy off his hands; and, against all expectations, there had been no rioting.

However, Boganda skilfully turned the Bokanga incident to his advantage. It occurred only five months before the parliamentary elections and proved a providential electoral argument. The Oubanguian people, who had suffered for so long from arbitrary sentences and imprisonments themselves, now saw Boganda not only as their leader, but as a veritable African Christ.

Boganda's Re-Election and the Colonists' Fronde

Boganda, however, still had to overcome several obstacles. The electoral rolls were restricted to 111,201 voters, that is, about one out of every six adults and most of the peasants supporting Boganda were still unenfranchised. Backed by the administration and the colonists, the RPF put forward Bella, a male nurse, as an 'independent' candidate, but Boganda's chances also seemed likely to be jeopardised by three other candidates, although they supported his policies. These were Antoine Darlan, who had joined the *Rassemblement Démocratique Africain* (RDA), Michel Galingui, known as Gallin-Douathé,[3] a socialist, and Eugène Friedrich, a French primary school-teacher, who was head of the education department.

With 31,631 votes, Boganda managed to outstrip Bella, who had 21,637, and Darlan who had 8,288; but in Haute-Sanga, Bouar-Baboua and Ouam-Pende, Bella gained three times as many votes as Boganda. In Chad, the second college had elected RPF candidates, and the white voters in Oubangui and Chad returned Malbrant, with 2,730 votes out of 2,956 votes cast. The RPF did not conceal its disappointment at Boganda's re-election, and the *Etincelle de l'*AEF wrote: 'The ex-Abbé cannot last much longer . . . with such a feeble victory . . . Profit while you can, Father, and rest in the House a while more. You are not likely to be returned a third time.'

The Europeans of Bangui, who had responded to Malbrant by trying to replace the ebullient Boganda by the insignificant and obliging Bella, gave vent to their indignation during the budgetary session of the *Conseil Représentatif.* On October 27, they accused the Oubanguian councillors of indulging in 'anti-French remarks' and 'threats', and of 'insulting ex-servicemen'. Seven resigned, on the grounds that they could no longer 'sit beside the adversaries of France'. They insisted that the Assembly 'had disqualified itself in the basest manner possible before an administration lacking in all sene of dignity because it had failed to protest when injurious accusations were levelled at France and its ex-servicemen'.

The administration resigned itself to accepting the logical and practical consequences of Boganda's return to office. In any case, since 1950, the French government had radically modified its policy toward many African countries. François Mitterand and his friends from the *Union Démocratique et Socialiste de la Résistance* (UDSR) had succeeded in wresting the RDA from the clutches of the Communist Party. In French Equatorial Africa, a considerable reshuffle of the administration followed the elections, and in July 1951, the head of Lobaye, and the head of the district of Mbaiki, who had been responsible for arresting the deputy, were both transferred. The legal proceedings were quietly dropped.

Finally, in October, the director of the Department of Political Affairs in the Ministry for Overseas France, Paul Chauvet, a friend of François Mitterand's, was appointed High Commissioner at Brazzaville, and the previous Governor, Aimé Grimald, the General Secretary of French Equatorial Africa, was placed in charge of the territory of Oubangui Chari. These two upright, level-headed men gave the administration firm injunctions to observe political neutrality. They were also plainly determined to put an end to the colonists' reluctance to introduce reforms. And on January 31, 1952, the first visit by a Minister for Overseas

83

France, Louis Jacquinot, took place and constituted a historical event for the much-neglected territory.

Towards Autonomy

Ineluctable Change

Boganda's success was equivalent to a defeat for the colonial administration and the recognition of the need for a medium term change of staff in 1952 was a significant step forward. Paul Chauvet, the Governor-General, recommended that the educated members of the population, who hitherto had been debarred from positions of responsibility by 'traditions, routine and even our own prejudices' should be granted easier access to 'administrative and advisory posts'. He regarded rapid promotion for African officials as essential if the change was to be made 'with us and with our guidance'; otherwise 'it would inevitably be achieved without us and against us'. But the task was far from simple. For years, no post higher than that of common clerk had been envisaged for any Oubanguian employee and the first promotions to posts of special agent, tax-collector and paymaster in the districts naturally proved disastrous. Bangui had no proper establishment for training officials at the time and no funds had been set aside to create one.

The Governor-General and the head of the territory also gave instructions[4] for traditional chiefs to be reinstated 'wherever possible', but this was a measure which came forty years too late. The only chiefs left in Oubangui Chari were administrative, the tax-collectors and game-keepers, who received their authority from the white official. Another idea was to de-centralise the administration, on the model of the reforms in Indo-China, and create a sort of local government under the direction of the secretaries of the heads of the cantons. But here again Chauvet and Grimald had to admit that the measure was impracticable in view of the total lack of competent men.

By asking the goverors and the administrators 'not to neglect the government of men on the pretext that the administration of things needed their full attention', the High Commissioner was

84

really admitting that the efforts of the colonial administration were largely limited to production.

Unprofitable Cultivation

Despite the political reforms and the colonial administration's good intentions as far as the African government employees were concerned, compulsory cultivation was still the rule throughout the entire cotton-growing zone. 'Persuasion, directed at the general interest and the need for production, along with plenty of technical advice, must gradually be substituted for constraint,' declared the High Commissioner. In 1949, an agreement had renewed the privileges of the four cotton companies over enormous areas. This included the administration's undertaking, dating from 1930, to supply the companies with cotton; thus the administration bore all the charges, while the companies enjoyed a comfortable profit, even during a bad year.

The companies became somewhat uneasy however, when the Boussac company offered to set up an enormous textile factory near the borders of Chad, Cameroun and Oubangui, in return for the lease of a zone for cultivation. They immediately exerted pressure on the local assemblies to have the project rejected, but they were only able to obtain a decision in their favour by promising to build a textile factory themelves close to the Boali falls in Ombella-Mpoko. The project was carried out as economically as possible and the factory, fitted up with second-hand equipment by the firm of Gillet-Thaon, soon proved a liability. The budget had to be stretched once again to find the money to modernise the plant, because the banks had refused to provide any more loans.

There were frequent clashes among peasants, guards, cotton-boys and foremen on the cotton-fields and in the markets. Flogging and even imprisonment was a common punishment for 'infringing phyto-sanitary regulations'. Sowing bonuses were distributed more or less arbitrarily and entire villages often found that the deferred remuneration never arrived. The practice of paying for the cotton as it was harvested gave rise to a lot of grievances. The price paid to the producer was kept abysmally low, while imported goods, and especially cotton fabric, cost more every year because of the fall in the value of money.

The federation derived considerable profits from this situation. In 1950, the cultivation of cotton in Chad and Oubangui provided more than 60 per cent of the revenue of French Equatorial Africa. When the agronomist, René Dumont, was invited to give a first-hand opinion of the position, he expressed his indignation at the way the producer's wage was kept at a minimum.[5] 'There is perhaps no commodity in the world so heavily taxed as cotton in French Equatorial Africa,' he wrote. 'In the winter of 1949–50, the cotton producer in Oubangui or Chad received 12 francs CFA for just over a kilo of cotton seeds, and the community got about 11 francs in the form of export duties, that is, 35 per cent of the market price, or 34 francs per kilo of cotton fibre plus 4 per cent of the cost price of the same cotton at port for the *Caisse de Soutien* [Emergency Fund].'

The cotton emergency fund used its resources to build and repair roads, and to construct hospitals and schools. Normally these expenses should have been borne by the state. Building was generally carried out in the two southern non-cotton-producing areas. The port of Pointe Noire itself was also partly financed by these funds. It was really a kind of 'bribery fund' at the disposal of the administration, and no longer a means of stabilising prices. In the producing zones, the meagre sums the peasants obtained from the sale of the crop were taken back the same day—sometimes even at the market itelf—in order to settle the capitation tax, calculated by village.

On October 7, 1952, Dr Aujoulat, the Secretary of State for the Ministry of Overseas France, grew alarmed at Boganda's continued protests and decided to pay a visit to the cotton zone of Ouaka-Kotto. The conditions under which this 'joyless unprofitable' system of cultivation was run deeply shocked him. Some time later after a series of bitter conflicts in Basse Kotto, Boganda published an article in the Parisian weekly, *France Observateur*, relating how a woman cultivator had been beaten to death. But it was hard labour which sustained the level of production, despite the severe soil erosion from over-cultivation without manure or other forms of fertilizer. The actual number of planters remained fairly stationary. In 1946–7, there were 335,748, and in 1952–3, 337,256, but the output of cotton seeds, almost 25,000 tons in 1946–7, rose to 36,000 in 1949–50, fell to about 26,000 in

1950–1, and was 41,280 in 1951–2, and 29,695 in 1952–3. As in all cotton-producing countries, the crop depended essentially upon atmospheric conditions.

The Governor of Oubangui Chari sent an urgent circular to the administrators informing them that their services would be appreciated in proportion to the amount of cotton picked in their districts.

Coffee Planters and Mine Owners

Outside the cotton zones, the Oubanguian economy was dominated by the mining companies and the European coffee planters. On November 4, 1947, the syndical Chamber for the mines of French Equatorial Africa stated that 'an increase in the output of the deposits in Oubangui was closely linked with the measures taken to augment the number of workers at the disposal of the companies'. The Governor decreed the maximum amount of labour that could be engaged over specific geographical areas, but in reality, the local authorities, and especially the armed guards sent out to recruit the men, interpreted these instructions as 'orders to supply labour', not as an authorisation to employ workers.

This of course made it much easier to exploit the mines. The yield soared from 87,226 carats in 1946 to 107,051 carats in 1947, 118,000 in 1948, 122,443 in 1949, 106,404 in 1950, 141,295 in 1951 and finally reached 146,148 carats in 1952. It fell temporarily to 128,880 carats in 1953. The progress and the future prospects of the production began to attract the attention of the United States, the principal importer of Central African diamonds. Malbrant had already tried to interest American circles in the economy of Oubangui Chari. 'In its desolation,' he wrote in November 1947, 'French Africa looks towards America as if it were the mother country.' In 1950, a series of conventions[6] were signed at the Quai d'Orsay, granting substantial American loans to the chief mining companies established in Oubangui. These agreements guaranteed the delivery of diamonds to the American government. One American company, Diamond Distributors Inc., also increased its holdings in the *Compagnie Minière de l'Oubangui Oriental* (CMOO).

Since the ravages of trachyeomycosis, the robusta and nana

coffee plantations in the south-west and along the banks of the Oubangui and the Mbomou had all been European, with a plentiful supply of African workers. The Europeans were anxious to preserve their monopoly over the cultivation and at the so-called production conference held in Bangui in 1950, they succeeded in preventing the development of plantations by Africans. Their arguments, such as the risk of theft on the European plantations, the danger of parasites through insufficient attention to hygiene, and the possibility of contaminating the 'methodical' plantations, were mere pretexts. The colonists really feared that if planting were introduced in the villages, it would deprive them of the labour they obtained at a strict minimum wage without even having to provide food.

This situation exasperated Louis-Martin Yetina, a member of the *Grand Conseil*. 'If I understand rightly,' he declared to the representatives of the European planters, 'the African plantations must be abandoned, so that you can be sure that the coffee sold by Africans has been grown by Europeans.'[7] Output remained more or less steady: 3,867 tons in 1946; 3,410 in 1947; 4,452 in 1948; 4,015 in 1949; 3,600 in 1950; 2,400 in 1951; and 3,180 in 1952, falling temporarily to 2,201 in 1953 after a drought.

The development of sisal plantations in the east, forestry exploitation in the west, and hevea in Lobaye, permitted the hope that the economy of Oubangui would be more varied in the future. What remained plain however, was that the spectacular drop in production predicted by the Chamber of Commerce in 1946 after the official suppression of forced labour, had not taken place. Credit for this must be given to the close vigilance exercised by the heads of the districts and the technical assistance agents in all fields of production.

A Few Colonists Go Over to Boganda's Cause

The détente in Boganda's relations with the administration in 1952 had already considerably disquieted the private sector and General de Gaulle's visit to Bangui in March 1953 seemed to confirm their worst fears. De Gaulle deliberately refrained from taking sides in the quarrel in Oubangui Chari, although he was received by the colonists, many of whom had supported Free France; Boganda had refused to meet him on the grounds that he was the leader of the RPF. The general's reticence was naturally interpreted as a disavowal of Malbrant's entire policy.

At the end of 1953, a number of Boganda's hitherto most determined adversaries, including Roger Guérillot,[8] a member of the *Conseil Représentatif*, and René Naud, the President of the Chamber of Commerce, attempted to contact the deputy through Hector Rivierez, a lawyer from French Guiana, whom Boganda had met in Paris at the *Ligue contre l'Antisémitisme et le Racisme* (LICA). Rivierez had been proposed by Boganda and elected senator of Oubangui Chari by the *Conseil Représentatif*. Since then, he had devoted all his energies to improving relations between Boganda and the Europeans.

Eventually, Boganda, Darlan, Rivierez, Naud, Guérillot and Chambellant came to an agreement by which the *Parti Radical Socialiste* (PRS) and MESAN would found an *Intergroupe Libéral Oubanguien* (ILO). The aim of this organisation was to place Boganda's relations with European private circles on a proper footing and also to arrange for an equal number of black and white dignitaries to be elected so that a united college could be established. When Louis Sanmarco, the chief administrator, whom Boganda had already met through Dr Aujoulat, was appointed head of the territory, there was every reason to hope that 1954 would be a year of quiet and general reconciliation.

The Riot at Berberati

Boganda had never been popular in Berberati where on April 30, 1954, a riot broke out when it was learned that a cook and his wife, both of whom worked for a European agent known for his brutal treatment of Africans, had died on the previous day. The families of the victims demanded immediate redress and the European's arrest, and within a few hours an enormous threatening crowd had gathered in the town. The head of the region was stoned and wounded and the head of the district, the local magistrate, and some other Europeans were molested. A goods-carrier, who was passing through, was killed. Finally a plane that was unable to land gave the alarm.

Brazzaville announced that parachutists would be sent and meanwhile the garrison at Bouar received the order to march on the town. Once again, the Baya drums gave out their old war signals

Central African Republic

and hordes of villagers rallied to the support of the demonstrators. The Governor, Sanmarco, hastened to Boganda and begged him to accompany him to Berberati in order to intervene. At last, on May 1, Boganda addressed a throng that had been growing steadily for the last twenty-four hours and assured them that 'the same justice would be administered to white as to black'. This speech seemed to satisfy the crowd who only a few hours earlier had been prepared to massacre every white man within reach, and people began to disperse. The French soldiers finally took up their positions without firing a shot.

The administration was highly indebted to Boganda for this remarkable achievement. The fact that an over-excited Baya crowd had agreed to go away quietly showed the deputy's ascendancy over all Oubanguians, even the hereditary enemies of his own race, who had voted against him in the elections. The inquiry eventually concluded that the cook had murdered his wife and then committed suicide. But the rioters were not forgiven after all and on May 8 the local court ordered the arrest and imprisonment of 158 persons.

The suddenness and the violence of the Berberati incident had greatly worried the High Commissioner. A report from the security department noted that the events had 'made it plain that many Europeans were hated by the great majority of Africans. They were regarded as oppressors, who persecuted the natives and called them niggers or baboons. . . .' The High Commissioner urged the Governors and all those in positions of responsibility to make every endeavour to 'enlighten minds' and 'to react firmly against all signs of what must be termed white racialism'. Chauvet, the Governor-General, also recognised 'an African racialism, going even deeper', but he admitted that the one was largely the product of the other. 'We must learn to realise,' he ended, 'that the feeling will never die down while the Europeans maintain their attitude of condescending and ill-tempered superiority, and refuse to understand that authority and dignity are not synonymous with scorn and contempt. This is one of the major political problems in Oubangui Chari, and it must be tackled with perseverance and determination.' But on September 1, 1954, the criminal court of French Equatorial Africa delivered a severe verdict on the rioters, some of whom were sentenced to five years penal servitude.

90

Two Peaceful Years

The Berberati riot had no sequel, and in the course of the next two years, the RPF were progressively disbanded and replaced by MESAN institutions in each district. Boganda declared to the Assembly that he 'recognised the services done to his country by the administration and the educational and health departments'. He added, 'doctors, administrators, and colonists are our friends', insisting, 'We are not as ungrateful as we are black. We know how much has been done for our country.'

Addressing the *Grand Conseil* at the end of the year, the Oubanguain deputy expressed his satisfaction at 'the High Commissioner's long-awaited understanding' and praised 'the sense of humanity of the Governor, Sanmarco'. He even went so far as to criticise his own political action. 'Oubangui Chari,' he declared 'has embarked on a positive undertaking at last, after years of negative grievances and sterile struggles, and a better future is ahead. While I speak to you, free men cultivate cotton and the administration encourages them in their work. The experts direct, guide and advise them and this is what we have been demanding for eight years.'

With the help of the administrative overseers, Boganda had set up a vast plantation of his own, and he invited all the villagers to do the same, wherever conditions would permit. Local councils were established in the districts and Boganda attended the meetings at Boda and Mbaiki in person, using the opportunity to urge all the councillors belonging to MESAN to collaborate closely with the European heads of district. All this seemed to indicate that a harmonious evolution and a more scrupulous application of the 1946 reforms would follow.

The arrangements drawn up under the *Code du Travail d'Outre Mer* (Overseas Labour Code) were automatically adopted by the big companies and the mines, but the coffee planters and some of the small traders were less willing to submit to all it prescribed. There was also considerable opposition elsewhere in the colony.

Boganda was voted by the people at the parliamentary elections on January 2, 1956. Although the electoral college had been enlarged, it still included no more than 271,577 Oubanguians, less than half of the active population, and it had been impossible to

organise polling booths in every canton. In the end, 42 per cent
abstained, but out of 176,182 votes cast, Boganda won 155,952—
84.7 per cent altogether. His only opponent, Jean-Baptiste
Songomali, an accountant from the Cotonaf, obtained 20,230
votes almost all from the towns. Thus, at a time when the Republican Front in Paris was drawing up a new programme of colonial
reforms, the only possible native spokesman in Oubangui Chari
was again Boganda.

On June 23, the National Assembly voted the *loi-cadre*, which
at last guaranteed a certain amount of autonomy for the colonies.
But by November, the colonists had made their first attempts to
seize control of the new institutions. On November 18, by-
elections were held in Bangui, where four-fifths of the Europeans
resided, and it was hoped that René Naud—the President of the
Chamber of Commerce—or at least one of the principal traders,
would be elected Mayor.

The administration divided the town into nine constituencies,
one of which would allow the administrative and commercial
sector to elect an exclusively European college. But Boganda
managed to outwit these manoeuvres by standing as a candidate
himself along with Antoine Darlan and opposing Naud and
Guérillot in the 'white constituency'. It was evident that the
Deputy would be elected Mayor and Naud had to be content
with the post of second-in-command. Twelve days later, the
Chamber of Commerce led a demonstration against the *loi-cadre*,
and the small traders organised a strike to protest at the high cost
of the new institutions, which the territories were expected to pay
for themelves.

The Organisation of the Loi-Cadre

From February to May 1957, the institutions were set up and
Oubangui converted into a semi-autonomous territory. The decree
of February 4 recognised the full civil status and financial autonomy of each country belonging to the federation of French
Equatorial Africa. In his capacity as head of the territory, the
Governor held the title of High Commissioner of the French
Republic. He controlled local affairs, and was the lawful President
of a *Conseil de Gouvernement* consisting of members, elected by
the Assembly either from among its own members or from outside.

The four territories formed a group under one General High Commissioner, who was assisted by a *Grand Conseil*. No arrangement was made for a federal executive.

On March 31, MESAN carried all the seats in the territorial assembly. Under the ILO agreements, Boganda had included a certain number of his European friends on the MESAN rolls to offset the suppression of the double college system. For the first time, there was a high percentage of voters, numbering 360,000, more than twice as many as on the previous occasion. Boganda, the Deputy Mayor, invited Hector Rivierez to be President of the new Assembly. After that, only the members of the *Conseil* and a vice-president, all of whom would receive the title of minister, still had to be appointed. The local departments they would direct were thus on the way to becoming ministries.

Goumba's Government

Boganda called upon a new man, Abel Goumba, to occupy the post of Vice-President of the *Conseil*. Goumba was a councillor for Ouaka-Kotto and the only African doctor actually from the territory. He was born on September 18, 1927, in Grimari and was the son of one of the best-known writer-interpreters in the colony, Michel Goumba, of Banziri origin. Boganda had noticed Goumba when the latter attended his catechism class and had at once appreciated his intelligence and honesty. After he graduated from Dakar, Goumba was first posted to the Middle Congo and not to Oubangui Chari, according to a long-established custom. He was thus well acquainted with the most inhospitable zones in the forest, where no European doctors were sent, and his experience had helped to develop his sense of vocation and public service.

The *Conseil de Gouvernement* set up on May 17, 1957, comprised only six ministers, for reasons of economy as well as efficiency. A young Mbaka primary school-teacher, David Dacko, was put in charge of Agriculture, Joseph Mamadou, also Mbaka, was given the Social Services, Health and Education, and Honoré Wilickond took over the Ministry of Labour. A qualified overseas doctor from Dahomey was placed at the head of Public Works, Transport and Mines, all grouped into one ministry. Roger Guérillot obtained a large Department, comprising all economic and administrative affairs. The Vice-President, Goumba, was in charge of

Finance and the Plan. The High Commissioner was President.
Boganda had decided not to participate in a government that
had a colonial governor as president. He became president of the
Grand Conseil of French Equatorial Africa in June 1957, after
being a councillor since April 1952. The *loi-cadre* was in fact only
one stage for Boganda. He considered that political action must
henceforth be conducted at the federation level and that a territorial framework was too restricted for his purpose.

Stability of Agricultural and Mining Output

During the three years 1954–6, no major political event had
troubled the life of the colony, apart from the brief insurrection
at Berberati. The low rate paid for cotton seeds, and the derisory
remuneration of the workers, discouraged any increase in pro-
ductivity. But in spite of varying atmospheric conditions, cotton
output kept above 40,000 tons, due to an improvement in the
plants and to supervised sowing.

Coffee production rose from 4,756 tons in 1954, to 5,786 tons in
1956. The Europeans had enlarged their plantations by about
6,000 hectares and almost 3,600 hectares were planted by Africans
under the supervision and with the aid of the administration.
Production of diamonds was maintained at about 140,000 carats:
147,103 in 1954, 133,543 in 1955 and 143,058 in 1956.

TOWARDS INDEPENDENCE

The Trials of Autonomy

Hardly was the first Oubanguian government established when
the fact that the territory was almost totally lacking in trained
personnel fully dawned upon Boganda. He was also irritated to see
that the majority of French officials and colonists were highly
sceptical about the future of Oubangui Chari as a viable autonomous state, though in fact their attitude was largely due to the
presence of Guérillot in the *Conseil*. His character and ambitions
made the administrators and technical assistants really feel
responsible only to the High Commissioner.

Guérillot immediately began trying to speed the departure of
the administrators, by encouraging Boganda in a violent campaign
against 'the officials, the saboteurs of the *loi-cadre*'. 'The world is

wide enough,' Boganda declared to the Assembly, 'so why shouldn't the colonial administrators leave. Let them leave our country and let our women and children send a fire-brand behind their plane . . . We shall throw fire-brands after their planes in farewell and curse their shameful memory for ever!' But during the same session, he admitted: 'We can begin to train men to work for us in four or five years time. But, gentlemen, where are the men we need today? When I said this in Bangui, I was nearly thrown into the river with a rope round my neck.'

Guérillot had also urged Boganda to Africanise the executive posts as quickly as possible, knowing that the resultant incompetence would merely strengthen the effective control of the colonists. But a few days later, speaking before the *Grand Conseil*, Boganda retracted a little by recognising the need to maintain the French administrative structure, though it would have to be given a new spirit. 'We must replace colonial methods with a new form of administration,' he stated, 'find a new attitude for the Ecole Coloniale and the rue Oudinot. We must free the overseas officials from the iron-collar of slavery and offer them a true French ideal'. He proposed transforming the districts into rural communes. 'The rural communities will be put in the care of a capable director, chosen from among members of the former administration, whom I know to be with us in this great revolution,' he declared. 'We all know their names, just as we know the real saboteurs, the men who do not wish to create Equatorial France.' Boganda seemed afraid of the isolation into which Guérillot and his accomplices were trying to lure him.

At the end of 1955, a study group was set up in Bangui to examine the prospects of building a railway from Bangui to Chad. The whole of south Chad had been included in the Bangui commercial zone for quite a number of years, but more plans were afoot to organise a Transcamerounian railway line leading to the same area, and this highly alarmed the traders in Oubangui. What was more, private investment had been dropping off considerably because of doubts about the political evolution of the country. Far too many firms, who were short of contracts, were encroaching upon the state's markets in order to supplement their earnings. The only way to rescue some of them was obviously

95

to give local trade a boost by embarking on some long-term scheme like the railway.

The idea of a railway gradually developed into an obsession, and the colonists persuaded Boganda and the other new ministers that it was a general panacea. The *Compagnie Générale de Transports en Afrique* (CGTA) was directly concerned, because it controlled the river transport from Brazzaville to Bangui, and Georges Bernard, its director in Africa, was one of the engineers. But only a rapid increase in production in the regions that would benefit from the railway could really warrant such an undertaking. Boganda asked Guérillot to work out a programme that would improve production and at the same time raise the standard of living of all Oubanguians. He had been particularly struck by a remark an important French official had made during a reception. 'Your country costs France far more than can ever be worth while.'

A Programme of Economic Recovery

While Boganda was thinking that one way of enriching the territory might be to follow the precepts which had enabled many colonists to make their fortunes, Athanase Saccas, a phyto-pathologist at the agronomic research station at Boukoko, had succeeded in obtaining seedlings of excelsa coffee-trees capable of resisting tracheomycosis. This was all Guérillot needed to imagine a vast plantation programme covering 100,000 hectares, with 70,000 excelsa trees growing on 133,000 family plantations, each comprising 8,925 square yards. He proposed paying the planters a four-year advance on the crop, constructing 77 small packing factories and engaging a certain number of 'inspectors', all of which would mean an outlay of about four thousand million francs CFA. He intended to finance this programme by floating shares on the private market. This, he said, would achieve an 'economic marriage' between European capital and African labour.[9]

As the private sector was not slow to voice its misgivings, Guérillot found he had to turn to the traditional source of public financing in France. The Governor, Paul Bordier, who had just taken up his post as High Commissioner, supported these requests for political reasons, but it soon became obvious that a substantial crop would not be available for several years. But Guérillot was not prepared to give up so easily. He considered that the necessary resources could still be obtained by doubling the cotton-growing areas and planting the remaining soil with ground-nuts every year.

To carry out these over-simplified plans of expanding coffee, cotton and ground-nut production, Guérillot elaborated a battery of economic sanctions and benefits. As part of his coffee programme, he decided that in the event of failure, the sums spent out of the national debt would be 'recuperated by higher taxation, penalising lack of goodwill'. For the cultivators who carried out his instructions to the letter, he envisaged tax exemption certificates, decorations, travel facilities and so on.

On December 30, 1957, the Territorial Assembly agreed to Boganda's request to give Guérillot a free hand. But in point of fact, the unrealistic scheme was seriously damaging to Boganda's reputation and to Oubangui as a whole. The full powers Boganda and the Assembly had granted to the minister outraged the Vice-President of the *Conseil*, Abel Goumba. Goumba was in close touch with the Oubanguian peasants and knew their state of poverty and misery better than anyone. He realised that it was quite out of the question for them to accomplish extra tasks under the present conditions and regarded Guérillot's ideas as a dangerous return to the concessionary system. Most of all he disliked the plan to set up regional economic recovery committees composed entirely of colonists and traders in each of the districts.

Goumba proposed a programme of popular education at village level, before more plans were started, with a *Commissariat pour le Développement Rural de l'Oubangui* (CODRO) to accomplish the preliminary tasks. He was only too aware that Guérillot's activities would simply exasperate a wretched people, who had been exploited far too long. He also saw that the final outcome would be a dangerous lowering of Boganda's prestige and new distrust of the *Conseil de Gouvernement*.

Guérillot wanted to organise 'work sectors' and place them in charge of the territorial councillors. He also recruited inspectors from among the unemployed whites in Bangui to supervise cultivation. They were to be assisted by large numbers of African auxiliaries also engaged from among the unemployed in the towns. These new guards would wear uniform. A number of demonstrations that broke out when the plans were made known obliged

97

Central African Republic

Boganda to travel all over the cotton zones to explain the meaning of the 'work crusade'.

Boganda Disheartened

While the Ministers, aided by the councillors and the heads of the European services set about administering the public offices as best they could, Boganda experienced a period of profound discouragement. In 1957, he had excluded Antoine Darlan, the councillor representing Oubangui Chari in the French Union, from MESAN. This had been Guérillot's idea and though the gesture was intended for Darlan, Boganda also agreed to exclude several other councillors from the east, whom the Europeans accused of being progressive, or even communist. Darlan retaliated with an impassioned attack, claiming that Boganda was entirely under the thumb of Guérillot and had betrayed the cause of 'Oubanguian emancipation'. There was general resentment all over Bangui.

Boganda finally let fly once more against the administrators, who were the supposed 'saboteurs of the *loi-cadre*', a statement which no one had forgotten. His relations with metropolitan France had become more strained in any case, although so far the new institutions had not met with any opposition. In February 1958, Boganda, Guérillot and MESAN became the object of a series of articles in *Le Figaro* which described Oubangui Chari as 'a poorly endowed territory among the very poor areas, which generally need a good two-thirds of their subsidies from France in order to survive'.[10] It was estimated that out of 100 francs spent in Oubangui, 70 came from the metropolis. The reporter alluded to the 'farcical' vicissitudes of local political life where 'some people met every day and were alternately bosom friends or inveterate enemies'.

The ambitious projects nurtured by Naud and Guérillot and over-hastily approved by Boganda, were ridiculed. 'It is a question of securing the strategic defence of the continent of Europe,' stated the *Figaro* article, referring to observations made by a Brussels economist, 'and we should risk a few thousand million in Africa if only to avoid a political vacuum. There are plenty of possibilities for workable undertakings, but when we are told that a railway-line from Bangui to Chari is indispensable to evacuate tungsten from Tibesti, or that in five years time, 230,000 square miles of bush will be flowering with coffee trees, even those who sincerely support the Euro-African idea, object to being taken for idiots!' The same journalist wished 'the best of luck' to the Oubanguian leaders who wanted to 'turn a few scraps of bush and a minuscule population with no apparent prospects of viability into a modern independent state'.

Boganda sought to fight his despair by going to the bush to spend a few weeks explaining to the people that now that the political era was over and they could no longer rely on France, the only hope for the country was to increase its agricultural resources. 'For twenty-three days,' wrote the Oubanguian deputy, 'I have driven personally through all the regions in the east to try to make the people understand why we need to work, because it is all I can offer, my life, my time, my freedom and my money.' He showed how deeply he had been hurt by the attacks from the press. 'You journalists, you professional politicians, colonialists, oppressors, rapacious vagabonds,' he wrote, 'we have all sorts of ways to take up your time. What's Boganda doing? He is planting coffee-trees all over Oubangui Chari. He has gone out of "politics". For the love of God, leave him in peace to work. What you really want is for us to remain a race of beggars for ever, so that we shall always be the laughing-stock of Europe.'

He recommended forbidding political activity in the territory altogether. 'The elections are over, the Assembly constituted, the government in place and the people are working. Any political propaganda must be regarded as a provocation and must be severely punished by the established authority, if there is one.' Boganda denounced the two-headed nature of the government and suggested broadening the responsibilities of the *Conseil*. But at that stage, in March 1958, he dared not even contemplate the nearness of independence, a word which never crossed his lips.

General de Gaulle's Return to Power and Oubangui Chari

While Boganda was occupied by his 'work crusade' and had temporarily given up politics, outside events accelerated the country's march towards independence. The Algiers insurrection on May 13, 1958, aroused violent emotion in French Equatorial Africa when General de Gaulle made it clear that the relations between France and the overseas territories were crucial to the settlement of the Algerian question. The federal structure he had advocated previously in his Bayeux speech was the only one which would still allow the harmonious evolution of all the countries.

Boganda was a little bitter at being left out of the Constitutional Committee and became profoundly aware of the disadvantages of his isolation from the African political scene. On his return from Paris in July 1958, he announced somewhat to the surprise of the Territorial Assembly that the *loi-cadre* was now outdated in Oubangui and in the whole of Black Africa. In the name of MESAN, he demanded 'the people's right to self-determination and a voluntary freely-consented independence. The ways of introducing it are to be examined'. On July 13, the Territorial Assembly, including the European councillors, adopted a motion to this effect.

Meanwhile, Boganda had been coming gradually more into line with Leopold Sedar Senghor's *Parti du Regroupement Africain* (PRA) and MESAN sent a delegation composed of Goumba, Dacko and Fayama to the constitutive congress at Cotonou. Goumba, who had risen from Vice-President to President of the *Conseil de Gouvernement*, stressed the need for economic de-colonisation.

The Bangui colonists hoped that the return of General de Gaulle would act as a brake on the political evolution in the territory, but Boganda predicted their disappointment. 'We recently heard at Bangui,' he declared, 'that with de Gaulle, we can win back the empire. I am not a spoilsport and I believe that illusions make life worthwhile. People should have illusions if that is what makes them happy. But I hope that this time they will be undeceived in the near future.' In effect, General de Gaulle admitted during his African trip in August 1958 that the territories able to choose an autonomous status under the new constitution, could also ask for independence if they wished.[11]

Boganda had altered his attitude at the presence of the word independence in the Constitution, distinguishing right and the use of right in this context. But General de Gaulle placed the African leaders, and Boganda especially, in an extremely difficult position, by stating that the rejection of the draft Constitution by any one territory would signify that territory's desire for immediate independence. He threatened to withdraw all French aid from the country making such a choice. Goumba was indignant at being put in this dilemma. He claimed that independence did not necessarily involve breaking the French connection and that freedom did not exclude co-operation. It was only on September 7, 1958, that Boganda finally gave his assent, evoking the 'dramatic days' the men of Black Africa had just experienced. Next, he went round to all the different centres in the country, explaining once again that the white men had to stay a little longer 'to set right the ravages of colonisation'. On September 28, Oubangui Chari declared its support of the Constitution by 487,031 votes to 6,085, that is, by a majority of 98.1 per cent of the population.

The Project of the Great Central African Republic

The fact that the great majority of the African territories agreed to the draft Constitution did little to alleviate their leaders' difficulties. A further delay of four months was announced, so that they could pronounce for or against a statute, which allowed the acceptance to be ratified by referendum and left the possibility of forming federations open. The text finally adopted placed the responsibility for the decision on the territorial assemblies. This meant there was a danger of a general 'balkanisation', but the risk was greatest of all in French Equatorial Africa. Last but not least, the Constitution guaranteed the safety of the oligarchies already in power, because it denied the popular vote.

Boganda was far from being unaware of the dangers of balkanisation and tribalism, which he always referred to as 'crimes against Africa', and was convinced that isolated independence would be catastrophic for Oubangui Chari. So in the short time allotted to him, he attempted in his capacity as President of the *Grand Conseil* to push through a proposal for a united state in Central Africa. 'On the political, economic and financial level,' wrote Boganda in a tract distributed at Brazzaville,[12] 'we are a minor people, but will metropolitan tax-payers always be so ready to play the pelican? Independence and national sovereignty mean doing without the help of others, and neither is possible so long as there is a tributary in one direction only and no counter current. A united state with a united government and a united parliament would reduce our expenses considerably. We could restrict the administrative budget and devote more of our resources to developing the welfare of our countries, so that all citizens would benefit, not just one privileged category. It is obvious that such an arrangement would encourage investment.'

Boganda imagined a central legislative assembly for the new autonomous state of French Equatorial Africa and a *Conseil* responsible to it. The territory belonging to the former federation would be divided into departments, and sub-divided into urban boroughs and rural communes. A Minister of State would execute the decisions of the government in each of the geographical zones corresponding to the former territories. The President would first be invested for one year only and could be from Oubangui Chari, the Congo, Gabon or Chad in turn. The new state could be called Equatorial Republic or Equatoria. Finally, the President of the *Grand Conseil* agreed to the name Central African Republic, which was geographically more logical for a state stretching from the Congo to the Central Sahara.

The United States of Latin Africa

Boganda regarded the new Central African Republic, which was a kind of resurrection of the French Congo before the foundation of French Equatorial Africa, as the first step on the road to a much wider achievement. In another address, he revealed the later stages of a project he entitled 'the United States of Latin Africa':[13]

> Next we would have to examine the question of the right bank of the Congo. Since the official historical frontier is the Congo and not the Oubangui, we must regard that area from now on as belonging to the Central African Republic. Thirdly, we must work towards reuniting the two Congos. The fourth stage will be to create the United States of Latin Africa, including the Central African Republic, the so-called Belgian Congo, Ruanda-Urundi, Angola and Cameroun.

Boganda was convinced of the urgency of the union of at least the four states of French Equatorial Africa. 'It is within our grasp,' he declared, 'and we must achieve it or posterity will judge and condemn us as traitors to our mission. . . . The Central African Republic must be built today, for tomorrow it will be too late. Our respective positions are plain now and we must commit ourselves. Chad and Oubangui Chari will surely be solicited by other voices and other means.' But the goodwill mission, led by Rivierez and Dacko, returned from the other three territories unable to obtain the adherence of Chad and without being received by the government of Gabon. In the Middle Congo, however, Jacques Opangault, the President of the *Conseil de Gouvernement*, declared his heartfelt enthusiasm. 'President Boganda,' he cried, 'you represent French Equatorial Africa, you must take up your responsibilities and wipe Oubangui Chari from the map just as we shall erase the Middle Congo. Make Gabon and Chad do the same.' The Congolese syndicates pronounced in favour of the project and a conference of Oubanguian and Congolese notables invited the elected representatives in both territories to draw up proposals for discussion as to how the fusion of the territories of the Middle Congo and Oubangui Chari was to be achieved.

But these territories were still far from being autonomous in practice and the last word, as usual, lay with the government and the High Commissioner. In the Congo, Opangault's majority hung on one vote and when that particular councillor went over to the Abbé Fulbert Youlou, strongly supported by a mafia of colonists, the situation was reversed. In Gabon, where the government was supported by the European companies, who wished to continue exploiting the forest and the mines in their own way, the leaders finally announced that they were opposed not only to the united state but to all forms of federation.

In such circumstances, the French government was unwilling to accept the responsibility and the risk of sponsoring a state or group of states, when the richest among them was to be excluded. On November 24 and 25 the High Commissioner called a meeting of all the leaders of the states of French Equatorial Africa to inform them that the letter and the spirit of the Constitution required each territorial assembly to make a separate choice by a certain date. Consequently, with a sinking heart, Boganda resolved to proclaim the Central African Republic as a member state of the Community, but restricted to the single territory of Oubangui Chari.

He gave it the flag he had devised for the Great United Central African Republic, blue, white, green and yellow with a horizontal red stripe and the star of MESAN, which was also that of King

Leopold's former state, in the upper left hand corner. This emblem deliberately mingled the tricolour of France with the three colours of the majority of the African states. The following months were occupied with disbanding the federation of French Equatorial Africa and tackling the difficulties presented by the composition of the Oubanguian government.

Boganda, President of the Conseil de Gouvernement

After the failure of the plan for a Great Central African Republic, Boganda hesitated to assume the leadership of the *Conseil de Gouvernement* in Oubangui. But his presence was regarded as indispensable, especially as the only European Minister in the government had managed the administrative and economic spheres so disastrously. Many French administrators and experts had left the territory because of Guérillot and the so-called economic recovery plan which had thoroughly discredited the *Conseil* both in Paris and in Brussels. In the bush there were frequent demonstrations, sometimes even in front of the Minister's offices; but the objectives were far from being attained. It was evident that Goumba had been right to condemn the entire project from the very beginning. Finally, in July 1958, Guérillot rather inadvisedly asked for a post of Senator and came up against Boganda, who was extremely annoyed at the way he had been canvassing among the members of the Assembly and in the African quarters in Bangui. In the end, Boganda appointed a councillor from the east, Etienne Ngounio.

There was now so much friction between the two men that Boganda decided to remove the over-powerful Minister from administrative affairs. Resolved to have him permanently out of office he sent him to Paris to assist the Central African delegate who was an independent deputy from Orne and a former Secretary of State. Boganda had rather rashly promised not to reduce his parliamentary privileges, although he had been defeated in the last elections, and had been finding the money from the budget.

Boganda was thus able to form a more homogeneous government on December 8, 1958. David Dacko was appointed to the Interior, and was also given the ministry of Economic Affairs, which was taken away from Guérillot. Pierre Maleombho replaced Honoré Wilickond, and Albert Sato was substituted for Joseph Mamadou, whose management had been severely criticised. Marcel Bouzims, the spokesman for Catholic youth, received the post of Minister of Agriculture; Abel Goumba remained in charge of the Finance Department and the Plan and was also made Minister of State, that is, Vice-President of the government.

An Interrupted Task

The first thing that had to be done was to endow the country with a constitution and to adapt the territorial administration to its new status within the French Community. The text was drawn up by a young auditor from the *Conseil d'Etat*, who merely modelled it on the French Constitution, but the preamble bore the personal stamp of Boganda. It included all the basic principles of democracy. 'In the Central African Republic, there are no subjects, no privileges of place, birth, person or family.' Both drafts were adopted by the Assembly on February 16, 1959. The Constitution listed a series of rights regarding the human person; the rights of freedom of expression, diffusion of opinions by speech, pen and picture, the secrecy of correspondence and postal, telegraphic and telephonic communications, the respect of belongings and the free movement of individuals, the inviolability of house and home, the rights of the family, the equality of rights among legitimate children and those born out of wedlock, the right to be educated, to work and to belong to a trade union, the right to freedom of conscience and to free profession and practice of religion. . . .

Boganda also drew up vast administrative and economic reforms, which included creating rural and urban boroughs on a non-ethnic basis, setting up district councils with wider powers and mutual development societies in the constituencies. Lastly, Boganda set about renewing the Assembly, which had to be made legislative. Large electoral constituencies were planned: western, south-western, Bangui and northern, east and north-eastern and Haut Obangui. He prepared the MESAN rolls and agreed to include five French citizens, either colonists or traders. Polling was fixed for April 5.

The Assembly, as defined under the Constitution, was elected for five years. It comprised 60 deputies, who invested the President of the government. The President appointed the ministers, was head of all the administrative departments, and could remain in office for the duration of the legislature. He could dissolve the Assembly by decree, but the Assembly could also unmake the government, if two-thirds of its members adopted a vote of censure and put forward the name of a successor. No project to revise the Constitution could be accepted if it endangered the Republican form of government and the democratic principles on which the Republic was founded.

On March 29, 1959, Easter Day, Boganda left Berberati on the North Atlas plane belonging to the UTA company which ran the regular mail service from Berberati to Bangui; the wreck of the aircraft was found the following day in the district of Boda not far from the Lobaye Valley. All the passengers were killed and the body of President Boganda was found in the pilot's cabin.

The whole country was stupefied by the news and many people suspected an assassination. The inquiry organised by the General Secretariat of Civil Aviation inspected the scene of the accident and a few weeks later, a Parisian weekly, *L'Express*,[14] revealed that an expert had discovered traces of a suspicious explosion in the fuselage. All the editions of the magazine were withdrawn as soon as they appeared on sale in Bangui, by order of the High Commissioner. However, apart from a minor incident in Mbaiki, where the crowd pursued and threatened a colonist, the population remained calm. The funeral took place in front of the cathedral of Notre-Dame de Bangui, thronged with thousands of Ouban-guians. Robert Lecourt was the Minister representing the French government and the General Secretary of the Community, Raymond Janot, also attended. Afterwards, Lecourt awarded the Central African President the *Ordre de la Nation Française*. However, the report of the inquiry never appeared in the French official gazette, and the circumstances of the accident remain mysterious.

Abel Goumba, Minister of State, and former President of the *Conseil de Gouvernement*, assumed the duties of President. On April 5, the elections for the Legislative Assembly were held in three constituencies as arranged, and the MESAN rolls were elected unopposed, although more than 45 per cent of the voters abstained.

On April 25, further polling took place in the fourth constituency. The seats of Boganda and Fayama, the candidates for the second constituency, were declared vacant.

David Dacko in Power

Goumba's interim lasted only a month. In spite of his assurances to the contrary, David Dacko, who had the backing of a coalition formed by the High Commissioner's administration, the Chamber of Commerce and the widow of the former President, decided to go forward as a candidate. He rather unwisely set himself up as the nephew and spiritual heir of Boganda. A press communiqué admitted that 'He inspired more confidence in the sectors of local private interests,' whereas Goumba was regarded as 'too nationalistic and xenophobe'.[15] Under these circumstances, Goumba, who was unwilling to divide the country, agreed to support Dacko, as he was already in such a strong position.

The Senator, Etienne Ngounio, replaced Boganda as Mayor of Bangui and President of MESAN, and Pierre Maleombho was elected President of the Assembly, as Boganda had hoped. Dacko kept Goumba as Minister of State, but soon removed him from the Finance Department. He completed his government by introducing two of his former colleagues, who had been assistant teachers.

David Dacko was born on March 24, 1930, at Bouchia in Lobaye. His father worked as a night watchman on a farm belonging to an important colonial company. When he finished his studies at the Ecole Normale of Mouyoundzi in the Middle Congo, he became one of the most brilliant school-teachers in French Equatorial Africa. First he took up a post in a mission of basic education, and then was made head of one of the principal schools in Bangui. Before becoming a member of MESAN, Dacko had been a militant in a teachers' trade union (*Force Ouvrière*), but he had none of the authority of Boganda, his so-called uncle.[16] He appeared before the Assembly at an unfortunate moment, and anxious to avoid any controversy over the large number of texts he had prepared to set up the new Republic, he risked asking for full powers. These were refused and from then on, crisis seemed not only likely, but imminent.

Discord within MESAN *and the Founding of* MEDAC

In July, Dacko announced that Goumba and Sato had resigned; in September, he relieved the European General Secretary of his functions and asked him to leave the country, accusing him of inciting Maleombho to oppose the government's action.

Now that he was no longer a Minister, Goumba was able to embark on a virulent campaign against what he termed the short-comings of the authorities in all spheres. On October 3, when a motion of censure proposed by Maleombho seemed likely to obtain the support of two-thirds of the deputies, Dacko immediately asked his European friends from the transport companies to fetch the peasants and the workers from Lobaye and have them placed round the Assembly. In the meantime, a number of deputies succumbed to bribes and withdrew their signatures from the censure motion. The defeat of the government was avoided, but it had been a narrow escape.

Dacko thus felt justified in making a number of significant alterations in his regime and in the party. When MESAN was created, Boganda had allowed several other political parties to continue to flourish, but although the African Democratic Rally and the African Socialist Movement enjoyed considerable influence in other territories, they had very few adherents in the Central African Republic. The exclusion of Antoine Darlan and several councillors from the east had not resulted in a strong opposition movement, as might have been expected.

With Boganda gone, the position was quite different. Dacko could not identify himself with MESAN and in any case was not even its President. He was also so overwhelmed by his administrative duties that he omitted to cultivate contacts among the people themselves. Goumba, on the contrary, had more and more meetings with deputies, trade unions and students. Ngounio and Maleombho were also highly annoyed at the way in which Goumba had been squeezed out of the government. All three criticised the President's authoritarian methods and accused him of violating the democratic procedure outlined in the Constitution.

On June 25, 1960, Goumba announced the creation of a new political party, the *Mouvement d'Evolution Démocratique de l'Afrique Centrale* (MEDAC), and fourteen deputies immediately joined. MEDAC claimed to inherit the doctrines of Boganda and MESAN, and Etienne Ngounio, the President of MESAN, announced his approval of the new movement. MEDAC rapidly widened its sphere of action to the interior, concentrating particularly on Mandjia country. Several branches were also founded in Bangui. Worried by this sudden popularity, Dacko hastened to condemn MEDAC as a dissident party, promising to revive MESAN, which had existed in no more than name since Boganda's death.

The Disintegration of French Equatorial Africa and the Isolation of the CAR

Internal problems, however, were far from being the most urgent. The federation of French Equatorial Africa had been in the course of liquidation since December 1958. On December 16, in Paris, President Boganda had urged his colleagues to search for another form of association as soon as possible. But on January 17, 1959, much against his will, he had had to relinquish his project of a United States of Latin Africa, and agree to the dismember-ment of the old federation. Two contradictory documents were signed, the first stating the 'unanimous will to safeguard the present economic unity among the states' and the resolve to set up a customs union to manage the railways and the navigable water-ways, and even a General Post Office, while the other created a 'liquidation commission' to dismantle all the remaining services in the federation and redistribute the federal possessions among the four territories.

Common institutions were not actually set up until the agree-ments were signed at Brazzaville on June 23, 1959, and in any case they hardly resembled a federal or even a confederal struc-ture. Provision was made for a Conference of Prime Ministers of the States of Equatorial Africa, an Equatorial Customs Union, a Transequatorial Communications Agency, an Equatorial Institute for Research and Geological and Mining Studies, an Equatorial Post Office and a radio station called *Radio Inter-équatoriale*.[17] For more than six months, the Gabon Assembly refused to ratify these agreements, but several of the new creations disappeared after a short time, such as the Geological Institute and later the Post Office, and many, including *Radio Inter-équatoriale*, were never even set up.

Central African Republic

In December 1959, General de Gaulle recognised the independence of the Federation of Mali. This event gave new impetus to plans in Equatorial Africa, because it was believed that France could not really grant independence to each territory separately. On February 22, 1960, the four heads of government met at Bangui, at a conference presided over by David Dacko. Dacko succeeded in obtaining the recognition that 'small states, which were still only slightly developed, could not claim effective independence and economic progress unless they belonged to some kind of general organisation'. But by the end of the conference all that the four Presidents had done was to create an Equatorial African States Study Commission. On behalf of his colleagues, President Dacko sent a disconcerting message to General de Gaulle on March 24 suggesting the application of the transference of competences principle to each of the four states. He outlined the basis of a Union, which might be constituted out of these states and which could receive national sovereignty. But even this timid project met with the opposition of Gabon.

A Charter establishing the Union of the Central African Republics (URAC) was examined at Fort Lamy on May 16 and 17, 1960. It dealt principally with associating Chad, the Congo and the Central African Republic, as Gabon had refused to have anything to do with it. The Central African Legislative Assembly ratified it on May 28 and Chad on June 10, but on June 22, the Congo began to change its attitude. On June 30, the Belgian Congo became independent and Abbé Fulbert Youlou in Brazzaville showed that he too had harboured certain ambitions particularly as he was backed by a number of important business circles. The failure of URAC had dramatic consequences for the Central African Republic because it condemned the former colony to the very isolation that Boganda had always sought to avoid.

A Significant Drop in Production

Each year the Central African budget had to assume new burdens as the country marched towards independence, but each year also saw a steady decrease in its resources. Production declined from 1957 onwards with the relaxation of the control exercised by the French administrators and the technical assistance force. The 'work crusade' intended to double the surface area of land for cotton growing proved totally ineffective. Output diminished in spite of additional plantations and technical improvements. It fell from 41,292 tons in 1955–6 to as low as 33,451 in 1959–60. This setback foreshadowed the steep fall that was to follow the declaration of independence.

The coffee output was fortunately maintained, due to the new yield from the European plantations started in 1950. Although it had fallen to 3,799 tons in 1956, it rose in 1958 and 1959 to reach 6,387 tons in 1960. In the mines there was also a worrying decline, with production dropping from 108,244 carats in 1957 to 69,662 by 1960. A number of mines even had to be closed and several companies contemplated leaving. The export of ground-nuts, on which Boganda and the Economic Recovery Committee had based their hopes, was no more than 1,773 tons shelled and 260 tons in husk in 1960. Sisal was affected by the general slump in market prices, and also by parasites, and disappeared from official statistics altogether, although it was still at 522 tons in 1958. Tobacco and rubber, with production at 360 and 690 tons respectively, began to look like possible substitutes.

All these different factors made the tasks of the Oubanguian government far from easy and rendered its position highly vulnerable, particularly after there had been so much boasting over the Economic Recovery Plan. At this point it is as well to remember, however, that the territory found itself in very special economic, financial and social circumstances after sixty years of colonial exploitation.

ILLUSIONS AND REALITIES

Limited Resources, Growing Expenses

In spite of the fact that the possessions of the former federation of French Equatorial Africa had been shared out among the territories, Oubangui Chari's resources were still very limited on the eve of independence. Fiscal duties had been heavily increased, but in comparison, the revenue for 1960 was still scarcely more than two thousand million francs CFA, 570,000 francs from direct, and 1,560,000 francs from indirect, taxation.

Metropolitan France had agreed to provide the salaries of the

European officials filling most of the administrative posts in Bangui but the working expenses of the country still amounted to 63 per cent of national funds and the deficit reached 600 million francs CFA. It was in these critical financial circumstances that independence was proclaimed. Output was even lower than it had been in 1944 and 1945, when the colony had far fewer burdens.

The situation was aggravated because the value of imports increased in proportion to the rise in prices in the industrialised countries, while at the same time a definite drop was registered in the selling price of tropical goods. The Central African Republic was at a great disadvantage in any case, because it was situated so far from the sea. In 1960, the value of the exports had not exceeded 3,427 million francs CFA, while imports, which reached 4,957 million francs CFA in 1960 were in the hands of five big trading companies, the heirs of the concessionary companies, who shared the exclusive representation of the different brands. The cost of transport was very high because of the *de facto* monopoly enjoyed by the *Compagnie Générale de Transports en Afrique*, and the margin of profit in Bangui was the highest in the whole of Africa.

There was also a decline in the degree of public and private investment in the territory since the end of the Second World War. No official statistics are available for private investment, but the French government's estimate was about 4,000 million francs CFA for the 1947–60 period. A quarter, almost 1,000 million went into equipment and the modernisation of the cotton ginning factories. The rest was consumed by building, mainly in Bangui, generally office blocks and a few shops, and by the mechanisation of one or two mine workings in the west. As this figure included the money spent on organising the coffee plantations, on prospecting expenses for permits, and on fitting up a few small factories for manufacturing consumer goods, such as a brewery, it is not an exaggeration to say that private investment was reduced to a minimum.

Public funds from France were more forthcoming. From 1947 to 1959, the territory of Oubangui Chari received 8,603,400,000 francs CFA from the *Fonds d'Investissement pour le Développement Economique et Social* (FIDES) as part of two plans, nearly 7,000 million francs CFA for economic development and some 5,000 million for the infrastructure, with almost 4,000 million for roads and ports. French enterprises had been benefiting from wide markets since 1949, one of them obtaining as much as 2,000 million francs CFA and these large-scale works had brought a period of temporary prosperity to trade. In 1960, however, all the great water-ways of the Central African Republic were still crossed by make-shift ferries. None of the roads was asphalted and the aerodrome, right in the centre of Bangui, was too small to accommodate the new long-distance mail planes. All kinds of equipment were still wanting, and road traffic had hardly increased at all in fifteen years. In 1958, statistics showed slightly more than 1,000 private cars and just over 4,000 utility vehicles, but these figures included all kinds of ramshackle contraptions. The transporters' turnover was mainly derived from conveying cotton at very high rates obtained through the convention procedure.

FIDES also devoted nearly 2,000 million francs CFA to encouraging production over the period 1947–59, 1,368 million of which went to agriculture. A total slump was avoided as a result of all these endeavours, but the zeal of the European foremen was matched by the planters' ill-will. However, improvement in the quality of the plants was obtained with the assistance of the Research Institutes and the studies of the geneticists and phyto-pathologists helped to remedy the erosion of the soil and check the invasions of parasites. Agriculture was still almost entirely directed towards the cultivation of cotton and it was precisely in that field that investment showed the most disappointing results.

A little over 1,000 million francs CFA in loans granted by the Central Fund for Overseas France had enabled a few shops and industries to keep their heads above water. Part of these loans went towards building the only hydro-electric plant in the country, but in 1960, it still only produced 8 million kilowatts.

The resources of the new state in 1960 were evidently totally inadequate to meet the expenses of administration. A budget for the provision of equipment was out of the question and all the investment in public works continued to be financed by external aid. It seemed likely that the country would have to assume additional burdens, despite the economic standstill, to deal with the management expenses caused by the aid itself.

The Central African Republic appeared to be trapped in a kind of cycle of misery. Aid from the new *Fonds d'Aide et de Coopération*

français (FAC) went up to 1,215,400,000 francs CFA in 1960, but
the French government still had to supply other forms of aid,
either directly or indirectly, such as the salaries of almost 500
technical assistants, the transfer of staff, research expenses, contributions to textiles, and sowing bonuses for the planters, as well
as the inevitable subsidies to balance the budget. In 1960, French
aid had reached about 3,000 million francs CFA, a sum equivalent
to the total value of the country's exports.

Education and Health

Without a definite increase in the population and an improvement in the standards of education, sanitation and nutrition, which
are the basic requirements for any substantial economic drive,
the chances of creating a body of senior or—even more important—middle grade officials to administer the country were
remote.

The health policy practised since the Second World War had
aimed primarily at extending the service of therapeutic medicine,
but resources were very limited. The entire health service consisted of about thirty French military doctors from the technical
assistance, one hospital in the capital with 450 beds, and a few
dispensaries, generally lacking in all essential medicines. Mal-
nutrition, poor hygienic conditions and infant mortality—200
deaths for every 1,000 births—really called for preventive medicine
or mass medicine, which would be less expensive, though would
require more staff and more nurses. Mobile health centres were at
least able to check the great endemic diseases which had already
cost thousands of lives in Central Africa.

By 1960, there were 27 European doctors, 4 African doctors,
who had graduated from Dakar, 4 chemists, 4 dentists, 16 public
health officers, 25 qualified women nurses, 12 midwives and 39
sanitary assistants. There were also 428 male nurses, who were
regularly sent to posts in the bush but who more often than not
had no training at all. Additional assistants were engaged to
distribute pills to the 65,000 lepers living in the colony.

In the field of education, the situation was even more serious.
In 1950, only 8 per cent of Central Africans attended school. Under
the *loi-cadre*, however, some attempts were made to increase
the number of pupils, which rose from 20 per cent in 1955 to 40

per cent in 1960, but there was still a shortage of teachers. For the 1959–60 school-year, the Central African educational services employed 679 persons, including secretaries and casual workers. There were only 26 primary school-teachers and 87 auxiliary school-teachers, none of whom held the *baccalauréat*. Secondary education was restricted to one *lycée* in Bangui, which had a staff of 19 European teachers, 12 of them with university degrees. No Central African had taught in this school since 1959 when an Oubanguian assistant left for Chad because Boganda reproached him for his socialist views.[18]

Nobody dared to compare the number of pupils who were successful in their examinations with the country's pressing need for educated officials. In 1959–60, there were still only 37,047 pupils in state primary schools and 24,361 in private schools, generally Catholic institutions. The number of secondary school pupils had increased—930 in state schools and 473 in private establishments—but the examination results were still appalling. In 1959, 906 Central Africans obtained a Certificate of Primary Education, 336 passed the entrance examination to the secondary school, 36 took a *Brevet élémentaire* (Secondary School Leaving Certificate) and three passed part one of the *baccalauréat*. Technical education was practically non-existent as the Chamber of Commerce had always put a brake on professional training. In 1959, only one person was awarded the Certificate of Professional Aptitude out of the 18 who sat for it. The following year the government opened a commercial school to provide instruction for office workers who wished to gain this certificate.

There was no institution to train pupils in public offices. In October 1960, the training of teachers for state education was limited to 82 pupils, 25 of whom were girls; in private teaching there were 81 pupils, and 3 girls. In 1959, the agricultural technical school of Grimari recruited 17 pupils out of 213 candidates, an exceptionally high number. French technical aid was needed to fill the gap until medium-level officials could be found. In 1959–60 there were still 54 French primary school-teachers employed in the Central African Republic. The cotton zone was in the charge of 37 European overseers, often engaged from the departmental agricultural colleges. All the overseers in Public Works, or on private undertakings, and all the agents on the coffee plantations were European. In view of the penury of technical schools, it was hard to see how these posts could be Africanised even on a medium term basis. \

The Masses Indifferent to Reform, a Privileged Caste

Boganda's disillusionment in 1958 was partly due to the over-rapid success of his campaign. He had managed to remove the abuses inflicted on the Central African population for generations. Oubanguians now headed the different administrative sectors in the country, but the framework of the administration on the eve of independence was still firmly controlled by the Europeans and there was no indication that this would change for at least another twenty years. When France finally granted independence, the Assembly voted it only five months after the death of the man who had incarnated the struggle for emancipation, and yet the mass of the Central African population remained totally unmoved.

Apart from a little excitement in Bangui, Dacko's seizure of power caused few reactions in the interior. The ordinary way of life remained unchanged in its essentials and the average yearly income of an Oubanguian, about 3,000 francs CFA, was still one of the lowest in the world. Outside the big towns, the old customs persisted, disturbed only by the burdensome task of supplying a crop of cotton each year. The peasant made a distinction between 'money work' imposed by the whites and their native employees, and 'village work' (*kwa to codro*) which followed ancestral laws.

The Central African Republic had become autonomous, then independent, but in practice it was little different from the colony of Oubangui Chari. In 1960, Oubanguian society was composed of just over one million peasants, 5,000 administrative officials and agents, 5,000 shop-assistants and 30–40 thousand labourers employed on projects managed by Europeans. Of the 5,000 officials, about 500 were politicians and these, it was hoped, would replace the 500 European officials still serving in the colony, as soon as possible, naturally retaining all the advantages these posts entailed, such as an expatriate's salary, accommodation privileges and sometimes cars and even servants.

Above this category were the 55 more or less uneducated deputies, men who had persecuted the villagers and to whom Dacko had to grant ministers' salaries in order to stay in power.

Once Boganda had gone, Central African political life centred entirely around this privileged caste, who seemed to be entirely indifferent to the low standard of living of the thousands in the villages.

Dacko urged the Ministers, deputies and privileged officials benefiting from the political evolution of the country, to use their remuneration, which he had increased tenfold, to buy back the European coffee plantations. He may have sincerely believed that this would further the economic development of the country—after all he had only the example of the European colonists to go on—and that his advice was sound: 'Every day, I tell our growing élite not to be ashamed of becoming the bourgeoisie, and not to be afraid of getting rich, provided they do not forget people who are in less fortunate positions than themselves.'

Abel Goumba, who continued to insist on the need for a programme of popular education, was regarded as a dangerous trouble-maker; his attempts to rouse the peasants to some awareness of their destiny was condemned as tribalism.

Independence, which a privileged minority would soon abuse, had ushered in an era of difficulties. Boganda's premature death now seemed a catastrophe: all the hopes of emancipation the great leader had managed to raise in even the tiniest village had collapsed when he disappeared. The clerks of yesterday, now Ministers of the Republic, were consumed with a thirst for power and took no interest in the miserable conditions of the ordinary people. Boganda had called this bourgeois élite *Mbounzou Voko*—the black whites.

4. Building a Nation

THE DECADE 1960–70 will stand in the history of the Central African Republic as the founding period of a nation by men who, however incompetent and ill-advised they may have been, fully assumed the responsibilities incumbent on them. A great deal can be gained by examining their achievements as objectively as possible and trying to appreciate the solidity of this initial framework.

THE EARLY STAGES

Independence Granted

The process of accession to independence began on July 4, 1960. The four Heads of State from French Equatorial Africa, each bearing letters reflecting their diverging opinions at this important stage in the history of their peoples, were received by General de Gaulle at the Elysée palace. 'Our four States,' wrote Presidents Mba, Tombalbaye, Dacko and Youlou, 'wish to preserve the advantages they enjoy in Central Africa, especially in the spheres of economy, finance and defence,' adding that 'we should like to participate in the necessary negotiations together, and we hope that independence will be proclaimed in each one of the republics.'

When the talks began on July 9, the Gabon delegation refused to sit beside the other three. But in any case the negotiations were a pure formality. Like the other territories, the Central African Republic expressed its desire to remain within the Community and its readiness to sign agreements similar to those France had proposed to the Federation of Mali and to Madagascar. These arrangements transferred all the competences set up to benefit the Community under Article 78 of the Constitution to the Central African authorities. At the same time, arrangements were made to form a co-operation which would palliate the immediate effects of the change. France thus retained the preferential trade system of the colonial period and Central African products were

118

guaranteed a privileged market in Europe. The disturbances in the former Belgian Congo influenced the decision of French Equatorial Africa to attempt to found a *Conseil de défense de l'*AEF with the approval of France, and to elaborate a 'common system of defence under a united command'.

During a short session from July 18 to 21, the Central African Legislative Assembly ratified the transfer agreements. The government had not imagined that independence would be granted so swiftly and so easily and was totally unprepared. Dacko's dismay was evident. 'In two years,' he declared, seeking to reassure himself, 'we have travelled at breakneck speed from a regime of an overseas territory of the French Republic to that of an independent sovereign state. At this rate of development, we must take care not to miss our target and condemn the Central African people to live in fear or misery instead of independence and freedom.'

Speaking on behalf of MEDAC, Goumba reminded the Assembly that he had supported the idea of an independence maintaining the French connection as early as August 11, 1958. He refused to vote the ratification of the agreements, however, on the grounds that they had been drawn up exclusively by France. 'Our "No" on the co-operation agreements,' he explained, 'means that our independence cannot and must not be established within the narrow framework of outdated institutions in Paris, but in Africa, and with Africans, through our sovereign people.'

On August 13, 1960, the ceremony of the proclamation of independence was held by torchlight before the former palace of the Governor. André Malraux, who had been delegated to sign the agreements, made a point of declaring: 'France bequeaths you her administration, because there can be no state without management.' The chaos still persisting in the Congo was at the back of everyone's mind. On the following day, a journalist reported that half the population of Bangui watched the other half parade through the streets. In the evening there was dancing at street corners. But the ordinary Central African as yet had no idea of what the event actually entailed, though a string of independences were being proclaimed. Conscious of the grandiose backcloth of the Congo at Brazzaville, Malraux exclaimed: 'You all know that an era is ending tonight . . . From now on, we speak the language of freedom . . . Our highest honour is to raise our joined hands

in the face of conflagration and misery . . . This is no transfer of
titles, it is the transfer of destiny.'

In May 1960, Dacko replaced Pierre Maleombho by one of his
former colleagues, Michel Adama-Tamboux, at the head of the
Assembly. When MEDAC was founded in July, the head of the
government decided to arrogate the leadership of MESAN and
lift it from oblivion. He took advantage of the absence of the
existing President, Etienne Ngounio, who was on tour in the east,
and summoned a meeting of the so-called MESAN militants. He
then composed a 'circular to the deputies of the west', enjoining
them to lend him their 'moral and material support' in order to
renew and revivify MESAN. On July 23, Radio Bangui announced
that Dacko had set up the head office of the *Union des Forces Vives
du Pays et de l'Indépendance* (Union of the Living Forces of the
Country and of Independence) and that this supposed movement
had asked him to take over the presidency of MESAN. Ngounio
protested indignantly at this flagrant act of political aggression.

Now that independence was proclaimed, Dacko began to be
more alarmed than ever at the growing propaganda from MEDAC
and refused to go forward with fresh elections, although the
government's new status demanded them. Instead he kept the
Assembly that had been selected in April 1959, limiting his alterations to organising by-elections to fill the seats left vacant by
Boganda and Fayama. In spite of governmental pressure, MEDAC
still managed to obtain more than 20 per cent of the votes cast
on September 25. Most of the support came from the Mandjia
area and a number of cantons in the cotton zone. In Bangui, 74 per
cent of the voters abstained.

On September 20, 1960, the Central African Republic, proposed
by France and Tunisia, was admitted into the United Nations
Organisation. Michel Gallin-Douathe was appointed permanent
representative and thus became the first Central African diplomat.
But it was essential for the country to choose a Head of State
without delay. On Sunday, August 14, the Assembly held a very
brief session and merely adopted a proposal 'to enable the President of the government to assume the functions of Head of State
and President of the Republic until the first President of the
Central African Republic is officially invested'. A select constitutional committee met in October 1960 to define the means of choos-

ing the first President. Goumba suggested that a minimum age of forty should be fixed, thereby putting both Dacko and himself out of the running, but the committee could not arrive at a decision. Dacko consequently felt more encouraged to work out his own way of staying in power, knowing he could count on the support of the French circles in Bangui, who were prepared to do all they could to strengthen his authority if it meant avoiding a crisis like that in the Congo.

In effect, over the last few months, Dacko had been drawing up a number of measures that were destined to put an end to the democratic regime Boganda had cherished so dearly. He declared in a speech on May 10, 1960, that 'our country needs a law to curb all the old subversive tendencies'. Oh August 14, invested with temporary powers, he expressed his eagerness to establish a strong regime, ostensibly to combat the threat of tribalism: 'Since I am responsible for the state, and for the security of the state, I solemnly declare that I shall spare no pains, however arbitrary, to prevent tribal hatred from dividing the country. I shall fight all those who claim that the Central African Republic, which is one and indivisible, is composed of two opposite camps, which would be contrary to all that the government wants.'

Suppression of Constitutional Liberties

Towards the middle of November, the issues the government wished to push through the Assembly were made known in Bangui: Dacko and the members of parliament were to be confirmed in office, while laws designed to set up an even more oppressive regime than the colonial system were to be introduced. MEDAC called a silent demonstration for November 17, but the Mayor prohibited it *in extremis*. On the morning of the 17th, the territorial guard and the police summarily dispersed all those who had gathered in front of the Assembly and a few stones were thrown.

The government laid four proposals before the House, one of which suppressed all 'acts of resistance and disobedience to public authority', another aimed at 'subversive writings' and yet another allowed the government the right to disband 'all political parties, trade unions, associations or organisations disturbing law and order . . .' and finally, a fourth permitted 'administrative measures' against persons whose actions might be regarded as 'dangerous to the public safety . . .' The French counsellors who had helped to prepare the documents were either police officers or former members of the police force.

Dacko himself was honest enough to admit the harshness of the new regulations. 'You say the colonial regime was more lenient. Of course it was,' he stated in the Assembly, 'but the present disorder would never have taken root if our regime had been harsher from the beginning. The only national crime I have committed is to have let the people slip back into anarchy.' Goumba fiercely attacked Dacko's effrontery. 'He has appointed himself,' he cried, 'it is unheard of. He has put himself in power. This has never happened in any country.' And he added, 'Now that he has a majority, he is showing his true colours. If he had the slightest trace of pride, he would never have taken advantage of it. He could have made a gesture to the world, and at least ask the Assembly to elect him.'

The conflict between the two men grew more and more acute, until finally Dacko deliberately provoked an incident which would show the population that he was not the tool of the French as his enemies claimed. Giving no explanations, he announced over the radio that he was breaking off all relations with the French High Commissioner, the Governor, Paul Bordier. To his Ministers he gave the pretext that the High Commissioner interfered unduly in administrative affairs. A conciliatory mission, entrusted to the former General High Commissioner, Yvon Bourges, was unsuccessful and Bordier flew discreetly to Bangui. By this manoeuvre, Dacko had won a political battle on the home front. At a time when all the district and regional heads were still French administrators, he had become the man who had 'driven out' the last Governor of Oubangui Chari. Henceforth, Dacko could act directly against his political rivals.

The opportunity soon presented itself. When the Heads of the new French-speaking African States met in Brazzaville, Goumba and several representatives of MEDAC went to the former capital of French Equatorial Africa with the intention of submitting a memorandum on the internal situation in the Central African Republic. This document dealt specifically with Ngounio's demonstration. On December 21, the President of the Ivory

Coast, Houphouet Boigny, headed a conciliatory mission to Bangui, where he was joined by the President of Upper Volta, Maurice Yameogo. Boigny merely announced that a goodwill mission would arrive on January 11 led by the President of Nigeria, Diori Hamani, while Yameogo declared his support of the 'ruthless condemnation' of all opposition parties. The Heads of State of the former French colonies were each concerned with consolidating their personal power in their respective countries and evidently condoned Dacko's authoritarian policies.

On December 23, Radio Bangui announced that the opposition had been disbanded. Dacko had recently entrusted the Home Office to his Prime Minister, Jean Arthur Bandio, who had a certain inclination for police intrigues. The same day, the President of the Assembly requested the Attorney General, a French magistrate from the technical assistance, to compose an urgent letter demanding the repeal of Dr Goumba's parliamentary immunity. Goumba was accused of having had a poster printed, inciting the population to demonstrate on November 17 and thereby 'participating in provoking an unlawful assembly'.

On December 24, the immunity of the former president of the *Conseil de Gouvernement* was repealed. Only six deputies had dared to vote against the motion. Nicolas Awoyamo, the deputy for Bambari, one of the first leaders of MEDAC to go over to Dacko, was elected Vice-President of the Assembly in place of Ngounio. The President of the Chamber of Commerce, René Naud, who, although he was a member of the Assembly, rarely intervened, thought it opportune to state that he 'solemnly and sincerely believed Dr Goumba guilty of wishing to cause trouble'. The leader of the opposition was arrested at the close of the session, but the magistrates were still uneasy. On Christmas Day, the local magistrate wrote a letter to Goumba to the effect that he need not obey the summons just sent, because he was a senator of the Community. The Minister of the Home Office put him under house arrest in order to be sure of his person. The same arrangements were made for Maleombho and Fatrane, but in Goumba's case, the measure was renewed until the trial finally opened in January 1962. On December 29, the Assembly repealed the immunity of seven deputies belonging to MEDAC: Maleombho, Sato, Gotoa, Kongo, Frameau, Ngawé and Metté. After settling that question, the members proceeded to examine what then seemed a matter of the utmost importance, namely, the sale-price of whisky, champagne and lemonade, and why the prices were different in the cafés in the town and in the bar attached to the Assembly.

On December 30, President Adama-Tamboux read out a third urgent letter from the Attorney General. The supreme magistrate once more demanded the repeal of Dr Goumba's immunity, 'for having formed and sustained relations with Heads of State and other agents of foreign powers during the conference held at Brazzaville' and for 'spreading injurious allegations against the Central African Republic and its government'. The new French Ambassador, Colonel Barberot, who had arrived on December 13 assured Dacko of the French government's support. Next, Ngounio made a public act of self criticism and thanked the Assembly for not depriving him of his title of Senator and for appointing him to the interparliamentary Senate of the Community (which was never in fact created). He then launched an appeal for 'wisdom, love and unity'.

The crisis in the Congo continued to be a determining factor in the evolution of Central African policy towards an authoritarian, if not totalitarian, regime. The European officials and the colonists who had settled permanently in the Central African Republic could think of nothing but the events next door. The mutiny of the police force had shown them how illusory it was to hope for protection from a native army, even when it was commanded by white officers. They considered that the safeguard of their possessions and their persons depended entirely on reinforcing a 'strong regime' and imprisoning all the 'politicians'.

The Europeans considered that one way of guaranteeing security would be to reconcile the officials and the private sector, by allowing the President of the Republic and the Ministers to tighten the reins and above all, making sure that all the key posts in the capital and in the centres in the interior were held by French administrators and experts. The almost total lack of competent men, which seemed to characterise the young Republic, favoured the execution of this plan.

Administrative and Financial Difficulties

For many months, administrative problems took precedence

over political and economic considerations. Officials and colonists
had hoped that the French would remain a little longer in the executive posts. And at the time the administrative life of the country
depended effectively on about fifty French administrators, who
were mainly graduates in law from the Ecole Nationale de la
France d'Outre-Mer. They were at the head of the districts and
the regions, and in charge of the Registry Office, revenue, the
supervision of production, and the upkeep of roads and bridges.
They also inspected the construction of public buildings, sub-
stituting their own experts or asking them to intervene when
necessary. They saw to the administration of justice, the management of Provident Societies, and settled numerous disputes
between individuals.

On January 1, 1961, Dacko decided to replace them all by
Central Africans, who for the most part had been no more than
clerks. He imagined that the French technical assistance would
provide each region or prefecture, and each district or sub-
prefecture, with French general secretaries. They could thus carry
out all the work of the former 'commanders in chief'. Dacko also
increased the number of management posts in the central administration in order to employ Central Africans, whom he recruited
this time from among the former colonial office staff. All these
promotions obliged him to ask for an even greater number of
French counsellors. The sudden Central Africanisation was an
added strain on the budget because it was planned to raise the
salaries of all the officials. More staff would also be needed in the
technical assistance sector.

The President's distrust of his Ministers and his Ministers'
counsellors, incited him to surround himself with a 'brains-trust'
of French advisers, whom he charged with supervising the ministerial departments. Each time there was a reshuffle of the government, the number of ministries augmented. Mutual Rural
Development Societies were also created in each district, but they
had not one accountant among them. There was such a shortage of
shorthand-typists and copy-typists that extra female staff had to be
engaged from Europe at high salaries.

An army had to be organised, embassies opened, a judicial
system set up, the police force and the gendarmerie augmented,
buildings constructed. In the meantime, premises had to be rented

at a high cost, equipment purchased, luxury cars provided for Ministers and officials, who were constantly being asked to attend conferences abroad and were almost permanently out of the country. The style of living of the new state soon imperilled the public finances. Taxes were increased from year to year at an alarming rate and by the beginning of 1962, the situation was critical.

The Drop in the Cotton Output

The first result of the disorganised administrative and technical services arising from the sudden Central Africanisation was a slowing down in the production of cotton. The worst years of all were 1961 and 1962, although atmospheric conditions had been normal. The crop from the 1961–2 season fell to below 28,000 tons for 310,400 planters, which put a great strain on the emergency fund. Meanwhile in neighbouring Cameroun, cultivation was showing spectacular progress.

Dacko's government agreed to accept the advice of Guérillot, now Commercial Attaché in Paris, and reintroduce the old cotton conventions, with very few modifications, thus holding the administration almost entirely responsible for the output. Fortunately this drop was slightly offset by a full yield from the European coffee plantations started in 1953. In 1961, 6,773 tons were exported and over 8,000 in 1962. But it was difficult for Central African coffee to compete in an already saturated market. In order to combat the slump, the Central African Republic, like other coffee-producing countries in Africa, had to agree to severely restricted quotas. It also had to agree to prohibit any extension of the cultivation, which meant sacrificing the only chance of developing much of the country. There were also increasing problems on the plantations themselves, especially in Haute-Sanga, where many berries were left unpicked because of shortage of labour.

'Diamonds, the Morphine of Central African Economy'

The economist, René Dumont, coined this phrase, to express his dismay at the diamond craze in a country that already had such a backward agriculture. The production of the mining companies established in the Central African territory had been falling since 1956. In 1960, it was no more than 69,662 carats and in 1961, 49,500 (26,749 of which were extracted in the west and 21,901 in the east). This decline was due to problems of labour and above all to the fact that Abbé Youlou had authorised free purchasing offices in Brazzaville. These were rapidly consuming all the diamonds from the Belgian Congo and from other countries. Dacko felt obliged to do likewise and on January 17, 1961, a law allowed the villagers to exploit diamonds outside the mining concessions and purchasing offices were established.

Diamond Distributors Inc. soon occupied a prominent position and encouraged an association of the major mining companies under their direction, the *Société Centrafricaine des Mines*, known as Centramines. They also set up the main purchasing office for locally extracted diamonds. Their production output exceeded all expectations, reaching 62,934 carats in 1961: In 1962, it was at 204,038 carats, bringing the total output to 111,484 carats in 1961 and 265,417 in 1962. The average price per carat attained 7,887 francs CFA at Bangui, against 1,398 francs at Brazzaville and 6,486 at Abidjan.

Possibly some of the diamonds actually sold came from the ex-Belgian Congo, but French mining experts admitted that a few river beds, where exploitation had been abandoned by the companies as unprofitable, were turning out to be richer than had been supposed. The intensive exploitation by the peasants—who were often former labourers—infected by the diamond 'fever', was more efficient than work by paid workers, who were housed and fed on the sites. But this system of local extraction caused a number of additional difficulties. In August 1961, some French traffickers created a *Société Centrafricaine du Diamant* (SCADIA), together with some Ministers, including the Minister of the Home Office, Jean Arthur Bandio. Dacko thought this a highly dangerous scheme and immediately expelled the promoters. But a few months later, he agreed to entrust a purchasing monopoly to a joint-stock company formed by Israelis and Central Africans, ICAD, and to allow it full exemption from export duties. This meant that needed revenue from the duties was lacking precisely at a time when the decline in cotton production was at its worst. In the diamond-producing zone, the social disintegration grew more and more worrying. Deserted villages and plantations extended for miles. Collectors often acquired the stones for sums much below their real worth, but the amounts earned in a few weeks still far surpassed anything a peasant could have gained from several years of cotton picking. The population regarded the wads of notes distributed in payment as 'the devil's money' which had to be spent immediately. Lorries stacked with wines and spirits went regularly to the diamond zones and new cars were found abandoned once they had run out of petrol. This wastefulness greatly alarmed the government, still grappling with an exceedingly limited budget. And in fact the diamond attraction constituted a powerful brake on agricultural production.

Corruption in Political and Administrative Circles

The Minister, the deputies and the prefects appointed by President Dacko were not all inspired with the same passion for public service. Often the reverse was the case and many considered their functions merely as a means of getting rich quickly. Dacko had at first thought this a normal reaction, but he was now obliged to recognise its evils. When he made a journey through the bush in 1961, he found that the people denounced the conduct of the Ministers and the members of the Assembly and sometimes even demanded the return of the colonial administrators. On October 2, the young President turned his anger on the Assembly:

> The agricultural campaign I have just carried out has allowed me to sum up our electors' opinion of us and I hope you will be able to find a remedy. They think that the deputies and the members of the government, especially those in charge of the ministries, do not shoulder their responsibilities. In the long run, this abuse of office will dishearten the people, who have placed their confidence in us. Another danger menacing our nation is alcoholism, and many of you are the worst offenders. You are intoxicated from morning till night, you lose all self-control, and reveal the business of your departments and your parties to all and sundry. It would still be a disgrace to the nation if you acted on your own account, but you do this in my name and in the name of MESAN, as if you too were indirectly undermining all that the government has achieved, and contribute thereby to the disintegration of the party. The Sango expression *mbi yeke gi kobe ti yanga ti mbi* (I search for food for my own mouth) must disappear forever, and must be replaced by a deeper, and truer national sentiment.

He recommended, 'no more demagogy, no more exploitation of the masses by the élite'. 'Yesterday, we were all beneath the yoke of the colonial system, fighting for our freedom and for the independence of our country. We used demagogy to destroy the colonists. Henceforward, the responsibilities of the nation are ours.' He added: 'The people speak of neo-colonialism, but the white man is no longer its practical author. Our own élite exploit their fellow countrymen, practise dishonest policies, and employ calumny and scandal, weapons with even sharper blades, to excite and trouble the people.'

The unfortunate prefects and sub-prefects, overwhelmed by their local duties or discredited in other ways, were made the scapegoats of both the members of the Assembly who were guilty of many abuses in their constituencies and the Minister of the Home Office, who merely intensified the number of transfers and imprisonments, whether they were justified or not. The Central African Ministers were mainly preoccupied with the exploitation—often hand-in-hand with the administrators who provided the equipment and the labour—of the plantations bought back from the colonists, with the management of bars and taxi-businesses, which they hardly took the pains to conceal, and with the construction of blocks of flats and villas, using money they either borrowed or robbed from public funds. Then they let the accommodation at exorbitant rents to other officials. In this way, they declared perfectly seriously, they were contributing to the economic development of the country.

The Task of Reviving MESAN

MESAN's existence had hung essentially on the magnetic personality of Boganda. Although tens of thousands of medallions were sold bearing the double effigies of Boganda and Dacko, the latter was still unable to make an impression on the masses. A few minor political groups, generally left-wing, continued to flourish on the fringe of MESAN, such as the MSA, the RDA, and the *Jeunesse Travailleuse de l'Oubangui* (Workers Youth). Dacko arrested the leaders of the youth group, supposedly on the grounds of their communist sympathies, but mainly because they maintained permanent relations with the small number of Central African students in France. The President was worried at being left behind by the young people in the country. On the night of June 26, 1961, he even announced the disbanding of the youth committees claiming to represent MESAN. Finally, failing to reconstitute the branches of MESAN Boganda had founded, he launched an appeal 'to all the political associations in the country' to unite to form a national movement. But every attempt to bring the members together obliged him to face the question of the MEDAC prisoners, whose trial was constantly postponed. No political reconstruction was possible until this abscess had been burst.

Dacko waited until the judiciary organisation of the country was set up before turning his attention to judging the leaders. The Supreme Court, presided over by Hector Rivierez, the former senator and President of the Assembly, was installed in 1962. It had the role of *Conseil d'Etat* and Supreme Court of Appeal.

The trial was fixed for January 26, 1962, but on the 23rd, the counsel for the defence, Marcel Manville, of the Paris bar, was held up by the police when his plane landed at Marseilles. The president of the bar intervened and the trial was postponed until February 9. The Swiss lawyer, Raymond Nicolet, was to defend Goumba, Maleombho and Fatrane, but the Central African Ambassador for France refused him a visa. The accused were finally defended by a lawyer from Bangui, a clerk, Maître Hirsch.

On February 22, the court, still composed of French technical assistance magistrates, accepted responsibility for sentencing the three men to life imprisonment. The verdict explained that 'it was neither judicious nor opportune to display the details of internal quarrels before the Heads of foreign States, however friendly they may be'. The accused were also proved guilty of 'provoking an unlawful assembly'. On May 28, Goumba, Maleombho and Fatrane attended by Maître Nicolet appeared before the Court of Appeal in Bangui, which confirmed the verdict of the criminal court. On June 7, the Attorney General appealed against the arrest, on the grounds that it was illegal, but the Supreme Court rejected it by a writ, which remained unpublished.

It was a perfect political trial. Everything went off as if the magistrates, who were embarrassed by the weak accusations, wished to exonerate the government for holding the accused in close confinement for the past eighteen months, discreetly termed house arrest.

The Equatorial Customs Union

As Boganda had foreseen, the position of each separate state of the former federation of French Equatorial Africa gradually crystallised until political alignment looked practically impossible. Dacko seemed to have taken up his stand; he denied any share in the responsibility for the failure of URAC and confirmed that his government had one single task ahead, namely 'to build the Central African nation', adding, 'Later, our descendants will think of conquering a greater Africa, stronger and united'. The ideal of African unity, so dear to Boganda, seemed to have been postponed indefinitely.

But if the French government allowed the political divergences to become more accentuated, it did not permit a similar situation in the field of economic co-operation. Every effort was made to set up a satisfactory customs union, which would guarantee the co-ordination of the four states and above all help to preserve the connections with metropolitan France. But first of all, the international agreement determining the equality of the commercial powers in the conventional Congo Basin had to be abolished.

On November 18, 1960, the four heads of government sent a letter to the French Prime Minister, explaining the reasons encouraging them to reject the St Germain-en-Laye convention of September 10, 1919. This letter had been carefully prepared beforehand by the French councillors. On March 21, the states begged the General Secretary of GATT to inform the contracting parties that they no longer regarded themselves bound by the commitments implied in that convention. This denial permitted a common external customs tariff to be fixed, though it did not apply to the other member states of the European Community. These countries could thus benefit from the same advantages as the former mother country. The French experts of the *Union Douan-ière Equatoriale* even envisaged a graduated tariff that would triple the minimum tariff because it could be applied to specific countries or to specific products. In order to encourage investments within the framework of former French Equatorial Africa, a common tax system was also adopted.

Thus in 1962, in spite of its failure to achieve some form of political association, the countries which once formed French Equatorial Africa found that they were linked by economic interests, also shared by France and the European Economic Community. These special circumstances seemed to be the condition under which technical and financial assistance could be obtained, and Dacko, more than any other, was conscious of his country's dependence on France in this respect. However, in its present state of under-development, the CAR had no alternative.

PERSONAL POWER, A UNITED PARTY

The Lessons of Two Official Visits

In June 1962, President Dacko made two official visits, to Israel and to France. When he saw how the entire Israeli population were participating in the construction of a modern state, he became even more aware of the deficiencies of his own country and of the appalling lack of public spirit. At the time the sole ambition of many young Central Africans was to have a career as a government official. 'Whatever the future of the Central African Republic may be,' Dacko declared on his return, 'the state will never have more than 5,000 administrative and political posts to offer. More than a million citizens will have to earn their living by exploiting our resources. We must encourage the people to work in agriculture, but we must also train them for other sectors of our new economy, such as commerce and industry.'

In France, Dacko had a different experience and confessed his surprise at the warm welcome he received from General de Gaulle and several other representatives. For three days, Paris flew the colours of the modest Central African state and Dacko was paid the same honours as all other Heads of State on an official visit. This convinced him that despite its economic and financial dependence, the Central African Republic was truly regarded as a sovereign state. Feeling that his political action was not only approved but upheld by the former metropolis, Dacko thought that he should take the French in the Oubanguian private sector to task for their feeble attempts to build the nation and he even criticised some officials from the Ministry of Co-operation.

'In France, they have a heart,' he declared. 'They are not the worm-eaten white men you meet here on the sites! Men who can see no further than their own immediate interests. Our struggle is to draw closer to the real France and destroy all those who are unworthy of our mother country.' For the benefit of the Central Africans, he added, 'A nation is not made in the street, in cafés, or in the public squares'. He stated that a number of special privileges, such as 'the best accommodation' would be granted to the Frenchmen from the technical assistance, but that even so, 'a certain purging would be necessary'. So, in June 1962, in the wake of Boganda, Dacko adopted a positive policy towards France itself, but remained adamantly opposed to a small number of Frenchmen and Central Africans he had chosen to make his scapegoats.

Dacko had been able to draw two political conclusions from his visits. On the one hand, he considered that the political structures set up in his country were but a caricature of French institutions and that the Central African people would never fit into the framework, and on the other, he decided that MESAN would have to be converted into a vast popular organisation, functioning on a national scale. In this way, there would be room for free discussion and it would represent the true voice of the people, while the President, the Assembly and the State would be mere emanations of its sovereign will. This conception was closer to the more fundamental Central African traditions which rejected the notion of personal power. 'Just as men and women in our villages traditionally participated in the decisions which the chief was to execute, so MESAN,' Dacko declared, 'will become a mass party uniting all of our people.'

But little in fact remained of Boganda's MESAN. The few delegates who had been summoned to Bangui in July 1959, to elect Dacko as leader of the phantom party, had represented no one but themselves. Dacko, however, was well aware of the situation and his next step was to ask the sub-prefects to appoint three delegates from each constituency to attend a national congress. The 114 so-called delegates were allowed to speak and vote, and about 400 other government officials, office workers, union members, and private citizens, were selected as delegates in an advisory capacity. Dacko assembled this crowd at Bambari in front of the offices of the prefecture in a session lasting from July 28 until August 1, 1962.

'We were amazed,' wrote a French observer[1] attending the

mock congress, 'at the rapidity with which the decisions were taken.' The various committees formed on Sunday July 29 had presented their conclusions to the General Assembly by noon on Tuesday, in an atmosphere of growing festivity as more and more beer was consumed. Beer was the only alcoholic drink officially allowed. In fact, there was really no mystery, because all the resolutions had been prepared beforehand with a few collaborators at Dacko's estate in Mokinda. Amid general approbation, Dacko adopted a motion 'to make MESAN a mass party', and 'to make a nation out of a colonial territory, and a united people out of all the tribes'.[2]

In the ensuing months, under cover of this resurrection, Dacko attempted to set up parallel machinery with the express purpose of protecting his office from the ambitions of the Ministers and members of the Assembly. First, he organised a management committee for MESAN as a sort of super-government, bringing together a number of prominent figures from Bangui and from the interior. They were chosen according to a variety of criteria, mingling ethnic and religious elements, the descendants of old leading families or former masters of a part of the country, Boganda's early companions, former officials and so on. The decisions taken by the committee were to be 'executed' by the government. In November 1962, the government declared that in order to lay the foundations of the country more efficiently all the other political parties would have to be disbanded and 'MESAN made into an institution'. The party was to fuse with the state and the whole population would automatically belong. The free discussion envisaged by Dacko remained theoretical, because apart from a shortage of senior officials, the Central African Republic was to an even greater extent lacking in local political leaders to organise the branches and the sub-branches.

For two years, Dacko and the management committee vainly tried to endow MESAN with a political doctrine, claiming that they were in favour of an 'African socialism based on African traditions, but which would benefit from Western ideas'. In the economic sphere, Dacko advocated state intervention in production and 'private enterprise' at 'the level of distribution and consumption'. In this, he was merely acknowledging the validity of the old patterns of trade the colonists had introduced. Dacko further stated that 'the harmonious means of developing the country and the improvement in the standard of living of the masses' could only be achieved 'with help from both socialism and capitalism'. Finally, in order to reassure the officials, who were avid for more privileges, he resolutely opposed those who claimed that 'the present generation must sacrifice itself for the future of the country'. He argued that the thesis of 'sacrificing generation after generation indefinitely was the product of a socialism that was doctrinaire, authoritarian and shortsighted.'

But in April 1963, MESAN, though in theory all-powerful, was still in its initial stages. Dacko increased his propaganda and the number of training courses, but the Central African people were still highly suspicious. The government had decided to levy subscriptions in the form of direct taxation, at a rate of '10 francs CFA per month for a child, 20 for a woman, 50 for a man, and 100 for militants and honorary members; parliamentarians, ministers, directors, heads of departments, and militants who occupied lucrative posts were to pay 10 per cent of their overall remuneration, after deduction of various other contributions of a family nature'. Dacko grew more and more uneasy over MESAN's lack of success and at the abuses practised by the deputies in the bush. He seriously began to consider holding a presidential plebiscite in 1964 to reshuffle the Assembly once again, as it was essential for him to regularise his own position as Head of the State. His official authority still rested on a series of compromises made with the deputies, whose period of office expired in April.

Dacko's New Economic Policy

By the end of 1962, Dacko realised that the country's interests were not necessarily the same as those of the foreign states and trading companies now firmly established in the Central African territory. The *Union Electrique Coloniale* (UNELCO) affair showed only too clearly that it was possible for the state, even when it lacked officials with an economic background, to replace the old colonial organisation by new structures. A paradoxical situation in production and in the sector for the distribution of electrical power had arisen after 1954. A firm affiliated to the French Electricity Company, the *Société Equatoriale d'Energie Electrique* (SEEE), produced the electric current which UNELCO bought and then sold back to the users at a comfortable profit, because their concession was held on very advantageous terms. At the end of 1962, the *Conseil des Ministres* decided quite logically, that the government ought to take over the concession and asked the SEEE to distribute the current direct to the users, as from January 2, 1963. An immediate drop in the price of electricity and the establishment of an investment programme followed. The decision also enabled a number of industrial projects in Bangui to be set up.

UNELCO and the colonial companies were quick to react, arguing that nationalisation of this kind was illegal under the co-operation agreements. But Dacko insisted on inspecting their out-dated plant, for which they were demanding substantial damages; eventually the French government agreed to help pay off the indemnity. Encouraged by this success, Dacko went on to work out the complete reorganisation of all the existing economic structures in the country, starting with the production sector.

The End of the Cotton Conventions

Dacko was aware that it was impossible to solve the cotton problem by sending deputies to the villages to preach 'work crusades'. The level of output continued to fall at an alarming rate, clearly revealing the growing dislike of administrative cultivation. The number of planters, however, remained much the same. Before independence, production had kept at around 40,000 tons, but now was down to below 30,000 tons. The last few years had shown: 1961–2, 27,452 tons; 1962–3, 33,353 tons; 1963–4, 27,456 tons.

The crisis came just when the European Economic Community decided to make a gradual return to world market prices, which were very unfavourable for cotton, and the emergency fund already showed a deficit. Some form of financial sacrifice would obviously have to be made by the government and also by the planters, as it was evident that the convention system could no longer sustain the producer's purchasing price in such circumstances. The fund started by demanding the suppression of sowing bonuses and a lowering of export duties.

Dacko took the business to heart. He was already weary of the unending grievances of the companies over lack of peasant labour and the shortcomings of the administration, and compared their attitude with the methods of the state-controlled *Régie Française: Service d'Exploitation Industrielle des Tabacs et Allumettes*, SEITA, (Department for the industrial exploitation of tobacco and matches). The cotton companies had never shown the slightest interest in the conditions of cultivation, whereas the tobacco company took over the whole sector, from sowing to drying the leaves. Moreover, when Dacko saw that production in Cameroun, unencumbered by conventions with privileged companies, had considerably outstripped the Central African Republic, he decided that the solution lay rather in a reform of the structures themselves than in an intensification of administrative pressure in the cotton fields. He sent Albert Payao, the Minister for Development, to Cameroun to study the methods of the state-controlled *Compagnie Française pour le Développement des Fibres Textiles Tropicales* (CFDT) which had been obtaining spectacular improvements.

In December 1963, negotiations were opened between the Central African Embassy in Paris and the cotton companies, who hoped to force Dacko to reject the conventions. Such a step would have involved arrangements to buy back the almost worthless plants at a very high rate, but the Central African government avoided the pitfall. Instead it proposed that a vast joint-stock company should be created out of the four existing companies and take charge of the whole sphere of production, ranging from cultivation to commercialisation. The cotton zones would be reduced to more manageable dimensions and a definite decrease in cost prices would be the result. A disagreement between two companies allowed the government to impose a clause obliging them to give up all claims to their former privileges and to agree to found the *Union Cotonnière Centrafricaine* (UCCA) in collaboration with the state. As the CFDT and the French Agricultural Development Office (BDPA) had also agreed to help, Dacko decided to entrust the general management of the UCCA, including the organisation of the planters, the ginning of cotton seeds and the commercialisation of cotton fibre, to the CFDT.

On April 23, 1964, Albert Payao opened the conference that was to determine the fate of the convention system. First, he asked the audience of businessmen and senior officials to pay a tribute to the victims of the old regime. 'In the Central African Republic we cannot speak of cotton,' he declared, 'without recalling the sorrowful days of the colonial period. How many of our mothers and our sisters, our fathers and our brothers knew the worst atrocities of slavery! How many died, crushed by privation, hunger and fear! In memory of these brave men, who are no longer with us, we must render homage as they deserve and observe a minute's silence.'

The cotton companies came out comparatively unscathed, as a new agreement guaranteed the reimbursement of the capital they had invested. But Dacko insisted that the new structure 'was an excellent transaction' for the Central African government, although a preliminary period would be necessary to test its efficiency. The concentration of the cotton zones needed to be organised and, as it happened, the wholesale support of the CFDT was not obtained until after another two seasons had passed, because the company had not reckoned with such speedy expansion. The losses shown for 1964–5 and 1965–6 were normal, considering the very small area involved. In 1964–5, there had been more than 29,000 tons and in 1965–6 more than 24,000. Dacko's courageous reform did not really show its fruits until 1967, and his successor reaped all the credit.

Reforms in the Mining Sector

Ever since the population had been authorised to prospect and exploit diamonds individually, a number of rather delicate problems had arisen. Dacko tried to define the limits of the sectors open to local prospectors and those reserved for the companies. In any case, the latter hardly needed to be told that it was impossible to go on holding rights over thousands of acres, even if they *were* uninhabited. They were also anxious to avoid any friction between their staff and the local diggers. Moreover, Dacko realised that only an increase in the diamond output could compensate for the drop in export duties arising from the agricultural standstill. At the end of 1963, however, he also noticed that part of the profits coming into the country from ICAD, the Israelo-Central African diamond monopoly, were much lower than the duties estimated and he decided it was time to put a stop to it. Like good sportsmen, the Israelis made no protest, observing that they preferred 'the friendship of the Central African people to diamonds', knowing perfectly well that they were still one of the country's principal diamond importers.

With the help of the French experts, Dacko set up a diamond stock market so that the government could base its taxes on the real value of the stones. But he was also anxious for the accredited purchasing offices to invest in the area and above all to establish a diamond-cutting firm. Diamond Distributors Inc. (DDI) agreed to this proposition and in less than six months, a joint economy company was created under the name of the National Diamond Counter (*Comptoir National du Diamant*—CND). Machines were fitted, specialists recruited from the German Palatinate and a training course begun. Ultimately, it was intended that the diamond-cutting factory, which was the first in Africa, should function solely with Central African personnel.

This new creation was part of a very large-scale arrangement under which DDI stipulated that the advice of the CND must be sought before any new purchasing offices could be licensed. Once they were certain that the Central African market would not be troubled by any interference from international traffickers, DDI made another agreement with the government to found a research syndicate called the *Grands Collecteurs*, with provision to dredge the great Central African rivers that were too deep for local exploitation. Half of the profits would go to the Central African Republic, although it had made no contribution of its own. In this way, the future of the state looked assured. The total output rose each year, from 265,417 carats in 1962 to 402,186 in 1963, and 442,281 in 1964. The companies' production seemed to have become steadier, with 61,319 carats in 1962; 73,782 in 1963; and 59,409 in 1964, while villagers contributed at least 86.76 per cent of the total national output.

Personal Rule

The authority that Dacko had acquired after a series of electoral successes enabled him to carry through these vast reforms in cotton and mining on a scale that the colonial administrators had never contemplated suggesting. On November 15, 1963, the Assembly made a slight alteration in the wording of the Constitution, stating that the President of the Republic would be elected by universal suffrage for a period of seven years. Dacko, the only candidate, received 682,822 votes out of a total of 686,929 and with 732,139 electors figuring on the rolls. This meant that 99 per cent of the voters supported him, an unheard of proportion in the Central African Republic. But in view of the comparatively restricted number of polling stations and the lack of transport, the regularity of the ballot was somewhat questionable. Dacko thanked the people for lending him the 'magical confidence' they had formerly placed in Boganda.

On March 15, 1964, a national roll drawn up by Dacko and accepted by the MESAN management committee bore the names of sixty candidates for the parliamentary elections. They were also successful, receiving 602,962 out of 613,600 votes cast and 728,981 registered. On March 21, Dacko made it clear that the new deputies' essential task was to try to rouse the rural population from its apathy. He also warned them against adopting too many European customs. On the 30th, he 'summoned' a third MESAN congress at Berberati, which proceeded in much the same way as the previous one and voted the motion that the party's recommendations should be passed on to the government. And as usual these had been prepared previously by the members of the government themselves. Foreign guests and ambassadors in Bangui had been invited to attend the congress. The Vice-President of the French National Assembly, André Valabrègue, did not hesitate to draw a comparison between Dacko and General de Gaulle: 'And you, ladies and gentlemen,' he declared to the members of the congress, 'you, who are the backbone of MESAN, must stand united behind President Dacko just as we unfailingly uphold the action of our leader, General de Gaulle.'

The congress added another advisory committee of six members to the management committee. This was intended to represent the National Assembly, the government, the employees, the youth movements and the women's associations, and was all part of Dacko's way of establishing his own personal rule. The whole point of MESAN's existence was that it would provide the support Dacko needed for his actions. The Ministers became his employees and he frequently reshuffled his government, occasionally removing a Minister whose wealth had become too blatant. In 1964, pretexting the needs of the agricultural campaign, he even confined the Ministers to a specific geographical area. Each was asked to travel to Bangui once a month on a particular date to attend the *Conseil des Ministres*. A circular was issued to the effect that 'the correspondence of the various ministerial departments should now be sent to the President of the Republic for his signature and approval.' Dacko was assisted in this formidable task by a young Central African administrator, Clement Hassen, a quick-witted and intelligent Fulani half-caste. Within a few months, Hassen had become the right-hand man of the regime and Dacko appointed him president of a number of institutions, including an Economic and Social Council, which was a kind of co-operative chamber with no powers.

President Dacko's Economic Projects

The plebiscites of January and March gave the Central African President sufficient authority to settle the problems that had arisen from the structural reforms in cotton growing and in the mines. But his firm intention was to tackle all the remaining sectors in turn. As early as 1962, he had realised that there was widespread opposition to industrialisation in any shape or form, when the French Minister for Co-operation sent out an expert, Henri Chrétien-Marquet, to draw up some preliminary measures for a few industries. The emotion these very tentative plans aroused among the Bangui traders merely strengthened Dacko's determination to contact French industrialists directly, in order to carry through at least some of the suggestions. The movement got under way in rather unspectacular fashion in 1964 with a milk and cheese factory at Sarki, a brick and pottery works at Bangui, a research unit for oxygen and acetylene packing, and a factory to produce plastic articles.

But Dacko was also anxious to encourage more important manufacturing industries that would augment the value of the products themselves. He planned a large textile factory, an oil and soap works, an ironworks to process the ore from Bogoin, a cement works for the limestone from Bobassa, and a factory to manufacture bags and sacking from rosella, a jute substitute found in the Bangui area. The Central African President regarded success in this field as a matter of personal pride, and he would not allow the various pressure groups involved to influence his choice. In 1962, the French government promised to construct a new international airfield in Bangui-Mpoko; the experts had simply suggested enlarging the existing one although it was in the centre of the city and landings were dangerous. To effect transport to the sea, Dacko opted for the construction of a railway from Bangui to Cameroun, though this would upset the entire network of communications in both territories.

He believed he could accomplish this programme in seven years of office, and even in the two years destiny allowed him, he managed to promote a number of projects submitted for study. He also contributed to transforming the *Union Douanière Equatoriale* into a real Central African common market, and it remains the necessary basis for any sound economic policy in Central Africa.

The Industrialisation of the Textile Industry

No development programme established by European experts had made any provision for new investment in the textile industry. Central African production was restricted to cloth manufactured by the factory of the *Industrie Cotonnière de l'Oubangui et du Tchad*, ICOT (Oubangui and Chad cotton industry); part of the four million yards produced were sold in Chad.

While he was reforming the cotton economy, Dacko also asked the directors of ICOT to contemplate widening the activity of their factory, with the aid of the government, to include the whole of the area under the UDE. But Cameroun and Chad had meanwhile made bilateral agreements for industrialisation that would provide the basis of a developed textile industry in both countries, and thereby directly threaten the Central African factory at Boali. Unknown to the government, the group controlling ICOT had taken the risk of condemning its own factory at Boali and, together with a German group, opened negotiations to carry out the Cameroun and Chad projects. Dacko reacted by contacting the Willot Brothers, a dynamic French group whose energy alarmed the members of the old syndicate of the *Industrie Cotonnière Française*. On January 8, 1965, Dacko signed an agreement with the Willot Brothers in Paris, which was not published for another month. It was planned to set up a large modern plant, a dyeing and printing works, a blanket factory and a factory to manufacture absorbents and surgical dressings.

A project on this level caused a stir in French industrial circles and in the Ministry for Co-operation. Thanks to Willot's offer to buy back the ICOT plants, Dacko was also able to enlist the help of the *Compagnie Française pour le Commerce Extérieure* (the French Foreign Trade Company) and the promise of a contribution from the *Fonds d'Aide et de Coopération* to supply the share of capital incumbent on the Central African state. By promptly creating the company envisaged in the agreements, Dacko was able to force the hand of the French government. The Willot group, later to become one of the leading European textile companies, agreed to follow up the effort in the following year with similar projects in Niger and Mali. The foundation stone of the future Central African factory was laid in August 1965. The ICOT affair had been a nasty jolt to French business circles interested in Africa. Several companies became convinced that, in future, French industry would be unable to retain its privileged African markets unless it agreed, once and for all, to participate in industrialising these countries.

Access to the Sea

Credit must be given to Dacko for having understood the urgent need for some improvement in communications to the sea if the country was to develop properly. He also saw that the construction of a railway from Bangui to Chad would do nothing to reduce transport costs between the Central African Republic and the Atlantic; on the contrary, it would merely strengthen the transport company's existing monopoly over traffic on the river. On June 4, 1962, the Central African and Camerounian governments drew up a plan for a railway-line from Bangui to Goyoum, one of the future stations on the Camerounian line. An investment of 16.5 thousand million francs CFA was initially estimated as necessary, plus about 2 thousand million francs worth of equipment. The line would cut right across the richest part of the Central African territory and result in a saving of more than 250 miles for travel between Bangui and the ocean. When the new plan was examined however, it posed a number of delicate political problems. Congo-Brazzaville was in danger of having its already limited resources curtailed even more if the river traffic with the Central African Republic ceased. As a result, the Central African

Republic decided to make overtures to the Special Fund of the United Nations Organisation instead of to France and Europe, where there was a certain reluctance to antagonise the Congolese. During its thirteenth session from January 11 to 18, 1965, the Special Fund agreed to grant a loan of 2,102,500 US dollars to study the economic potential of the regions that would be affected by the project and to determine the course of the prospective railway link. Even if Dacko had been unable as yet to wrest a definite decision in favour of the project, he had at least managed to stimulate large-scale research in the regions of Lobaye and Haute-Sanga.

Plans and More Plans

During 1964 and 1965, Dacko devoted himself personally to establishing further schemes. After failing to persuade an industrialist from the north, to whom he had granted a purchasing monopoly over ground-nuts and sesame, to build an oil and soap works, Dacko turned to the *Société Industrielle et Agricole du Niari* (SIAN), which had connections in the French milling trade. They agreed to the project, intending to finance it with loans from Germany. Next, with the Willot group, he also set up two joint economy companies to create a rosella spinning and weaving factory to produce sacking and bags for transport and storage. Previously these had been imported at great expense. Loans from Israel resulted in the creation of the *Comptoir Israelo-Centrafricain* (CIC) to direct a series of research units.

Dacko also opened relations with the *Etablissements Leroy de Lisieux* to start a wood-peeling and plywood factory. The Central African forest had so far remained intact because of its isolation, but now it was beginning to attract prospectors from Europe who were uncertain about the future of the over-exploited forests in the Ivory Coast and Gabon. Within a few years, experts from the Woods and Forests Commission had drawn up an inventory of the entire forested zone. The *Centre Technique Forestier Tropical* (CTFT) counted about 2.5 million acres of valuable forest. In return for the promise to industrialise, Dacko proposed to grant concessions in Haute-Sanga and Lobaye to two big French groups.

The de-populated eastern zones had become valuable reserves for African fauna and the enormous variety of species attracted hunters from all over the world. It now remained for the Central

African government to develop hunting as a tourist attraction; in Kenya it had already proved an important source of foreign currency. But Dacko suddenly grew annoyed at the casual attitude of the guides, especially when they omitted to ask him to receive several of their clients who belonged to European royal families. In 1963 he prohibited hunting altogether, but the following year he granted two vast concessions for the development of hunting as a tourist industry in the eastern part of the territory.

At Dacko's request, the agricultural experts resumed their previous research with a view to encouraging vast plantations of oil palms and hevea in Lobaye. A national company, the *Société Nationale d'Exploitation Agricole* (SNEA) was created to plant two consecutive areas of almost 5,000 acres each. But although the experts had planned the project down to the last detail, it sank into oblivion in Paris and Brussels. At about the same time the *Fonds d'Aide et de Coopération* and the *Fonds Européan* were proceeding with similar but more ambitious projects in the Ivory Coast and Cameroun. Finally, technical difficulties and staff problems jeopardised the launching of the SNEA altogether. Dacko, however, managed to conclude a satisfactory arrangement with the *Régie Française des Tabacs* to found a *Société Franco-Centrafricaine des Tabacs* (FCT) for the production and export of almost a thousand tons of high quality tobacco.

In 1964, he turned to the organisation and training of the peasants. With the help of the French BDPA he created a few *Offices Régionaux du Développement* (ORD), which meant that the over-worked Central African prefects and sub-prefects could hand over their economic departments to the new directors, who were all from the French technical assistance. The number of experts available was nevertheless restricted and some departments were still unable to settle the debts they had run up over several years of co-operative activities.

The *Jeunesse Pionnière Nationale* (JPN) was an attempt to create centres on the lines of the kibbutzim in Israel, and several youth camps were founded in the villages and placed under the direction of Israeli officers. However, not only did the experiment fail to stimulate the peasants, it even roused them to anger, as they felt strongly about what René Dumont called 'a new category of privileged rural castes', The 'rural public service' was an expensive

145

failure. Each of the villages had cost from 25 to 30 million francs CFA to organise and the budget had no reserves that could possibly meet this sum. Somebody had misunderstood the lesson taught by the disastrous 'paysannat' system of village administration during the colonial period.

Uneasiness at Home

The revolution in Brazzaville from August 13 to 15, 1963, made a profound impression on Dacko, particularly as the French government did nothing to prevent the overthrow of Abbé Youlou. He determined, however, to persevere with the decisions taken at Berberati, first creating the *Union Générale des Travailleurs Centrafricaines* (UGTC) in an attempt to control trade union activities which had been responsible for the uprising in the Congo. Next Dacko obliged Central African students in France to form a government controlled association. He also took great pains to conceal the numerous difficulties in the sub-prefectures and prefectures and the frequent conflicts among officials, Ministers, notables and leading members of the party.

A decree issued on November 6, 1964, set up 'vigilance committees' in each sub-prefecture for the purpose of settling the growing differences between MESAN and the representatives of the government. On the 20th, a law made it possible for a representative of MESAN to assume the functions of village chief or mayor. It was also stated that the presidents of the sub-branches and the branches of MESAN automatically became presidents of the local councils in the sub-prefectures or prefectures. These measures revealed that in practice there was really no proper state or party structure left, just a vast network of taxation benefiting the State and MESAN and fusing their respective funds. A great part of the sums collected simply lined the pockets of the General Secretary of the party, Charles Ondomat, and a few other official members. The peasant population was literally dispossessed of all that it managed to save and as usual their sole means of defence was inertia. They dissociated themselves more and more from 'money work' and above all from the cultivation of cotton. If a peasant improved a plot of land, he was a prey to the rapacity of the tax-collectors of the administration and of the party. Under these

conditions the 1965–6 cotton season proved disastrous. The estimate was finally made after the regime had fallen: 24,445 tons.

President Dacko also re-imposed a form of forced labour. On
April 9, 1965, he launched the operation *kwa to kodro*, meaning
'village work'; when he declared: 'I want to see each man, each
labourer, peasant, government official and trader use his own hands
to build a house, repair a road, and plant trees,' he was really
prescribing a return to the generalised hard labour of the colonial
days to carry out projects in the general interest.

Salaried workers and traders had been compelled to save a certain amount of money in order to subscribe to a national loan in
aid of social and economic development; in these circles the
feeling of discontent was even stronger. The inhabitants of each
sub-prefecture were invited to pay subscriptions. In practice the
system worked through deductions made from the government
employees' salaries, and in the case of the rural populations, by
tax-collection similar to the capitation tax. All these factors
aggravated the general dissatisfaction, especially as the Ministers,
members of parliament and members of the management committee continued to live in a very grand manner.

But Dacko threatened to come down once again on the heads of
the administrative departments. On May 13, 1965, he declared:
'It is unthinkable that at the very moment when the *Conseil des
Ministres* evolves a series of measures to put an end to such crimes
as the increasing misappropriation of the funds of the state, certain
directors should publicly squander our money. What better proof
is there of their total irresponsibility. Look at our peasants, who
earn their living by the sweat of their brow, and tell me if you do
not feel the need to come to their aid. How is it then that the money
reserved to improve the lot of these hard-working people can be
taken and ruthlessly dissipated? From now on there will be no
mercy. Those who deceive us and rob us are placing our entire
development in peril. They must be punished as an example and
condemned to the hardest labour.'

These threats were proof of Dacko's distress. There was growing
dissension among the deputies; the President of the Assembly,
Adama-Tamboux, who had just published a collection of his own
speeches (taken down by a devoted councillor), no longer concealed his desire to replace the Head of State. Tamboux had been

147

to France and Europe on a number of occasions to show his friendliness towards the former metropolis and the countries of the European Economic Community. The young officials rebelled against Dacko's accusations and threats. 'Nobody can weigh the present embezzlements,' wrote Bamboté, the leader-writer of *Terre Africaine*, 'against the future of the country, that is, against its youth, who are the ones who will inherit the national administration.' He taxed Dacko with plotting an appeal to the members of the foreign technical assistance in order to extricate himself from a tricky situation.

Dacko read this article while he was in France. He had suddenly decided to take a fifty-day trip abroad with a suite supposedly representing the diverse elements of the population. This impromptu visit caused some embarrassment in the Chancelleries, and Dacko finally felt obliged to leave out London because the British government did not seem sufficiently pressing in its response to his desire to visit the country. In Rome he was received by the Pope. On his return to Bangui, he organised a popular meeting at the Boganda stadium on August 1. But it seemed as if the school-master had already lost control of his class.

A Rash Foreign policy

As Head of a comparatively diminutive State, directly dependent on France for constant financial and technical assistance, Dacko was not in a position to contemplate an adventurous foreign policy. The all-powerful trading companies always kept an eye open for any new departures likely to harm their privileges. Therefore, when Dacko opened negotiations with the Soviet Union in 1960 his action provoked such an outcry that he put off taking any further decision until a more opportune time. However, when he attended the OAU conference in 1963, he was struck by the fact that many other African Heads of State had acquired much more freedom of action in the field of diplomacy.

A number of events in 1964 led Dacko to essay a new diplomatic policy. First there was General de Gaulle's recognition of the Chinese People's Republic, followed by the speedy departure of French troops from the Central African Republic; then a message from Nkrumah suggesting Bangui as the seat for a future government of a United Africa. On January 22, 1964, a popular republic had been proclaimed in Zanzibar, and on February 4, Chou En-Lai had made a speech in Mogadishu expressing his delight at the 'excellent revolutionary situation' existing in Africa. On February 5, Dacko declared that 'it was natural to recognise a country that had 800 million inhabitants'. Yet, a few days later, he applauded the intervention of French parachutists at Libreville to reinstate President Mba. In August, he sent a mission to Moscow and Peking, led by Ferdinand Bassamongou, the new president of the Economic Council. The mission was still in North Korea when he sent another delegation to South Korea and Taiwan. On May 15, the Central African government had signed a treaty with Chiang Kai-shek's Taiwan regime. On September 29, Dacko signed another agreement, this time with a representative of Peking who had come to Bangui specially for the purpose, with a view to obtaining an interest-free loan of one thousand million francs CFA. The French Ambassador was extremely annoyed at not being informed until October 9. 'If we widen our horizons, this does not mean that we forget our old friendships,' Dacko insisted, 'but we shall be able to count on fresh support for our plans.' However, the Central African Republic was just a little too near to Congo-Kinshasa for the opening of a Chinese Embassy at Bangui to pass without comment. Dacko seemed to have been banking on the success of the pro-Chinese regimes at Brazzaville and Stanleyville and was eager to open relations with Peking before the proximity of these left-wing tendencies affected the situation in his own country.

The intervention of Belgian and American troops at Stanleyville on November 29, 1964, both irritated and worried Dacko. 'How can we speak of foreign policy,' he asserted angrily, 'without expressing our sincere distress at the tragedy overtaking our brothers across the Oubangui. Since Tuesday, what was once the eastern province of the Congo has been transformed into a blazing furnace where American and Belgian imperialists burn, kill, and murder. Their very presence kills the defenceless humble peasants, and hundreds of hostages have perished because of their aggression. Perhaps the so-called insurgent Negroes defend their exploited lands too fiercely, perhaps their nationalism is too selfish, and innocent whites are sacrificed in the name of occult interests, that no one understands. These men, who have given their lives, prove once again that the independence of the old colonies is still too frail for the luxuries of division and demagogy. The day we too begin to fight among ourselves, others will intervene under any pretext because their sole desire is to show the world that Africa has got off to a bad start[3] and that Africans are adolescents, incapable of building a country.'

On December 22, 1964, Dacko tried to swing away from Washington by signing a treaty with Moscow over the partial prohibition of nuclear experiments. But 1965 ushered in all kinds of diplomatic problems. One of China's foremost African special- ists, Mieng Yeng, was posted from Zanzibar to Bangui. While the French troops were being withdrawn, Chinese missions began to arrive on both a temporary and a permanent basis, much to the dislike of the traders, who thought the Chinese took too great an interest in the people's everyday life. A great Chinese fair was organised for the end of the year. Dacko had not realised that Frenchmen in Africa were not necessarily anxious to share their trading profits with the Chinese, even if their government had recognised China. When Houphouet Boigny, Leon Mba, Tombal- baye and Ahidjo all declared their hostility to the China of the Peking government, Dacko found himself comparatively isolated. The elimination of Ben Bella and Colonel Mobutu's seizure of power in Kinshasa, made him wonder whether he might not have been too hasty in playing this Chinese card.

In November 1965, he requested the Chinese Ambassador to pay the second portion of the loan in cash and not in kind as had been arranged; but the Peking representative refused point blank. Suddenly Dacko saw that all the foreign nations involved in Africa—and above all in the Congo—put their own interests first, and that there was no greater danger for a weak African government than to try to take advantage of all of them at the same time.

A Common Market in Central Africa: the UDEAC

During 1963, 1964 and 1965, a series of conferences was held to try to transform the *Union Douanière Equatoriale* into a true Central African common market. There were evident advantages in such an arrangement for France and the European countries who supplied and bought products from the equatorial territories. In a region which was dominated by vast densely populated states like Nigeria, the Sudan, Mali and the Congo, the only way to obtain security for investment and the development of communications and industralisation was to have some kind of organisation along these lines. The government of Gabon and its councillors took an active part in elaborating a closer economic union to link the states of former French Equatorial Africa and Cameroun.

One of the major problems to be solved was the distribution of duties among the five states. The lack of customs frontiers between them and the fact that the same trading companies dominated the import trade in each, meant that in the end the existing systems were never put into practice. A large number of commodities went through customs in the Congo and were afterwards forwarded to the Central African Republic and Chad duty-free. Finally, the states agreed to create a common fund, to comprise the inclusive contributions from each state and distribute them yearly according to statistics. This method provoked all sorts of complications, and both the Central African Republic and Chad claimed that they suffered under the arrangement.

Another source of friction was transport; three of the countries still depended on the river for their trade. In Bangui, the traders hoped that a railway line would replace the road and connect the river with Chad. In Cameroun a railway was already being built across the country and would eventually reach Chad and the Central African Republic. Any change would mean that the association for the *Union Douanière Equatoriale*, the *Agence trans-équatoriale de communications* (ATEC), would have to revise its structures, but as the whole project seemed likely to upset a number of interests, it was eventually dropped.

A treaty setting up the *Union Douanière et Economique de l'Afrique Centrale* (UDEAC) was at last signed at Brazzaville on December 8, 1964, and Dacko succeeded in locating the main office of the General Secretariat at Bangui. This agreement guaranteed an alignment on an economic level, which was close to what Boganda had desired in the political field. In spite of the difficulties likely to arise from the distribution of the duties, the co-ordination of transport and the distribution of industries, it seemed a positive achievement in so far as the economic development of the Central African Republic was concerned. The Brazzaville treaty was to be enforced on January 1, 1966, and a former

151

Central African Republic

Camerounian Minister, Charles Onana Awana, who had been appointed General Secretary, took up residence in Bangui.

Dacko and the Diamond Traffickers

Dacko had been very cautious up to 1965 over the question of allowing professional persons of doubtful character to enter the Central African diamond market. He had agreed that the National Diamond Counter should be consulted before licences for purchasing offices were granted; but in September 1965 a number of licences were obtained by persons who had not completed these formalities. The old accredited purchasing offices decided to ask Dacko to reconsider this form of authorisation and he hastily decided to suspend it altogether. The general excitement in the diamond world caused a lot of misunderstandings and on December 21, a friend of Dacko's, Jean Hubler, one of the former administrators of Overseas France and director of a purchasing office since 1961, was ambushed and murdered near Bangui.

Dacko Ready to Give Up

When Dacko presented the Assembly with budget proposals for 1966 reducing expenditure by about two thousand million francs CFA, he knew he was committing political suicide. For more than seven years, the privileged class of politicians and officials had been living on a very grand scale compared with the prospects they had known under the colonial regime and they were still not prepared to make any sacrifices. Colonel Jean-Bedel Bokassa, who had taken over the Ministry of War on his own initiative, went to the Assembly in person to protest about the reduced allocations to the army.

The officials' union planned a general strike and the President of the Assembly, Adama-Tamboux, hastened to reveal his long-cherished desire to become President of the Republic. During the last *Conseil des Ministres*, Dacko admitted his utter weariness of power and declared that he would resign. But there were so many men with such diverse ambitions that the only outcome would be chaos, and he was eventually persuaded to remain in office a little longer. In what was to be his last speech to the Assembly, he enjoined his collaborators not to yield to Western customs and to abstain from all festivities during the Christmas period.

152

5. Military Leadership

A Soldier in Power

New Year's Eve

The events which took place on the night of December 31, 1965, verged on the fantastic. First there was a telephone call from Izamo, the Chief of Police, to the Chief of Staff, Colonel Bokassa. The two men had not been on speaking terms since the budget debate as Bokassa considered the army had been sacrificed to the police. Izamo now invited Bokassa to a New Year's Eve cocktail party, but Bokassa had been warned that this was a ruse to have him arrested. In fact, both men seem to have been hatching a *coup d'état*.[1] Bokassa outwitted Izamo by asking him to call first at the camp at Roux to sign some documents that had to be completed at the end of the year. When Izamo arrived at about seven o'clock he was placed under arrest. At about eleven, in accordance with a plan which had been minutely prepared by Captain Banza, the army entered the administrative centre of the town and surrounded the palace. Dacko was dining in town with friends. When he learned of the crisis he set off for his native district, only to be arrested by Lieutenant Seremale and brought back to the presidential palace. At 3.20 next morning Colonel Bokassa made him sign a statement handing over all powers.

Meanwhile, there was violent shooting between soldiers and police, and the villas occupied by Ministers were sacked. Bonfires of their clothes were made, and the Ministers themselves were bundled into lorries and driven off to the military camp. Firing continued until next morning. The airfield was put out of action making it impossible to land or take off. Officially the shooting caused eight deaths, including that of Maurice Dejean, a former Foreign Minister. In front of the radio station lay the body of the night-watchman who had attempted to stave off automatic fire with his bow and arrows.

During the morning of January 1, Bokassa announced over Radio Bangui: 'Since 3.20 this morning the government has been

153

taken over by the army. President Dacko and his ministry have resigned. The hour of justice has sounded. The bourgeoisie is no more, and a new era of equality between all citizens is beginning.' The whole city was stupefied, but most amazed of all were the French inhabitants of Bangui, who had been overtaken by events as they were ushering in the New Year. The gates of the prison were thrown open and the prisoners mixed with the crowd which had gathered as the news spread. The end of the Dacko regime was greeted with relief. Bokassa claimed that Izamo and his 'pro-Chinese accomplices' had planned to seize power, and that only his own prompt intervention had saved the President's life.

Colonel Jean-Bedel Bokassa and the Conspirators

The man to whom Dacko was forced to cede power was a relation of Boganda's. He was born on February 22, 1921, in the village of Boubangui, in Lobaye. When he was six, his father had died as the result of official ill-treatment, and his mother committed suicide from grief. Bokassa, like Boganda, was brought up in Catholic missions in Mbaiki, Bangui, and Brazzaville. In 1939 he joined the French army. On December 1, 1956, after seventeen years of faithful service, he was promoted second lieutenant under the *loi-cadre*. On January 1, 1960, he returned to Bangui with the rank of lieutenant to form President Dacko's war cabinet. In 1963, when a major, he was appointed Chief of Staff at the Ministry of Defence.

The first steps he took after the *coup d'état* shed some light on the putsch, which was described as a 'hold-up of the Treasury',[2] and he revealed the names of those who had taken part in the conspiracy. On January 2 he announced a series of new measures. The Assembly could be regarded as dissolved as there would be new elections. Parliament would continue to function. The Chinese were to be expelled.

During the night of January 2–3, a new government was formed and adopted the name of Revolutionary Council. The list of Ministers left no room for doubt as to who had organised the putsch. It now appeared that the army had followed the lead given by certain of Dacko's Ministers and various senior officials. But all three categories of conspirators were equally represented in the new government. There were three army men: Captain Alexandre

Banza (Finance and Ex-Servicemen); Lieutenant Timothée Malendoma (Economy); and Police Lieutenant André Magalé (Health and Social Affairs). There were three former Ministers, including Jean Arthur Bandio, Dacko's Home Secretary, now returned from France, where he had been for the last six months supposedly taking a cure, the Foreign Minister and Dominique Guéret, National Education Minister. Lastly there were three young civil servants: Ange Patassé, inspector of the regional development offices (Minister of Development); Antoine Kezza, director of public offices (Labour); and Maurice Gamana-Leggos, prefect at Bangui.

A Temporary Regime

On January 4, Bokassa enlisted the aid of Dacko's legal adviser, who hastily drew up two constitutional documents to serve as the basis of the new regime. The first authorised the President to deal by decree with circumstances as they arose; the decrees were to be discussed by the *Conseil des Ministres*. The constitution of November 20, 1964, was abolished and was to be replaced by a new one 'submitted to the will of the people'. The second document set out the structure of the provisional regime in fourteen rather sketchy articles, the thirteenth of which 'took note of' the dissolution of the National Assembly, the Constitutional Council, and the Economic and Social Council.

Apparently Colonel Bokassa did not intend to remain in power long. Visiting the *Jeunesse Pionnière Nationale* in the camp at Kolongo, he told them he had acted in order to put an end to 'the extravagant policies of the previous regime which were frittering away the national income'. He said in conclusion: 'I want the Central African people to know that as soon as order is restored and the economy is on a firm footing again, I, who am a soldier not a politician, shall feel it my duty to put forward President Dacko as candidate in the elections. If he wins, he will return to power. If another Central African is elected, then *he* will take over. But until then, President Dacko must stand aside while I try to bring the situation back to normal.'

Although the population as a whole were completely uninvolved in the *coup d'état*, there were many examples of their satisfaction at being freed from the contributions levied on them by MESAN.

In all his speeches Bokassa was careful to make a distinction between Dacko—whom he referred to as his 'cousin and his guest'—and his entourage. He attacked 'certain members of the government' who had 'lost all national conscience' and 'indulged in all kinds of exactions, malpractices, theft and embezzlement'. He called the National Assembly 'a lifeless organ no longer representing the people'. The heads of the general secretariat and the management committee of MESAN were 'a band of thieves and swindlers'. The Ministry of Home Security 'had become a people's army'. Certain senior civil servants used their offices to meet their lady friends. And so on. He dwelt on the fact that the peasants had been dispossessed by the agents of the party. But despite his attacks on what he called the 'privileged bourgeoisie', he was careful to conciliate them by denouncing the reduction in civil service salaries, the abolition of student grants, and the retrenchment on foreign missions. He blamed the country's constant recourse to foreign aid on the misdeeds of the Dacko government.

'The abuses of the government,' he asserted, 'have so aggravated our economic position that there is practically nothing left of the state's reserves. Yet we were always asking for more money from France, America and more or less everywhere. What we must do is work and produce our own money before we ask the help of others.' The army was rewarded for its action. Officers received promotion and increases in their salaries. Many were decorated. As proof of a plot against the army, Bokassa presented to the population about 100 rifles and almost 300 ordinary and machine pistols, said to have been found on the premises of the Home Security Ministry, managed by Jean-Baptiste Mounoumbaye, a police officer, who was Dacko's faithful body-guard. He had managed to escape, and Bokassa, calling him 'chief of secret police', put a price of 5 million francs CFA on his head. The Central African radio was entrusted to Edouard Fatrane, the former general secretary of MEDAC; each day it gave the population new details of the previous regime's corruption. Bokassa was presented as 'the warrior who had given himself to the service of his abandoned people'. This was an evident attempt to appeal to the ancient traditions of the country to vindicate the new Head of State.

The New Year's Eve *coup d'état* soon proved beneficial. The dismissal of the deputies and the notables of MESAN, who were mostly incompetent and incapable, facilitated the government's task. Banza, who was promoted to the rank of Lieutenant-Colonel, had been offered the Ministry of Finance, and showed all the authority that was required in the circumstances. He belonged to the powerful Baya race, whose members had so far been excluded from governmental circles. Dacko had often regarded his Ministers as mere executors of his will, but Bokassa let them assume full responsibility for their departments during the first six months of 1966.

His choice of men, moreover, was happier than that of his predecessor. Two young directors, Ange Patassé and Antoine Kezza, who had been educated in France, were responsible for the priority sectors: development, public offices, and labour, comprising peasants, workers and office employees. No pains were spared and within a few weeks, the situation in their respective domains had vastly improved. The Lieutenant appointed to the administration, Timothée Malendoma, was promoted Captain and held the post of Minister of Economy. He was honest, intelligent and industrious, and equal to the considerable task ahead of him. However, the new Ministers only represented two-thirds of the government; the remaining section from the preceding regime had been appointed merely to ensure a transition between the two systems.

Restoration of Foreign Relations

After the initial surprise, reactions from the neighbouring countries and the rest of the world seemed to place Colonel Bokassa's regime in a kind of quarantine. It was generally considered that it could not last more than six months. The explanations given in Paris and at the meeting of the Ministers of OCAM by Guimali, Minister for Foreign Affairs of both the old and the new regimes, had not been convincing. Bokassa saw himself obliged to resort to a subterfuge in order to obtain recognition, which was long in forthcoming. On February 1, he invited the French Ambassador, Jean Français, the general secretary of UDEAC, Onana Awana, and several journalists to hear a statement made by Dacko, brought from the house where he was more or less a prisoner: 'It was impossible to go on working when every day I was told—you will be assassinated—I wanted to resign . . . Colonel Bokassa is merely pursuing the policies of my own government . . . all the other African Heads of State who have been deposed have been killed and yet here I am after 32 days, at the side of the new President and the members of his new government.' After this declaration, Bokassa embraced his predecessor. On the following day, *Terre Africaine*, the organ of the government, published an article by an anonymous 'patriot' heaping insults on the 'satanic' Dacko and his gang, and expressing the hope that they might never be heard of again.

This play-acting fooled nobody. On the contrary, it caused serious misgivings as to the real intentions of those now in power. The new regime received some support from unexpected quarters. The Chinese diplomats had been requested to leave on January 6, but the Bokassa government now appointed Nestor Kombot-Naguemon, a friend of Dacko's and one of the promoters of the Chinese alliance, to be their general secretary. On February 8, the government announced its acceptance of the American offer of fifty-seven peace force volunteers. Bokassa hoped this might produce some reaction from the French government, which—although General de Gaulle had sent personal messages to Bokassa—still maintained its displeasure over the *coup d'état*. All decisions for new projects under the Aid and Co-operation Fund had had to be postponed. On January 15, with the aim of speeding up recognition from the UDEAC states, Bokassa announced the establishment of diplomatic relations with Congo-Kinshasa.

At last in early March, after a meeting between President Bokassa and President Tombalbaye at Bouca in the Central African territory, the Chad government recognised Bokassa's regime as 'the only legal government of the Central African Republic'.

'We are no longer alone and we shall never be alone again,' said *Terre Africaine*, which had greatly resented a reference in the French newspaper *Le Monde* to 'diplomatic isolation'. Soon afterwards the French planning mission which had been set up in 1965 arrived in Bangui and was warmly welcomed by President Bokassa. But it was not until the first fortnight in April that the four states of the Entente and Togoland accorded *de jure* recognition to the Bokassa government. This was the first time there had been so much difficulty over recognising an African government after a *coup d'état*.

Lieutenant-Colonel Banza, Bokassa's second in command, passing through Paris in May 1966, gave a clear and precise account of the reasons for the coup and the aims of the new regime, and succeeded in reassuring French political and economic circles. He said that 'if today the French President were to ask the Central African people to confirm the vote they gave on September 28, 1958, their answer would be the same, and it would be given with the same enthusiasm'. After the welcome given to Banza, Colonel Bokassa was able to pay a private visit to France in July. He took the opportunity to relate the achievements of his government in the six months since it came to power. The new regime now seemed to have every chance of lasting and was universally recognised. In spite of all this, the French President asked Colonel Bokassa to release ex-President Dacko, or at least guarantee his safety.

Continuity in Economic Policy

All through January plane-loads of people who had been expecting something of the kind to happen for months, flew in to Bangui. Those to whom the situation was most propitious were the international diamond traffickers, who came to pick up buying licences before the new Ministers had found out too much about them. By the end of the month it looked as if Bangui would soon be a centre for all kinds of dealers in diamonds, fire-arms and mercenaries—often the same people. But Captain Malendoma took vigorous steps, and in April various adventurers of different nationalities were given forty-eight hours to leave Central African territory. This measure saved the country's economy.

In June Malendoma revived the project, left in abeyance by Dacko and his Minister Ayandho, to set up an *Office National du Diamant* (National Diamond Bureau). The Bureau was established by decree on June 20, and put in the charge of the Director of Mines. An agreement of August 6 allowed Diamond Distributors Inc. to form an international consortium made up of four specialised companies—American, French, Dutch and Israeli. Forty per cent of the commercial profits made on the international market were to be paid to the Bureau: in 1967 and 1968 respec-

159

tively the Central African government derived additional revenue of 166 and 174 million francs CFA from this source. The total national revenue from diamonds had thus more than doubled since 1965: in 1965 it was 390 million francs CFA; in 1966, 450 million; in 1967, 700 million; and in 1968, 875 million. With national diamond cutting output in 1968 at 35,000 stones weighing 4,000 carats, the prospects of the industry were healthy.

In the cotton sector the structural reform carried out by Dacko was to prove its worth. Moreover, in 1966, new varieties had been introduced over some 111,000 acres, and just over 23,000 acres were cultivated either mechanically or by animal-driven ploughs. The people welcomed the decision to abolish all taxes except that on produce. The Aid and Co-operation Fund's grant of a fleet of lorries to the *Union Cotonnière Centrafricaine* meant that cost price could be reduced without any reduction in the price obtained by the producer. Such a reduction had been feared because of the deterioration in world markets. There seemed every reason to hope that the Ministry of Development's target for 1970–1 (60,000 tons) would be achieved.

Another special concern of Patassé, Minister of Development, was the rationalisation of coffee-growing and its commercial exploitation. His reorganisation of the Central African producers' co-operatives soon enabled them to pay off their debts. In collaboration with the importers of Le Havre, he reformed the commercial organisation of the coffee trade with the result that the price paid to the producer increased, although European producers continued to predominate. The Minister tried unsuccessfully to free some of them from their dependence on the exporting companies. But some of the planters were in debt; most of them wanted to sell their plantations as soon as possible; and chronic misunderstandings had arisen among them. All this made the government's task a difficult one. However, the firm attitude it adopted within the *Organisation Internationale du Café* enabled Central Africa's entire output to find a place on the world market within the quotas allowed. It was therefore no longer necessary to build up stocks, which would only have been an additional burden to a country already handicapped by its remoteness.

The years 1966–8 were satisfactory for all three principal products and for a number of secondary activities as well. Cotton production was about 39,000 tons for the 1966–7 season, and reached a peak of a little over 49,000 in 1967–8. The coffee crop for the same two seasons was 9,127 and 8,207 tons, while rough timber production in 1968 was over 7 million cubic feet. Diamond output continued to rise: 540,599 carats in 1966; 520,628 in 1967; and 609,327 in 1968. Traffic through the port of Bangui in 1967 exceeded 195,000 tons. But low prices received for its own products and the rise in the cost of imports increased the country's trade deficit. In 1967, with imports at 10,908 million francs CFA and exports at 7,166 million, the deficit stood at 3,741 million.

At the beginning of 1966, Colonel Bokassa insisted that since the search for uranium carried out by the *Commissariat Française à l'Energie Atomique* (CEA) had proved positive, a processing plant should be constructed.

A Taste for Power

As the months went by Colonel Bokassa showed less enthusiasm for going forward with presidential and parliamentary elections. He liked to style himself 'absolute monarch' and forbade mention of the words democracy or elections. On October 15, 1966, he declared that he wished to continue as the nation's 'guide'. 'I am everywhere and nowhere,' he said, 'I see nothing yet I see all. I listen to nothing and hear everything. Such is the role of a Head of State.' Some Ministers were uneasy at the prolongation of what was supposed to be a temporary regime, but others, like Jean Arthur Bandio, Home Secretary, flattered Bokassa's monarchist leanings, and a court began to grow up at Bangui.

His visits abroad during the second half of 1966 showed President Bokassa that the regimes of many African states had in fact become monarchical. In 1968 he made himself a two-star general, and some of his entourage compared him with the President of France. His portrait appeared on school exercise-books, and many public buildings were named after him. Even the agricultural campaign was called 'Operation Bokassa'. Dacko's successor clearly wanted to be thought of as another Boganda. When he flew back from Chad he had himself carried off the plane on a litter, before a respectful crowd, as if he were the resurrected founder of the Central African Republic.

On January 2, 1966, the Central African government announced the release of all political prisoners with the exception of Jean Gautier Ledot, a former Minister against whom Bokassa seemed to bear a personal grudge. At the end of February Mounoumbaye was denounced by a peasant woman in Lobaye, arrested by Lieutenant-Colonel Banza, and condemned to death and shot at the army camp in Bangui. The French press gave the details of the particularly horrible circumstances in which the execution was said to have been carried out.[3]

Some members of Dacko's government and administration, and of the MESAN management committee, still remained in jail. Several times it was announced that Dacko was about to be released, but he continued to be kept under guard night and day in a house with closed shutters near the Presidency. In August 1967 the question of his release was discussed again by the *Conseil des Ministres*. But the deaths or secret executions of some of his friends made this a delicate matter. The trials flamboyantly promised in 1966 never took place. An auditing commission had examined the former government's accounts and found evidence of misappropriation by certain officials. But the MESAN accounts were not made public, and Colonel Bokassa merely said that Dacko had misappropriated 'hundreds of millions'. The business of the political prisoners was a state secret which the new President seemed particularly determined to keep to himself.

Skilful Domestic Policy

'Our policy is popular, realistic, and revolutionary', said Colonel Bokassa at a press conference in April 1966. Some of the decisions of the first two months directly affected the lives of the people. Bokassa was aware of the considerable influence exercised by the *Union des Femmes Centrafricaines*, led by the dynamic Madame Franck, and one of his first acts was to abolish legal polygamy. Also, though there were not really enough schools to make it feasible, he raised the school-leaving age for girls to twenty. He started building a covered market in the centre of the capital to replace the wretched stalls which had served before. Bangui was one of the few African towns without any public transport, and Bokassa placed an urgent order with France to provide it with buses. One of his earliest official visits was to the in the Bangui hospital, and he made the spectacular gesture of donating to it his first month's salary as President. He expressed indignation when he heard of the salary paid to Dr Ngaro, recently graduated as a surgeon from Montpellier, and ordered the figure to be doubled. He also took an interest in the Central Africans' leisure time, setting up and subsidising two national orchestras, Centrafricain Jazz and Vibro-Succès, for whom there arrived a plane-load of instruments. On the other hand, he banned tom-toms on weekdays, and forbade public figures to enter bars, dance-halls and markets. Nor were the problems of Bangui's food supplies beneath his attention. To avoid a meat shortage he went himself and paid in cash what was owing to Chad cattle-breeders by Central African butchers. Conscious of the influence of the Christian missions over a large section of the population, he made frequent appearances in church, sometimes pronouncing lengthy prayers in front of the statue of the Virgin Mary.

Measures and acts such as these, and the speeches every day on the radio, made Europeans smile, but they succeeded in establishing contact between the government and the people. Colonel Bokassa did not make Dacko's mistake of thinking political problems could be settled by the intervention of the management committee of MESAN, or even Congress. On February 4, 1967, he called together some members at MESAN headquarters and told them: 'Nobody has exploited you for a year. MESAN will no longer be an organ of exploitation. Its mission is to lead the Central African people to happiness.' Then he proclaimed that MESAN was immortal, which meant it could safely be forgotten for a while. It proved more difficult to neutralise the only union, the *Union Générale des Travailleurs Centrafricains* (UGTC), which made no secret of its disappointment at having been left standing by the army in December 1965. In February 1966 Maurice Gouandjia, president of the UGTC, said that the working-class movement should always be in the vanguard of revolution, and that while the army had only done its duty in the *coup d'état*, the UGTC should really have taken the initiative. Gouandjia was arrested on Bokassa's orders a few months later after a strike during the construction of the new airfield at Bangui-Mpoko. But he was soon released. Bokassa had tried to set workers and peasants and even officials and students against one another. In

February 1967 he declared that those people who were asking for higher salaries 'ought to hear the cry of poor peasants, civil servants with nowhere to live, and students whose grants were too small'. Kezza, Minister of Labour, considered that the army and the workers shared a common cause. On August 5, 1967, *Terre Africaine* solemnly announced 'A great consolation for the proletariat! Comrade Jean-Bedel Bokassa is now one of the 55,000 union members of the Central African Republic'. Bokassa appointed the president of the UGTC, on October 11, 1968, as Foreign Minister in place of the equivocal Bandio. He realised that from now on clashes of interest between classes just coming into being were likely to be of more importance than racial rivalries. He was relying on such developments to keep himself in power as long as possible. On the purely political plane, Bokassa tried to win the support of former members of MEDAC, and had Pierre Maleombho, former president of the National Assembly, made chairman of the very tribunal which had sent him to prison in February 1962.

An Incoherent Foreign Policy

Colonel Bokassa was annoyed by the isolation inflicted on his regime for several months in 1966, and during the latter half of that year he left the country in the care of Lieutenant-Colonel Banza and made a series of visits in Africa and Europe. He went to Cameroun, Gabon, and Madagascar for the OCAM meeting, Congo-Kinshasa, where Colonel Mobutu gave him a warm and carefully calculated welcome during an official visit lasting thirteen days, and finally to the Sudan. Both in the Congo and in the Sudan he said some things which must have worried his partners in OCAM. In Kinshasa he posed as Boganda's successor, proclaiming the need for the 'sister republics' to unite. In the Sudan he agreed to a draft plan to extend the railway from Port Sudan to within the Central African Republic. He announced that the Central African radio would in future broadcast in the three languages of the Organisation for African Unity: French, English and Arabic.

At the 1966 meeting of the OAU at Addis Ababa he asked for full powers for the secretary-general, and called for the establishment of an African peace-keeping force, which perhaps he hoped to command. Paris followed this flood of frequently contradictory speeches without worrying too much; a good deal was set down to the Colonel's personality. But a photograph in *Paris-Match* for August 20, 1966, showing Bokassa festooned in decorations, nearly caused diplomatic relations to be broken off. But the appointment of Jean Herly, a former colonial administrator, as the new French ambassador, helped to restore harmony, as a result of which financial and economic relations between the two countries improved. Bokassa agreed to the five-year plan and the prudent objectives the Maumon mission had devised. He also agreed that a financial aid mission should be sent to set his budget right.

But in the course of 1967 and 1968, Bokassa began to think that French aid was not sufficiently substantial and, moreover, that the control exercised on the use of the sums granted was too restricting, although he had obtained a number of free gifts such as aeroplanes, defence equipment and transport, all of which helped to reduce the expenses of the state. He had even been allowed a number of personal favours such as the construction of his own aerodrome in the village of Boubangui, where he was born, although it was only about 50 miles from the capital. But what rankled was the fact that France would not allow him to mint his own money. When 10,000 francs CFA were issued as paper money by the *Banque Centrale des Etats de l'Afrique Equatoriale*, Bokassa was flattered, but still not satisfied. So in order to obtain additional financial help, he determined to raise the question of the *Union Douanière Equatoriale* once more, knowing perfectly well that France and the European Economic Community set great store by this institution.

Pressing for Re-Alignment

In 1966 and 1967, there was serious friction within the UDEAC. Both Chad and the Central African Republic were faced with treasury difficulties and considered that they suffered unduly from the inclusive distribution of duties as arranged under the treaty. They frequently refused to allow goods which had already gone through the customs in another state to enter their territories duty free. In December 1966, an agreement was signed to establish the rebate due each quarter to Chad and the Central African Republic. But in September, Tombalbaye and Bokassa expressed their annoyance again because foreign aid went in preference to the states with better access to the sea. On December 22, however, the Conference of the Heads of State of the UDEAC made a number of resolutions to strengthen the Union. The United Nations *Commission Economique pour l'Afrique* (CEA) and the *Banque Internationale pour la Reconstruction et le Développement* (BIRD) were both asked to set up a sub-regional branch for the UDEAC. This type of regional association was suggested as a model for other African states.

In February 1968, Tombalbaye, Bokassa and Mobutu suddenly decided to create a *Union des Etats de l'Afrique Centrale* (UEAC) which implied the wholesale reconversion of foreign trade in Chad and the Central African Republic. French interests were seriously endangered by this arrangement because the economy in Chad was controlled by a cotton company closely connected with banking and economic circles in Brussels and for some time, the Chad government had been represented by retired Belgian officers in several international economic conferences. Colonel Bokassa did not hide his wish to move out of the franc zone and to create a Central African coinage linked to the Congolese zaïre. On April 22, 1968, the Central African President went even further and officially denounced the Brazzaville treaty.

The UEAC drew up a charter, but within six months the deterioration in relations with France placed Bokassa in a difficult position. The period of colonial competition in Central Africa was over and the government saw that it was quite useless to speculate for long on a division of interests among the Western powers committed in Africa. Colonel Mobutu also realised that in fact he had nothing to gain by intervening on the right bank of the Oubangui and the Congo. In October, various pretexts were put forward for the delay in setting up the UEAC, and the UDEAC institutions functioned as usual. The other countries of OCAM thought the steps taken by the Central African Republic and Chad were madness.

Fishy Financiers

Less than six months later Bokassa and Banza opened negotiations with a number of bankers whose standing in international commercial circles was not of the highest. 'Anyone can raise 20 million pounds if he is in a position to get someone to stand security for him,' wrote *The Sunday Times* (London) on June 12, 1966, in an article exposing the methods used by 'one of the most durable of fishy London financiers', who had duped first the Libyan and then the Malawi governments. But the London paper did not reach Bangui, and Bokassa was soon receiving a gentleman who introduced himself on behalf of a bank in the Bahamas. On October 15, the Central African President agreed to accept a loan of 50,000,000 US dollars in order to construct a hospital, a cement works, a blast-furnace, a hotel plant, a coffee factory, a factory to treat cassava, air and river transport companies and 400 new flats. In return, he promised to grant the English 'benefactor' a forestry concession 'which could be as much as 15,500 square miles', in other words, the whole of the Central African forest.

The same month, another bank from the Bahamas, operating mainly in Nigeria and the Lebanon, made similar agreements with Lieutenant-Colonel Banza. The President and his treasurer thus hoped to solve all the economic problems that were pending, but they were soon reminded that this was precisely the sphere in which their independence was limited. 'Advice' from France was not long in forthcoming and soon convinced Bokassa that it was advisable to give up the injudicious arrangements.

At the beginning of 1967, Bokassa transferred the Minister of Economic Affairs, Captain Malendoma, who had strenuously tried to protect his country from adventurers, to the Ministry of Ex-servicemen, and gave Economic Affairs to Banza, who already held the Finance portfolio, but in 1968, some rather undignified quarrels over Public Works cost Banza both his posts, though he remained a Minister of State and was eventually put in charge of the Department of Health.

Fear of Plots

A curious tract had been put in circulation on December 15, 1966, informing the people that a *Front de Libération Nationale de la République Centrafricaine* sentenced Colonel Bokassa to death. Strangely enough, it also published the names of the future revolutionary government, under the leadership of Lieutenant-Colonel Banza. This clumsy provocation fooled few people. By September 1967, Bokassa was so obsessed by the fear of plots that he began to believe that only the return of French troops could prolong his reign. On the 21st, he made a trip to Paris to ask for this aid, on the pretext that it would enable him to protect the 25,000 Sudanese refugees of the Zande race—who lived in the eastern part of the Central African territory—from any attacks by 'Muslim activists'. On November 10, 80 French parachutists of the 11th division discreetly arrived in Bangui. The *New York Times* publicised the operation and *Le Figaro* replied by explaining that it was merely a routine acclimatisation manoeuvre in tropical countries for a small number of troops. In any case, co-operation agreements between France and the Central African government made the application for military aid legal.

About the same time, a few Central African officers were invited to attend a training course abroad, and in April 1968, President Bokassa reshuffled his government. This was when Lieutenant-Colonel Banza lost the Ministries of Finance and Economic Affairs and was given the Ministry of Health. The French military contingent, later on doubled, in effect removed the danger of mutiny in the small Central African army, which numbered only a thousand men. Part of the army had been billeted to Bouar, about 380 miles west of Bangui. The more restive elements were sent 750 miles away to the east, ostensibly to supervise the Congolese and the Sudanese frontiers. The regime seemed to have won a year's respite.

Although the return of French troops to Bangui had been discreet and very restricted, it was severely criticised by the Ministers. The composition of the government had been far from harmonious since the Minister of Education, Dominique Guéret, had left for France when the Colonel held him personally responsible for the poor results obtained in the *baccalauréat* examinations. A few of the younger Ministers were affected by the attitude of Central African students in Paris, who condemned the 'military fascist dictatorship' in Bangui. And almost everyone was worried about President Bokassa's inconsistent foreign policy. Ruptures and spectacular reconciliations were the main feature of Bokassa's relations with other African Heads of State and when, on May 20, 1968, he learned to his horror that General de Gaulle had left Paris, he announced that he would take the first plane 'to give his hand to his companion in arms'. In October, fresh rumours of plots obliged Bokassa to ask for a second military contingent.

On the 11th, he dismissed his Minister of Foreign Affairs, Bandio, who was in favour of the UEAC. It began to look as if Bokassa's entire policy was taking a new direction.

The Central African Republic Re-Enters the UDEAC

A meeting of the general committee of the six countries belonging to the European Economic Community, the associated African countries and Madagascar was held in Brazzaville from October 14 to 17. General Mobutu, however, was unwilling to go to a country which had broken off diplomatic relations with his own after Pierre Mulele's execution and refused to participate. Chad and the Central African Republic followed suit. The Congolese Minister of Foreign Affairs, Justin Bomboko, declared at Bangui that Congo-Brazzaville had become a centre of training camps for guerrilla warfare for the Congo, Chad and the Central African Republic.

The situation was reversed a month later, when the Minister for Co-operation visited Bangui and on November 8, Bokassa announced that the *Commissariat de l'Energie Atomique* (CEA) had decided to begin exploiting the Bakouma uranium deposit. On November 24, he refused to attend the celebrations of the third anniversary of the Congolese Republic at Kinshasa, nor would he allow Congolese aeroplanes to land at Bangui. Radio-Kinshasa declared: 'France threatens to turn off the tap and the children are afraid of dying of thirst. That is the sad thing about still being dependent'. Relations with Chad were not improving either. Presidents Tombalbaye and Bokassa spent their time covering each other with insults and the Central African President even summoned the notables of Bangui to the graveyard to attend the mock funeral of his counterpart in Chad, publicly accusing him of murdering Boganda.

On December 9, the Central African Republic dramatically suspended diplomatic relations with Congo-Kinshasa and decided to re-enter the UDEAC. This action was based on specific economic and financial factors; it exonerated Bokassa's government from having to pay for the supplies and equipment which had been bought on credit from the Congo over the past two years. When Bokassa forbade the forwarding of goods to Chad and the transit of Chadian cotton in Central African territory, the quarrel seriously endangered the position of the European trading companies. Chad's exports through Nigeria were hampered by the civil war and the whole country was threatened with suffocation. Some thought, however, that this was just an excuse for staging Chad's return into the UDEAC as well.

In December, France announced that General Bokassa would pay an official visit from February 11 to 13, 1969. The man who had fought for Free France had been waiting for this invitation, the highest honour that could be paid to an African Head of State, for almost three years. Bokassa made a preliminary trip to Paris in December to make arrangements for his visit. 'Is an invitation to Paris the reward for a return to hegemony in the former states of French Equatorial Africa? Or is the return a direct consequence of the invitation? African diplomacy is too secret and too abstruse for a European to hazard a straight answer.' These were the questions *Le Monde* posed in its leading article on February 12, 1969.

The sumptuous receptions offered to the Heads of African States in Paris were veritable historical events. In 1962, being received at the Elysée palace had allowed President Dacko to speculate on his new prestige and inaugurate an ambitious political and economic programme. In 1969, President Bokassa felt that the friendship displayed by General de Gaulle authorised him to cling to power for a little longer, but in spite of repeated requests from France, he still delayed in setting Dacko free, although he continued to promise to do so. In April and May, however, two unexpected decisions gave his shaky regime, which was increasingly worrying to all the foreign powers, a new lease of life, at least for the immediate future.

'Arrested on the night of April 10 at Bangui, tried and sentenced to death on the 11th, Lieutenant-Colonel Banza was shot at dawn on the 12th in conditions that some will not hesitate to describe as a political assassination,' wrote *Le Monde Diplomatique* in May 1969.[4] The *Agence France-Presse* correspondent was accused of having leaked news of 'internal affairs' without the government's approval. Bokassa put him under arrest and threatened him with a court martial.

The execution of his second in command revealed a situation which the President had been ingeniously trying to conceal for months. The solitary exercise of unlimited power was no longer enough for Bokassa and for a long time he had been anxious to dissociate himself from the man whose remarkable organisation on December 31, 1965, had enabled the army to take power. The people were informed that one of the officers, Mandaba, had managed to restrain Lieutenant-Colonel Banza when he was inciting the army to murder the Head of State, intending to seize power himself. Bokassa implicated the Ministers in the responsibility for the judgement passed on the man he had come to regard as his rival. The repugnant circumstances of his death were never revealed; several other men of standing, who had been close to him, were also executed in secret.

Since he enjoyed full powers, Bokassa felt he should manage the natural resources of the country and the budget, which was drawn up and 'distributed' by the *Conseil des Ministres*. He had attempted to mint his own money, and had made all the necessary arrangements to have notes bearing his portrait to be printed abroad. He even planned a ceremony for the occasion. When the plan came to nothing, he tried to gain control of the diamond trade, claiming that it did not bring the state enough profits.

The head of the Department for Mines and Geology, Blaise Ouayo, one of the most scrupulous of Central African officials, had been reluctant to consent to the operations demanded of him in December 1968. Like all those who challenged the whims of the Head of State, he was thrown into prison. Bokassa's next step was to disregard all the previous agreements and grant a licence for a new purchasing office, which would be managed by a Minister, Kombot Naguemon.[5] Once again, Bangui attracted the international traffickers, and the National Diamond Bureau soon found that it could no longer function satisfactorily.

However, other products of Central African sub-soil were also being exploited. On April 29, 1969, a *Compagnie des Mines d'uranium de Bakouma* was created in Bangui. The government only had to contribute 20 per cent of the capital, because the Atomic Energy Commission and the *Compagnie française des mines d'uranium*, already functioning in Gabon and Niger, each provided 40 per cent. The unusual nature of the ore, which was in the form of phosphates, necessitated setting up a new process treatment. The exploitation envisaged at the Mpatou deposit was to last about twenty years and represented an investment of some 8,000 million francs CFA. The opening of the factory, which will have a capacity of 1,200 tons a year, is planned for 1972. The decision to go ahead has created a great many technical problems, but the Central African government considers the project to be one of vital importance.

In June 1969, Bokassa accused ex-President Dacko of corresponding with the Chinese Embassy at Brazzaville and moved him to the condemned prisoners' cell. Once again his trial was announced, but it was cancelled a few weeks later when after making his self-criticisms, Dacko was taken back to his own village and placed under supervision.

On his return from Congo-Brazzaville in August, Bokassa announced that he wished to establish 'scientific socialism'. The Chad insurrection, which was spreading to Sara country worried him as much as the disturbances at Brazzaville, because reports from the sub-prefects and the prefects all spoke of growing discontent in the villages, especially in Baya and Banda areas. Two of Dacko's former Ministers and a deputy belonging to the same ethnic groups were quietly set free.

Although in the first instance, Bokassa had regarded his office as temporary, it soon transpired that he was evidently ready to adopt any policy that would keep him in power.

The Expulsion of the French Technicians

In September 1969, Bokassa realised that the Centradiam Society was engaged in some rather doubtful financial undertakings and was not bringing him in sufficient revenue. Furthermore, the consortium in charge of the National Diamond Bureau had, since the creation of Centradiam, considered the 1964 agreements as void and postponed their annual payment. Bokassa ordered the police and army to surround their offices and the consortium was forced to give way.

Encouraged by the success of this operation, Bokassa then released Ouayo, head of the Department of Mines; and on October 28 he ordered the mining societies which were exploiting the use of mining permits to pay a sum of several hundred million francs CFA. This figure represented the renewal rights for the permits, but raised to an impossibly exorbitant rate (415 times higher).[6] Failing to obtain satisfaction, Bokassa arrested all the European technicians employed at the mining works and expelled them from the country. In all, some forty persons (including dependants) were involved, mainly French but also some Belgians. A decree was issued revoking all the mining permits and forcing the three mining companies to close down. The President of France made a formal protest and the French press were highly critical of General Bokassa, whose singular methods of government were on this occasion revealed to the whole world.[7]

On New Year's Eve the Central African President rescinded the order for expulsion and declared that he was ready to discuss the situation with the mining society representatives.

In December 1969 an imposing Central African delegation assembled in Moscow, but in spite of the concessions offered them the Russians were prepared to make only a very modest financial commitment. The events of November and December had been a great blow for Central Africa's prestige and finding himself more and more isolated on the international level, Bokassa now sought to renew his ties with his central African neighbours.

1970 was a difficult year for Bokassa. The closing of the mines had been badly received by the Baya and the Banda. Furthermore, several agricultural co-operatives were in serious financial difficulties due to fraudulent misappropriations by the management. Put on the spot, Bokassa dissolved all state systems in the field of production and expelled more than 60 French experts in the Agricultural and Livestock Breeding Services.

These new expulsions irritated the French government and put the whole rural development of the country in jeopardy.

Bokassa hoped that the Eastern countries would supply the technicians he needed and he also believed that Rumania would build a railway to Cameroun. He was sorely disappointed.

The death of General de Gaulle gave him an opportunity to try to get out of the straits he found himself in. He hoped that the tears shed publicly at Notre-Dame and at Colombey-les-deux-Eglises would suffice to have his flirtation with the communist bloc forgiven him. To show goodwill, he demoted the Foreign Minister, Kombot Naguemon, and announced that he would return the mines to the companies to whom they had previously belonged.

But the financial balance-sheet at the end of 1970 was still heavily in the red. The budgetary deficit of the Central African Republic was of the order of 2,500 million francs CFA and the total of unpaid bills reached the 2,000 million mark.

General Bokassa's flights of fancy are severely judged by a great part of French public opinion and requests for aid are now scrutinised very carefully. The attitude of Central Africa's Head of State has furnished the opponents of the policy of co-operation with African states with plenty of ammunition.

6. After Ten Years' Independence

GENERAL BOKASSA was the last African 'sovereign' to be received by General de Gaulle with all the customary pomp. However, the diplomatic tenor of the usual speeches made on these occasions barely concealed the anxiety felt in France about the fate of this precariously situated territory, so poorly equipped for independence. 'Some pessimists forecast that the new arrangements would cause serious friction between our peoples,' General de Gaulle declared on February 11, 1969. 'They said that France would wish to retract, or even that your young Republic would prove incapable of government. Well, they are all wrong. We have respected the right of your country to self-determination, and Bangui, under three successive Heads of State, has admirably assumed its national duties, in spite of all the internal and external difficulties.'

Today, the pessimists decried by de Gaulle do not seem so wrong. The situation had been gradually deteriorating in Oubangui.

At the start of a new decade of de-colonisation, it is perhaps worthwhile to attempt an objective summary of the events of the past ten years. In 1946, when René Malbrant fought so unremittingly to retard the application of the reforms in Oubangui Chari, he warned his audience of the 'tyrannies of tomorrow'. Today, his words have a prophetic ring. Four months after independence was proclaimed, a great number of public liberties were suppressed and the principal political party in opposition was disbanded. The Assembly turned into a mere instrument of the Head of State, and the one party was merely the organ of general approval for governmental action, levying heavy subscriptions to strengthen the privileges of the ruling classes.

In 1966, after the members of the Assembly and the party officials had been dismissed, there remained only the Chief of Staff, who occupied the office of Head of State for an unstated period. The few Ministers in the government were appointed, revoked, and even executed at his will. The administrative edifice built up on the advice of the colonists had crumbled away and the orders of the Head of State alone had force of law, overriding all the accepted legal conventions. But the most striking thing about the political evolution of the country was the Central African population's comparative indifference to the successive upheavals. Even after a decade, and in spite of all Dacko's efforts, the political regime remains superimposed on a people who continue to live according to their ancestral codes.

Political life in Central Africa unfolds like a play, in which only a few of the 4,000 officials and agents have a part, that is, only those who feel directly concerned in what is going on. Those who occupy the white men's offices and villas and ape the colonial administrators as best they can, have such a totally different existence from the peasants, that one wonders what will be the future of this remote country, so poorly blessed by nature. At the end of the nineteenth century, Jules Ferry had protested that to occupy a country by placing a tricolour flag in the hands of two or three Senegalese sharpshooters 'was not founding a colony, it was playing at colonisation'.[1] At the moment, it looks very much as if someone is playing at de-colonisation and that a true Central African state has still not got beyond the stage of good intentions.

On August 13, 1960, André Malraux had declared that France bequeathed 'its administration' to the Central African Republic, indicating presumably that French officials would remain in charge of the actual machinery. But less than eighteen months later, the government decided to put Central Africans in almost all the administrative and advisory posts, appointing clerks and auxiliaries who were ill-prepared for the responsibility. The French system was soon disrupted, and the tiny number of Central African students made it very unlikely that competent officials would be available before at least another ten years. The creation of a local *Ecole Nationale d'Administration*, recruiting students at far too low a standard and functioning with the help of officials from the Ministry of Co-operation posted to Bangui, was only a temporary stop-gap.

The chronic shortage of staff was largely because before 1945 only about 5 per cent of local people had benefited from school education and the attempts made to improve the situation in the years preceding autonomy had been very feeble. The main features of the territorial administration were abandoned roads, lack of public funds and abuse of public offices. Although the military regime condemned the disorder, it proved incapable of setting matters right. The financial rules introduced by the French have by now almost all disappeared. Those responsible for misappropriating public funds have not been imprisoned, but sometimes promoted to better paid posts, on the grounds that their higher salaries will help them to pay back what they owe. So far, the fact that France still controls the issue of paper money has prevented total bankruptcy, which seemed the most likely outcome of the situation; in 1970, internal disorder was kept in check by a number of restrictions placed on the national budget, which, it should be remembered, is less than the working capital of any large Parisian store.

In October 1957, Boganda had realised that his country could not quickly train the officials it needed. But in August 1960 the problem of the future of the Central African nation was again posed in terms of education and this time with dramatic urgency. President Dacko, who had been a head-master, devoted a great deal of energy to improving conditions and the number of pupils attending primary schools rose from 67,500 in 1960 to 135,000 in 1966. Attendance at secondary schools increased from 1,899 to 4,846. The state also assumed all the charges for private education. By 1966, some progress had been made in the field of technical education, but there were still only 742 pupils in 32 different branches; and the entire programme had to be carried through with a limited number of inadequately trained members of staff. From October 1958 to October 1960, the number of African primary school-teachers dropped from 30 to 10. Most of Dacko's former colleagues had been made ambassadors, Ministers, and directors, as there was no one else to fill these posts, and this consequently reduced the teaching staff. In 1960, assistant teachers in elementary schools numbered only 145 and in the secondary schools, all the posts were held by Europeans. As it was essential to train teachers as quickly as possible to take charge of the newly-created classes, the examination results suffered. The present figures for the country show that about ten Central Africans per year pass the *baccalauréat* and 300 obtain the *brevet* (secondary school leaving certificate).[2] At this rate, the country will obviously not even be able to provide officials to fill the posts held in 1960 by the Europeans, let alone the rest, for a good many more years. *Terre Africaine* pointed this out in October 1968: 'If we are to wait for the elementary schools to be reorganised in order to train our officials, the Central African Republic must give up its ideas of independence until the present pupils have graduated.'

/Schools should not, of course, be regarded as mere factories to produce officials and politicians, for they obviously play an important role in the evolution of the people. And it is useless to wish to make Central Africa a responsible self-governing state before the whole of the population is educated. While the few scattered European schools produce a privileged caste, each Central African village continues to give its younger generations the remarkable social education provided by the initiation societies. These traditional schools do much to preserve the stability and cohesion of rural society and the primary school will never become really popular unless there is some sort of osmosis between the initiation societies and the Western type of education. This is a very delicate task which can only be tackled by leaders who are in close touch with the people and with their traditions.

Missionary activity got off to a difficult start in Oubangui Chari. The Fathers of the Holy Ghost began by buying back the slaves and creating 'villages of freedom'.[3] Former slaves were thus the first to receive religious instruction and education, but it was a method which actually retarded the evangelisation of the people at large. Later on, the tax exacted by concessionary company agents undermined much of the work of the missions, but despite their very restricted means, they succeeded in educating the principal political leaders in the country, including of course, Barthélémy Boganda.

Although the symbol of Christ the Redeemer spread among this unhappy persecuted people far beyond the spheres of influence of the missionary posts, the narrow-mindedness of a number of priests, their tolerance of the colonists, and the invective some of them poured on the ancient traditions, tended to delay the movement of conversion. The Protestant ministers, who were less numerous but better equipped, limited their aims to demanding the observance of a few basic rules, such as sobriety. However, the natural religious sense of the natives helped the missionaries' task.

At the hour of independence, the Churches too had to change their status, and many missionaries of the old school were obliged to leave, full of misgivings about the future of the country where they had worked for twenty or thirty years. Mgr Joseph Cucherousset, a French archbishop consecrated in 1948, had understood the human realities of the country perfectly, and remained at the head of Central African Christianity until 1969. On January 5, 1969, a Central African, Joachim Ndayer, the son of a catechist was consecrated bishop in front of the cathedral of Notre-Dame de Bangui. Aged thirty-four, he was the youngest bishop in the world.

Problems of leadership were just as acute in the Churches as in the field of administration and for a long time most priests, ministers and nuns were foreigners. Both Catholics and Protestants were in a minority in the territory, because the rural populations were still deeply attached to their ancient rites. The recent internal transformation of Western Churches however, seems likely to facilitate a revival of the missionary movement. The 'over-zealous' missionaries described by the African priest, Father Chouanga, 'who destroyed the tom-toms, snatched amulets from the people's necks to replace them with miraculous medallions, and thrashed the neophytes guilty of executing a few dances, in order to make them mend their ways', are now a thing of the past.[4] As in the secular domain, a kind of osmosis is necessary between the ancient cults and the religion brought by the white men. This is not as impossible as some may think, because it is precisely what happened in the Upper Nile where Negro-African Christianity lasted ten centuries. In the Central African Republic where all aspects of life are thoroughly permeated with religion, such an evolution could be accomplished without undue friction. If the new faith can be grafted on to the basic religious traditions, Christianity may indeed prove a long term means of remedying the advance of more materialistic civilisations.

After ten years of independence, the thorny problems of religious instruction and education still have priority and their solution depends largely on the progress made in the sphere of public health. Unless something is done in this direction, all efforts to educate and evangelise the people are bound to be ineffectual.

The number of doctors in the country, nearly all of whom are

179

Europeans, has scarcely increased in the last fifteen years. At present there are about thirty, which is clearly insufficient and makes it impossible for any new hospitals to be built. Furthermore, an increase in staff would mean an additional strain on the budget which already has a hard task to find the salaries for government officials. The mobile medical services concentrate on the endemic diseases, such as sleeping-sickness and smallpox—which almost succeeded in annihilating the Central African population before the Europeans came—but it is essential that 'mass medicine' be organised without delay.[5] 'We consider that while it is practically impossible for a doctor to run before he can walk,' wrote Goumba, 'there is, on the contrary, one field where immediate action is possible, and necessary: we must train large numbers of auxiliaries and extra-medical staff in as short a time as possible. Health agents, technical assistants, qualified male nurses, female nurses, sanitary engineers and so on are all urgently needed.' In the villages, the mortality rate is still high and unless priority is granted to mass medicine all the efforts to develop the country are likely to fail. The promotion of industry to the detriment of subsistence crops and the resultant decline in hunting and fishing, have undoubtedly created new problems of under-nourishment.

In the last analysis, sixty years of colonisation and ten years of de-colonisation have aggravated the plight of the Central African peasant. The explorers' accounts all attested to the various tribes' remarkable talent for agriculture, but rubber gathering and whole-sale requisitioning of labour have totally ruined this ancestral activity and cultivation of cotton by the administration has pre-vented its revival. The present situation is a tragic paradox, with more than half the active population cultivating cotton all the year round. 'A peasant's life,' stated Goumba, 'is worth a month and a half of that of a member of Parliament.' He also pointed out that a clerk's monthly salary of 15,000 francs CFA corresponded to three years' work by a cultivator. The result of this situation is that the people are forced to work the land merely to pay dues to a mysteri-ous and unknown state.

Village work outside of the monetary sector is on a very small scale and there is a general regression in material standards. Dwellings are in a deplorable state, insufficient subsistence crops

are grown—sometimes only cassava—and the local crafts have
been permanently ruined. To escape from this dreary round, a
young Central African has no alternative but to leave his family.
His chances of success are few: he can work on a plantation or in
the mines, he can become a free diamond prospector, a servant,
a government employee or a chauffeur. Many of these young people
swell the numbers of the urban proletariat where they have no
prospects of employment whatsoever. Once they have cut themselves off from the protection of the traditional village framework,
they are deprived of all form of social security.

Operations subsidised by foreign aid benefit only a few privileged persons who inhabit the costly model villages in the 'modernisation' sectors. The enormous task yet to be accomplished is far
beyond the capacities of the leaders of the country, but it would be
unfair to reproach them for failing in a field where the colonial
administration proved equally unsuccessful. The mere fact that the
Central African territory has now become an independent political
entity, will not work miracles; the great problems generally
affecting the economy of the Afro-Asian world are more accentuated in this particular area. This territory with its tragic heritage
has so far aroused little interest in foreign countries, other than
France. Experts blame the people's lethargy or the lack of economic training of most of the leaders, but they also admit that they
have no magic recipe to suggest.

The meritorious efforts made by President Dacko in the
economic field between 1964 and 1966 are, nevertheless, beginning
to show some results. Some even believe that the country will not
start to make real economic progress until the next century.

If no spectacular mining or oil discoveries are made, perhaps
a new policy of co-operation could be tried to remedy the instability of Central African society for which colonisation and its
corollary, de-colonisation, must bear the blame. Once the unfortunate terrain for the concessionary undertaking, this region might
possibly serve yet again as a guinea-pig for new experiments.
In 1946, the first 'progress volunteers'—France's version of the
American Peace Corps force—were sent out, but unfortunately,
despite the well-meaning efforts of the young pioneers, the
achievements have been inconclusive. Everyone realises that the
fundamental problem is at the level of the masses. The wheels

can only turn again gradually, as past ravages are repaired and effaced; it is unfortunately too easy simply to ignore all that the people suffered in the colonial era.

Some object that the destiny of a million and a half Central Africans will probably have no effect on the future in the rigorous accounts of world economy. Yet it would still be possible for co-operation policies between richer and poorer countries to seize this unique opportunity and show that they are not just another form of neo-colonialism. 'No policy has a higher vocation,' recalled Robert Delavignette, 'because it aims at the ideal of world peace by aiding the countries which are still developing.'[6] The real road to co-operation might perhaps lie through the villages, but this too would require careful study and a true understanding of a society which must be given the credit for having survived for thousands of years.

The preliminary stage towards fruitful co-operation would perhaps be to abandon the balkanisation policy, for which the persons skilfully placed in power in the richest territories are at present responsible. When Réne Dumont studied the possibilities of development in Central Africa, he could think of no better 'viable economic entity' than a huge area stretching from Camer-oun to Burundi.[7] He declared: 'Unite or perish, this should be the slogan of all the small African states.'

Ten years after Boganda's death, the plan for the United States of Latin Africa, which to some still appears Utopian, remains the Central African people's only path to salvation. The populations of this vast area may unite one day, but so far, the jumble of agreements made by transitory governments with limited means at their disposal, has produced few results. This first step towards true sovereignty was written out in full by Boganda in the Central African Constitution, but conditions are so unfavourable at present that none of the Heads of State considers it seriously. Illiteracy and a total absence of information prevent the masses from siding for or against such a unification, which is so vital for their future.

The gravity of the situation is most blatant in the Central African Republic. The greater part of the population remains ignorant of the concepts of state, property and profit, and takes refuge in an attitude of indifference or mistrust. This may be an ancient reflex of a people subjected to a centuries-long persecution, or it may be wisdom. The time spent on 'money work' is still, in their eyes, time wasted for a people who have, for better or for worse, remained closely attached to nature.

The 'internal and external difficulties' of the administrative unit created by colonisation and baptised 'Central African State', cannot possibly arouse the interest of the people who constitute the nation while it is so poorly adapted to the true realities of the country. If the whole population could be made aware of the irreversibility of the European impact, there would be a tremendous step forward, infinitely more valuable than an increase of foreign aid. At the moment, the sums supplied almost exclusively by the European Economic Community and France, guarantee the functioning of the existing undertakings, and avoid the political vacuum which would jeopardise the balance of power in the continent.

The whims of the government and the incompetence and corruption of a number of officials in positions of authority threaten to exhaust the patience of the peasant population. The question arises whether in this country where the inhabitants do not really distinguish between the colonial regime and the government that came with independence, a new political stage might not in fact be reached very soon. The answer rests not only with the new generations in Boganda's homeland, but also with the young people of neighbouring territories who, one day, will be called upon to unite in the building of a common future.

Notes and References

1. THE COUNTRY AND THE PEOPLE

1. W. G. Browne, *Travels in Africa, Egypt and Syria from the year 1792 to 1798*, London 1799

2. B. Aubreville, *Climats, forêts et désertification de l'Afrique Tropicale*, Société d'editions géographiques, maritimes et coloniales, Paris 1949

3. R. Sillans, *Les savanes de l'Afrique centrale*, Le Chevalier, Paris 1958

4. R. Dumont, *Le difficile développement agricole de la République Centrafricaine*, Institut National Agronomique, Paris 1966

5. Castelli and Jolivot, *Annuaire statistique de la République Centrafricaine*, Bangui and Paris 1964

6. See A. M. Vergiat, *Moeurs et coutumes des Manjas*, Payot, Paris 1937

7. F. Eboué, *Les peuples de l'Oubangui-Chari*, Comité de l'Afrique française, Paris 1933

8. R. P. Teilhard de Chardin, 'L'Afrique et les origines humaines' in *Revue des Questions Scientifiques*, Vol. XIV, 5th series, January 20, 1955

9. R. de Bayle des Hermens, 'Premier aperçu du Paléolithique inférieur en République Centrafricaine' in *L'Anthropologie*, Vol. LXXXI, 5-6, Paris 1967

10. P. Vidal, *La civilisation mégalithique de Bouar*, Firmin-Didot, Paris 1969

11. R. Cornevin, *Histoire du Congo-Léo*, Berger-Levrault, Paris 1963

12. See Lopez-Pigafetta, *Description du royaume du Congo et des contrées environnantes*, translated from the Italian and annotated by Willy Bal, Université de Lovanium, Kinshasa 1963

13. Mgr Confaliomeri, *Histoire du Congo*, Vatican Library, Rome, Codex Vat. lat. 12.516, folios 103-25

14. M. Delafosse, *Essai sur le peuple et la langue sara*, André, Paris 1897

15. E. de Dampierre, *Un ancien royaume bandia du haut-Oubangui*, Plon, Paris 1967

16. S. Santandrea, *A Tribal History of the Bahr el Ghazal*, Nigrizia, Verona 1963

17. C. R. Lagaé and V. H. Vandenplas, *La langue des Azandé—*

Introduction historico-géographique, Editions dominicaines, Gand 1921–5

18. See *Black Ivory and White, or the Story of el Zubeir Pasha, Slaver and Sultan, as told by himself*, translated and put on record by H. C. Jackson, Oxford 1913; Negro University Press
19. J. Hilberth, *Les Gbaya*, 1962
20. H. Faure, *Contribution à l'étude des races de la région de Carnot*, Brazzaville, Société de Recherches Congolaises, 1928
21. G. Toqué, *Essai sur le peuple et la langue banda*, André, Paris 1904
22. A. de Calonne-Beaufaict, *Azandé*, M. Lamertin, Brussels 1921; J. Leyder, 'Note préliminaire a l'étude des grandes migrations de l'Afrique centrale' in *Revue de l'Institut Sociologique*, No. 13; Mgr B. Tanghe, 'Pages d'histoire africaine' in *Aequatoria*, VII, 1944
23. H. A. MacMichael, *A history of the Arabs in the Sudan and some account of the people who preceded them and of the tribes inhabiting Darfur*, Cambridge University Press, 1922; Barnes and Noble, 1922
24. A. M. Vergiat, *Les rites secrets des primitifs de l'Oubangui*, 1936
25. B. Boganda, 'Faisons le point' in *France—Outre-Mer*, Paris, September-October 1957
26. P. Vidal, *L'initiation dans l'éducation traditionelle (population Gbaya-Kara)*, (in Roneo) Paris, Le Havre 1962

2. THE COLONY OF OUBANGUI CHARI

1. El Tounsy (Sheikh Mohammed ibn Omar), *Voyage au Darfour*, Paris 1845, and *Voyage au Ouadai*, Paris 1851. Translated from the Arabic by Perron
2. Julien, 'Mohammed Senoussi et ses états in *Bulletin de la Société de Recherches Congolaises*, Brazzaville 1925, 1927, 1928 and 1929
3. Fresnel, 'Notice historique et géographique sur le Ouaday' in *Bulletin de la Société de Géographie*, Vol. XI, Paris 1849
4. E. Berlioux, *La traite orientale*, Guillaumin, Paris 1870
5. P. Potagos, *Dix années de voyages dans l'Asie centrale et l'Afrique équatorial*, Leroux, Paris 1885
6. B. Hassenstein, *Friedrich Bohndorffs Reisen in Zentralafrika 1874 bis 1883*, Petermanns Mitteilungen, Vienna 1885
7. Dr W. Junker, *Reisen in Afrika 1875–1886*, E. Mölzel, Vienna 1889. Translated into English by A. Keane as *Travels in Africa*, Chapman and Hall, London 1892
8. F. Lupton, 'Letters to the London Geographical Society' in *Proceedings*, October 1886

9. P. Pauliat, *La querelle internationale de l'Oubangui* (typewritten), Sorbonne, Paris 1966

10. H. H. Johnston, *The life and work of a great traveller, G. Grenfell and the Congo*, Hutchinson, London 1908; Kraus Reprints

11. L. P. Monteil, *Souvenirs vécus—Quelques feuillets de l'histoire colonial—les rivalités internationales*, Société d'éditions géographiques maritimes et coloniales, Paris 1924

12. M. Michel. *La Mission Marchand (1895–1899)*. Ecole pratique des hautes études, Paris 1968

13. P. Leroy-Beaulieu, *De la colonisation chez les peuples modernes*, Guillaumin, Paris 1902

14. C. Mangin, *Souvenirs d'Afrique—Tournée d'inspection au Congo 1908*, Denoël, Paris 1936

15. F. Challaye, *Le Congo français*, Alcan, Paris 1909

16. M. Violette, *A la veille d'Agadir—La N'Goko Sangha*, Larose, Paris 1914

17. J. Saintoyant, *L'afflaire du Congo*, L'Epi, Paris 1960

18. *Dossiers Concessions 1900–1920*, Archives Nationales, Section Outre-Mer, Paris

19. See *Une étape de la conquête de l'AEF, 1908–12*, published by Etat Major des Troupes, Brazzaville

20. E. de Dampierre, *Un ancien royaume bandia du haut-Oubangui*, Plon, Paris 1967

21. R. P. Daigre, *Oubangui-Chari. Témoignage sur son évolution 1900–1940*, Dillen et Cie, Issoudun 1947

22. *Journal Officiel de l'AEF*, December 1, 1921

23. See his article in *Atlas des Colonies Françaises*, ed. by G. Grandidier, Société d'éditions géographiques, maritimes et coloniales, Paris 1934

24. A. Gide, *Voyage au Congo*, Gallimard, Paris 1927

25. A. Londres, *Terre d'Ebène, la traite des Noirs*, Albin-Michel, Paris 1929

26. M. Michel, *Les débuts du soulèvement de la haute Sangha*, Brazzaville, Centre d'enseignement supérieur, 1966

27. P. Kalck, *Réalités Oubanguiennes*, Berger-Levrault, Paris 1959

28. J. and J. P. Lenormand, *L'or et le diamant en France métropolitaine et dans l'Union Française*, Editions SEF, Paris 1952

3. EMANCIPATION OF THE CENTRAL AFRICAN PEOPLE

1. Report in *L'Etincelle de l'AEF*, Bulletin of the Rassemblement du Peuple Français, Brazzaville

2. *Pour sauver un peuple*
3. At present Ambassador for the Central African Republic in France
4. Haut Commissariat de la République française en AEF, *Circulaires de base (1952–56)*, Imprimerie Officielle, Brazzaville 1956
5. R. Dumont, *Les possibilités d'accroissement de la production cotonnière en AEF*, 1950
6. Under the title Marshall Aid
7. Report of the Production Conference, Bangui 1950
8. Roger Guérillot, at present Ambassador for the Central African Republic in America
9. Report of the Committee of Economic Affairs
10. M. Olivier-Lacamp, 'Afrique Noire 1958—En Oubangui-Chari, parti unique' and 'Administration déchirée entre des obligations contradictoires', articles in *Le Figaro*, January 31, and February 3, 1958
11. Speech at Brazzaville
12. J. de Dreux-Brézé, *Le problème du regroupement en Afrique Equatoriale*, Librairie Générale de Droit, Paris 1968
13. P. Decraene, 'M. Boganda voudrait faire de la République Centrafricaine le noyau de l'Afrique latine', article in *Le Monde*, Paris, January 22, 1959
14. 'L'enquête sur la mort de M. Boganda', article in *L'Express*, May 7, 1959
15. *Index*, Paris, May 5, 1959
16. He merely belonged to the same ethnic group, the Mbaka or Ngbaka
17. J. F. Gillet, *Les organismes communs aux Etats de l'Afrique centrale*, Brazzaville 1965
18. Antoine Bangui, at present Minister in the Tombalbaye government in Chad

4. BUILDING A NATION

1. A. Bussiere, *La RCA sans Boganda*, (typewritten) Paris 1963
2. J. P. Rougeaux, *Le parti unique en République Centrafricaine: le MESAN*, Faculté de Droit et des Sciences Economiques, Paris 1968
3. René Dumont, *L'Afrique noire est mal partie*, Editions du Seuil, Paris 1962

5. MILITARY LEADERSHIP

1. The night of December 31, President Dacko dismissed his servants and burnt all his papers, and according to witnesses intended to

hand over the reins of power to Izamo. The plot might have been revealed to Bokassa by a chauffeur

2. J. P. Térivé, 'Analyse d'un coup d'Etat' in *France—Eurafrique*, No. 171, Paris, March 1966

3. *Paris-Presse, L'Intransigeant* and *France-Soir*, February 24–9, 1966

4. P. Decraene, 'Après l'exécution du colonel Banza, menaces d'instabilité en RCA', article in *Le Monde Diplomatique*, May 1969

5. President and director general of the Centradiam Society. General Bokassa and the Minister, Ayandho, appeared on the list of administrators

6. Decreed by an order of June 6, 1967, which has never been applied in view of its unrealistic contents

7. See P. Decraene, 'République Centrafricaine—les autorités justifient l'expulsion d'une quarantaine de ressortissants français', article in *Le Monde*, November 28, 1969; and R. Lanteri, 'Centre-Afrique— les carats font la loi', article in *L'Express*, December 1, 1969

6. AFTER TEN YEARS' INDEPENDENCE

1. G. de Courcel, *L'influence de la conférence de Berlin de 1885 sur le droit colonial international*, Faculté de Droit, Editions internationales, Paris 1936

2. By a decree passed on November 12, 1969, General Bokassa created a university bearing his name and comprising four faculties. However, it seems unlikely that this project can be realised before the country becomes better equipped scholastically

3. R. P. C. Tisserant, *Ce que j'ai connu de l'esclavage en Oubangui-Chari*, 1955

4. Mgr Tchidombo, *L'homme noir face au christianisme*, 1963

5. A. Goumba, *Evolution de la politique de santé dans les Etats d'Afrique Centrale*, Faculté de Médecine, Bordeaux 1968

6. P. Kalck, 'Robert Delavignette et la décolonisation, in *Bulletin de la Société française d'histoire d'Outre-Mer*, Paris 1967, Vol. LIV, Nos. 194–7

7. 'Le difficile développement agricole de la République Centrafricaine' in *Annales de l'Institut national Agronomique*, IV, Paris 1966

8. *French Aid*

(a) The Co-operation Aid Fund (*Fonds d'Aide et de Coopération*, FAC) 1959–68 (grant): 186,708,000 French francs (9,330,000,000 francs CFA) plus the salaries of 586 officials from the French technical assistance programme (as of October 1, 1968)

(b) Central Bank of Economic Co-operation (Caisse Centrale de

Coopération Economique, CCCE): 982 million francs CFA in loans plus 3,723 million francs CFA in investment, for the same period.
European Aid
  (*a*) European Development Fund: 15,776,000 dollars
  (*b*) Second European Development Fund: 15,688 dollars, plus 1,678 million francs CFA (for production and diversification)
American Aid
  786 million francs CFA (in equipment and work projects)
German Aid
  514 million francs CFA (in loans), plus suppliers credit
Chinese aid
  An interest free loan of 1,000 million francs CFA (1964)
Soviet Aid
  Books and student scholarships (no figures available)
Israeli Aid
  25 million francs CFA (loans) plus 200 million francs CFA (investment)
United Nations Aid
Special Fund: 2,102, 500 US dollars
IDA: 8,500,000 US dollars (road works 1965–70), plus food and assistance to Sudanese refugees

Bibliography

Adama-Tamboux, M., *4 ans de législature*, Imprimerie Centrale d'Afrique, Bangui 1964

Adloff, R., *West Africa: The French Speaking Nations* (*Yesterday and Today*), Holt, Rinehart and Winston, New York 1964

Alis, H., *A la conquête du Tchad*, Hachette, Paris 1891

Anguilé, A., and David, J., *L'Afrique sans frontière*, Bory, Libreville and Monaco 1965; preface by Henri Rochereau

Augouard, Mgr P., *44 années au Congo*, Poitiers 1934

Aymerich, Général, *La Conquête du Cameroun* (*1er août 1914–20 février 1916*), Payot, Paris 1933

Balandier, G., *Sociologie actuelle de l'Afrique Noire*, Presses Universitaires de France, Paris 1955

Banza, A., 'La remise en ordre d'un Etat' in *Europe–France–Outre-Mer*, No. 444, January 1967; Press Conference of May 13, 1966, Communiqué No. 16, Embassy of the Central African Republic Press Service, Paris

Bayle des Hermens, R. de, 'Premier aperçu du Paléolithique inférieur en République Centrafricaine' in *L'Anthropologie*, Vol. LXXI, 5–6, Paris 1967

Berlioux, E., *La Traite orientale, histoire des chasses à l'homme organisées en Afrique depuis 15 ans pour les marchés de l'Orient*, Guillaumin, Paris 1870

Biarnès, P.; Decraene, P.; and Herreman, P., *L'Année politique africaine 1967*, Société Africaine d'Editions, Dakar 1967

Boganda, Barthélémy, 'Faisons le point' in *France–Outre-Mer*, Nos. 334–5, September-October 1957; *Enfin on décolonise*, Imprimerie officielle, Brazzaville 1958; 'Logique, justice et raison' in *Terre Africaine*, No. 4, November 1958

Bokassa, J. B., Press conference held at Bangui on April 21, 1966, published in *Terre Africaine*, May 1, 1966; extracts published by *Souvenir et Devenir*, No. 21, September-October 1966

Borella, F., *L'évolution politique et juridique de l'Union Française depuis 1946*, Librairie générale de Droit et de Jurisprudence, Paris 1958

Bourget, M., *Merveilleux pays; République Centrafricaine*, Delroisse, Versailles 1968

Britsch, A., *Histoire de la dernière mission Brazza*, Davy, Paris 1958

Bruel, G., *Bibliographie de l'Afrique Equatoriale Française*, Larose, Paris 1914; *L'Afrique Equatoriale Française*, Larose, Paris 1918

Brunschwig, H., *Mythes et réalités de l'impérialisme colonial français 1871–1914*, Armand Colin, Paris 1960; *L'avènement de l'Afrique noire du 19 ème siècle à nos jours*, Armand Colin, Paris 1963

Bussière, A., *La R.C.A. sans Boganda*, (typewritten) Paris 1963

Calonne-Beaufaict, A. de, *Azandé*, M. Lambertin, Brussels 1921

'Centrafrique: le réveillon de Bangui—le parti unique aboutit à l'armée' in *Jeune afrique*, Paris, January 16, 1966

The Central African Republic, Hour of Independence, Information and Press Service of the French Embassy in the United States, New York 1960

Challaye, F., *Le Congo français*, Alcan, Paris 1909

Chavannes, C., *Le Congo français*, Plon, Paris 1937

Chauleur, P., *Le régime du travail dans les territoires d'Outre Mer*, Encyclopédie d'Outre Mer, Paris 1956

Chevalier, A., *L'Afrique Centrale française*, Challamel, Paris 1907; 'La culture cotonnière au Congo belge et en Afrique Equatoriale Française' in *Revue internationale appliquée et d'agronomie tropicale*, XXIX, 1949

Comité directeur du Mesan-Comptes-rendus des réunions 1962–1963, Imprimerie Centrale d'Afrique, Bangui 1962-3

Congrés du Mesan—1962–1964, Communiqués finaux, Bangui 1962, 1963, 1964

'La Conjoncture économique en RCA après 6 ans d'indépendance' in *Marchés Tropicaux*, Paris 1966

Coquery-Vidrovitch, C., *Le Congo français au temps des grandes compagnies concessionnaires*, thesis, Mouton, Paris 1971

Cornevin, R., *Histoire de l'Afrique*, Payot, Paris 1962–6

Dacko, D., Opening speech at the ordinary session of the Legislative Assembly on May 10, 1960, Imprimerie Centrale d'Afrique, Bangui 1960; Press conferences of June 27 and 30, 1962, on his official visits to Israel and France, Imprimerie Centrale d'Afrique, Bangui 1964; Opening speech at the Budgetary Session, 1964, Imprimerie Centrale d'Afrique, Bangui 1964

Daigre, H. P., 'Les Bandas de l'Oubangui' in *Anthropos*, No. 26, 1931, No. 27, 1932

Dampierre, E. de, 'Coton noir, café blanc' in *Cahiers d'Etudes Africaines*, Paris 1960

Decraene, P., 'L'Oubangui-Chari entre dans la Communauté sous le nom de République Centrafricaine' in *Le Monde*, December 3, 1958; *Le panafricanisme*, Presses Universitaires de France, Paris 1959;

Après Léopoldville et Cotonou, Bangui' in *Le Monde*, January 2–3, 1966; 'République Centrafricaine, sombres perspectives in *Feuilles d'Avis de Lausanne*, January 28, 1966; 'La RCA réintègre l'UDEAC. Une nouvelle union morte-née' in *Le Monde*, December 11, 1968; 'Le général Bokassa, un soldat, sorti du rang' in *Le Monde*, February 12, 1969; 'Après l'exécution du Colonel Banza, menace d'instabilité en RCA.' in *Le Monde diplomatique*, May 1969

Delafosse, M., *Essai sur le peuple et la langue sara*, André, Paris 1897

Delavignette, R., *Afrique Equatoriale française*, Hachette, Paris 1957; *Du bon usage de la décolonisation*, Casterman, Paris 1968

Demesse, L., *A la recherche des premiers âges, Les Babinga*, Paris 1957

Deschamps, H., *La fin des empires coloniaux*, Presses Universitaires de France, Paris 1950; *L'eveil politique africain*, Presses Universitaires de France, 1952; *The French Union*, Berger-Levrault, Paris 1955; *L'Afrique noire précoloniale*, Presses Universitaires de France, 1962

Devèze, M., *La France d'Outre Mer. De l'Empire colonial à l'Union Française*, Hachette, Paris 1948

Dreux Brézé, J. de, *Le problème du regroupement en Afrique Equatoriale*, Librairie générale de Droit et de Jurisprudence, Paris 1968

Drouillon, R., *La caféiculture en Oubangui Chari*, Imprimerie Centrale d'Afrique, Brazzaville 1957

Dumont, René, *Les possibilités d'accroissement de la production cotonnière en AEF (Oubangui–Tchad)*, (in Roneo) Paris 1950; *L'Afrique Noire est mal partie*, Seuil, Paris 1962; 'Le difficile développement agricole de la République Centrafricaine' in *Annales de l'Institut national Agronomique*, IV, Paris 1966

Dybowski, J., *La route du Tchad*, Firmin-Didot, Paris 1893

Eboué, Félix, *Les peuples de l'Oubangui-Chari*, Comité de l'Afrique Française, Paris 1933; Circular on local politics, Brazzaville 1943; *Economie et plan de développement en République Centrafricaine*, Ministry of Co-Operation, Paris 1963

El Tounsy (Sheikh Mohammed ibn Omar), *Voyage au Darfour*, translated from the Arabic by Perron, Duprat, Paris 1845; *Voyage au Ouadai*, translated from the Arabic by Perron, Duprat, 1851

Erhard, J., *Le destin du colonialisme*, Eyrolles, Paris 1958

Evans-Pritchard, E. E., 'The Ethnic Composition of the Azande of Central Africa' in *Anthropological Quarterly*, XXXI, 1958

Faure, H., 'Contribution à l'étude des races de la région de Carnot, in *Bulletin de la Société de Recherches Congolaises*, Brazzaville 1928

Flassch, A. M., 'La République Centrafricaine, un jeune état en pleine renaissance' in *La Cité*, Paris, October 1968.

Ganiage, J.; Deschamps, H.; and Guittard, O., *L'Afrique au 20 ème siècle*, Sirey, Paris 1967

Gaud, F., *Les Mandja*, Brussels 1911

Gauthereau, R., *Le développement de l'action rurale au Tchad et en Oubangui Chari dans le cadre du plan d'équipement*, (in Roneo) Paris, June 1957

Gauze, R., *Oubangui Chari, paradis du tourisme cynégétique*, Imprimerie Ozanne et Cie, Caen 1958

Gentil, E., *La chute de l'Empire de Rabah*, Hachette, Paris 1902

Gide, Andre, *Voyage au Congo*, Gallimard, Paris 1928

Gillet, J. F., *Les organismes communs aux Etats de l'Afrique Centrale*, Imprimerie Nouvelle, Brazzaville 1965

Girard, R., *Projet de chemin de fer Bangui Berberati*, (in Roneo) Bangui, May 23, 1958

Gonidec, P. F., *Droit d'Outre mer T 1: de l'empire colonial à la Communauté*, Paris 1959; *T 2 Les rapports actuels de la France métropolitaine et des pays d'Outre mer*, Montchrestien, Paris 1960; *Les systèmes politiques africains*, 2 vols., Paris 1970 and 1971

Goumba, Abel, *Rapport sur l'activité générale du Conseil du Gouvernement et la marche des services territoriaux*, (in Roneo) National Assembly, Bangui, December 5, 1957; *Evolution de la politique de santé dans les Etats d'Afrique Centrale*, Faculty of Medicine (thesis), Bordeaux 1968

Guena, Y., *Historique de la Communauté*, Paris 1962

Guéret, F., *La Formation de l'unité nationale en République Centrafricaine*, Faculté de Droit et des Sciences Economiques, (typewritten) Paris, October 1970

Guillemin, R., *L'évolution de l'agriculture autochtone dans les savanes de l'Oubangui*, Bangui 1955, published by the Inspection générale de l'Agriculture de l'AEF, Nogent-sur-Marne 1956

Guigonis, G., 'La forêt centrafricaine à peine exploitée est une des plus riches' in *Europe–France–Outre-Mer*, No. 444, January 1967

Hilberth, J., *Les Gbaya*, Upsala 1962

Histoire militaire de l'AEF, Imprimerie Nationale, Paris 1931

Homet, M., *Congo, terre de souffrance*, Montaigne, Paris 1934

Hugot, P., 'République Centrafricaine—du plan intérimaire au plan quadriennal' in *Industries et Travaux d'Outre-mer*, Paris, January 1966

Hutereau, A., *Histoire des peuplades de l'Uele et de l'Oubangui*, Goemare, Brussels 1922

Iddi-Lala, R., *Contribution à l'étude de l'évolution socio-politique en République Centrafricaine*, thesis, Faculté des Lettres, Paris 1971

Jannaud, G., and Kellermann, J., *La mécanisation de l'agriculture en*

Central African Republic

République Centrafricaine, Secrétariat d'Etat à la coopération, Paris 1967

Johnston, H. H., *The life and work of a great traveller, G. Grenfell and the Congo*, Hutchinson, London 1908

Julien, Cpt.,'Mohammed Senoussi et ses états' in *Bulletin de la Société de Recherches Congolaises*, Brazzaville 1925, 1927, 1928, 1929

Kalck, P., *Réalités Oubanguiennes, préface de Barthélémy Boganda*, Berger-Levrault, Paris 1959; 'Géographie, Histoire, institutions nouvelles de la République Centrafricaine' in *Encyclopédie Africaine et Malgache*, Larousse, Paris 1964; 'Paul Crampel, le Centrafricain' in *L'Afrique littéraire et artistique*, No. 2, Paris, December 1968; *Histoire centrafricaine des origines à nos jours*, Vol. I: Des origines à 1900; Vol. II: De 1900 à nos jours, (typewritten) Faculté des Lettres et des Sciences Humaines de Paris (thesis) Sorbonne, Paris, June 11, 1970; 'Les savanes centrafricaines' in *Histoire Générale de l'Afrique noire*, Vol II, ed. Hubert Deschamps, Presses Universitaires de France, Paris 1971; 'La République Centrafricaine' in *Encyclopédie Politique et Constitutionelle*, série Afrique, ed. P. F. Gonidec, Institut International d'Administration Publique and Berger-Levrault, Paris 1971

Korableff, G., *Contribution à l'étude de la géologie et de la géologie appliquée de l'Oubangui*, Lib. Soc. Econ., Paris 1940

Lagaé, C. R., and Vandenplas, V. H., *Le Langue des Azandé—Introduction historico-géographique*, Editions dominicaines Veritas, Gand 1921–5

Leboeuf, J. P., *Bangui (Oubangui-Chari)*, Editions de l' Union Française, 1951

Legris, M., 'Esquisses centrafricaines 1) Les Mandarins de Bangui; 2) 500.000 carats à fleur de terre', in *Le Monde*, January 4, and February 5, 1966; 'Le nombre des réfugiés en rca a triplé' in *Le Monde*, January 13, 1966

Legum, Colin, *Pan Africanism: A Short Political Guide*, Pall Mall, London 1962

Lenormand, J., and J. P., *L'or et le diamant en France métropolitaine et dans l'Union Française*, Editions SEF, Paris 1952

Leroy-Beaulieu, P., *De la colonisation chez les peuples modernes*, Guillaumin, Paris 1902

Leyder, J., 'De l'origine des Bouaka' in *Bulletin de la Société Royale Belge de Géographie*, I, Brussels 1936

L'Huiller, J., *Le café dans la colonie française de l'Oubangui-Chari*, Imprimerie Humbert, Paris, August 30, 1933

Lotar, R. P., *La grande chronique de l'Ubangui*, Institut Royal Colonial

Belge, 1938; *La grande chronique du Bomu*, Institut Royal Colonial Belge, 1940

MacMichael, H. A., *A History of the Arabs in the Sudan and some account of the people who preceded them and of the tribes inhabiting Darfur*, Cambridge University Press, 1922

Magalé, A., 'Un gros effort est fait dans le domaine sanitaire' in *Europe–France–Outre-Mer*, No. 444, January 1967

Malendoma, T., 'Les problèmes généraux de l'économie centrafricaine' in *Europe–France–Outre-Mer*, No. 444, January 1967

Maistre, C., *A travers l'Afrique Centrale*, Hachette, Paris 1895

Mangin, C., *Souvenirs d'Afrique—Tournée d'inspection au Congo 1908*, Denoël et Steel, Paris 1936

Maran, R., *Batouala*, Albin Michel, Paris 1921

Marcilly, J. de, 'La République Centrafricaine, pays aux possibilités intactes' in *La Revue Française*, Paris, April 1967

Maurienne, C., 'Barthélémy Boganda, prophète d'une oeuvre inachevée' in *Jeune Afrique*, No. 275, Paris, April 3, 1966

Mehellel, A., 'RCA—L'ère des marchands de sable est passée' in *Jeune Afrique*, No. 227, April 11, 1965

Mehl, R., *Décolonisation et Missions protestantes*, Société des Missions Evangéliques, Paris 1964

Meinrad Hegba, R. P., *Personnalité africaine et catholicisme*, Présence Africaine, Paris 1963

Menthon, J. de, 'En Lobaye, sur les traces d'André Gide' in *Combat*, Paris, December 13–20, 1954

Mercier, J., *L'économie et les transports du Tchad, de l'Oubangui et du Nord Cameroun*, Institut du Transport Aérien, Paris 1956

Moussa Bartoumé, G., 'Le problème de la santé en RCA' in *Devenir et civilisations*, No. 9, Paris 1962

Muracciole, L., *Les constitutions des Etats africaines d'expression française*, Librairie générale de Droit et de Jurisprudence, 1961

Olivier-Lacamp, M., 'Afrique noire 1958, En Oubangui' in *Le Figaro*, January 31, and February 3, 1958

Ouayo, A. B., 'L'essor remarquable du diamant' in *Europe–France–Outre-Mer*, No. 444, January 1967

'Oubangui-Chari' in *La Documentation Française, Notes et Etudes Documentaires*, No. 898, Paris, May 1948

Patasse, A., 'La production agricole et ses perspectives' in *Europe–France–Outre-Mer*, No. 444, January 1967

Plan intérimaire biennal 1965-1966, Bangui 1963

Plan quadriennal 1967-1970 de la RCA, Industries et Travaux d'Outre-mer, Paris, September, 1967

Plan triennal provisoire de développement économique et social 1960-1961-1962, Bangui 1959, 2 vols.

Portrait et profil de S.E. David Dacko, président de la République Centrafricaine, Direction Information et secrétariat général du MESAN, Bangui 1964

Poutrin, G., *Esquisse ethnologique des principales populations de l'*AEF, Masson, Paris 1914

Prevost, P. L., 'L'Union Douanière et Economique de l'Afrique Centrale' in *La Revue Française d'études politiques africaines*, Paris 1968

'La République Centrafrique' in *Documentation Française, Notes et Etudes Documentaires*, No. 2733, December 29, 1960

'La République Centrafricaine 1966' in *Perspectives Africaines*, No. 190, April 21, 1966

'La République Centrafricaine' in *Bulletin Commercial d'information africaine pour la Suisse*, SESAF, Geneva, July 1966

'La République Centrafricaine' in *Jeune Afrique*, Supplement to No. 309, Paris, December 11, 1966

Ritter, K., *Neu Kamerun*, Iéna 1912

Romeuf, J., *Vues sur l'économie de l'Oubangui-Chari*, Publications Economiques et sociales, Paris 1968

Romieu, J., *Mouvements coopératifs en Afrique Noire—L'exemple de l'*AEF, Montpellier 1953

Rougeaux, J. P., *Le parti unique en République Centrafricaine: le* MESAN, (typewritten) Faculté de Droit et des Sciences Economiques, Paris, October-December 1968

Rendu, P., *L'opinion publique et la mission d'enquête de Brazza*, (typewritten) Sorbonne, Paris 1950

Saintoyant, J., *L'Affaire du Congo, 1905*, L'Epi, Paris 1960

Sautter, G., 'Le Chemin de fer Bangui—Tchad dans son contexte économique régional' in *Etude de l'économie des transports au Tchad et dans le nord de l'Oubangui-Chari*, Institut de géographie appliquée de l'Université de Strasbourg, Bangui 1959

Sillans, R., *Les savanes de l'Afrique Centrale*, Lechevalier, Paris 1958

Sinnassamy, G., *La suppression de la justice pénale indigène en Afrique Equatoriale Française*, (in Roneo) Faculté de Droit, Aix-en-Provence 1953

'Situation économique et mise en valeur de l'AEF' in *Documentation Française, Notes et Etudes Documentaires*, No. 1461, Paris, April 9, 1951

'Situation sociale de l'AEF' in *Documentation Française, Notes et Etudes Documentaires*, No. 1816, Paris, November 15, 1956.

Stengers, J., 'Léopold II et la fixation des frontières du Congo-Bruxelles' in *Revue Belge des questions politiques et littéraires*, 1963

Suret-Canale, J., *Afrique Noire, Géographie, civilisations, histoire*, Editions sociales, Paris 1958

Tanghe, Mgr B., 'Pages d'histoire africaine: essai de reconstitution des liens de famille paternelle qui relient entre elles les populations soudanaises du nord du Congo' in *Aequatoria*, VII, 1944

Tchidombo, Mgr. *L'homme noir face au christianisme*, Présence Africaine, Paris 1963

Tempels, R. P., *La philosophie bantoue*, Présence Africaine, Paris 1963

Tessmann, G., *Die Baja, ein Negerstamm in mitteleren Sudan*, Strecker und Schroeder, Stuttgart 1934–7

Térivé, J. D., 'Analyse d'un coup d'Etat' in *France–Eurafrique*, No. 171, Paris, March 1966

Teulières, A., '*L'Oubangui, face à l'avenir*,' Editions de L'Union Française, Paris 1953

Thomas, Jacqueline, *Les Ngbaka de la Lobaye*, Mouton, Paris 1963

Thomas, R. S., *Fondation de l'Etat indépendant du Congo*, Office de Publicité, Brussels 1953

Thomson, V. and Adloff, R., *The Emerging States of French Equatorial Africa*, Stanford University Press, California, and Oxford University Press, 1959

Thuriaux Hennebert, Arlette, *Les Zandé dans l'histoire du Behr el Ghazal et de l'Equatoria*, Institut de Sociologie, Brussels 1964

Tisserant, R. P. C., 'L'agriculture dans les savanes de l'Oubangui' in *Bulletin de l'Institut d'Etudes Centrafricaines*, New series, No 6, Brazzaville 1953; *Ce que j'ai connu de l'esclavage en Oubangui Chari*, Plon, Paris 1904

Toqué, G., *Essai sur le peuple et la langue banda*, André, Paris 1904; *Les massacres du Congo*, Paris 1907

Vergiat, A. M., *Les rites secrets des primitifs de l'Oubangui*, Payot, Paris 1937; *Moeurs et coutumes des Manjas*, Payot, 1937

Verplancke, H., *La République Centrafricaine*, Imprimerie officielle Congo-Tchad, Brazzaville 1962

Vidal, P., *L'initiation dans l'éducation traditionelle—population Gbaya-Kara*, (in Roneo) Bangui and Le Havre 1962

Wallerstein, I., *Africa—The Politics of Independence: an interpretation of modern African History*, Vintage Books, New York 1959; *Africa: The Politics of Unity*, Pall Mall, London 1968

Weinburg, H. K., *Entkolonisierung und Föderales*, Dunker and Humblot, Berlin 1968

Weulersse, J., *L'Afrique noire*, Fayard, Paris 1934

Central African Republic

Willequet, J., *Le Congo belge et la Weltpolitik 1894–1914*, Presses Universitaires de France, 1962

Zieglé, H., *Afrique Equatoriale Française*, Berger-Levrault, 1952

Ziegler, J., *La contre-révolution en Afrique*, Payot, Paris 1963

Zuylen, P. van, *L'échiquier congolais ou le secret du roi*, Dessart, Brussels 1959

Index

Abéché, 36
Abiras, 55
Adama, Modibo, 22
Adama-Tamboux, Michel, 120, 124, 147, 152
Adamawa, 2, 8, 12, 39, 48
Addis Ababa, OAU at, 164
AEF, see French Equatorial Africa
Ahidjo, 150
Algiers, 49, 99–100
Aloa, kingdom of, 19
Antonetti, Raphael, 60
Anziques, see Boubangui
Aouk, R., 1, 5, 23, 34, 36, 48
ATEK, 151
Aubé, Robert, 77
Augagneur, Victor, 60
Augouard, Father, 42
Aujoulat, Dr, 86, 89
Awana, Charles Onana, 152, 157
Awoyamo, Nicolas, 123
Ayandho, 159

Baboua, 8, 12, 70
Baguirmi, 17, 23, 33–4, 36, 48–9
Bahara tribe, 24, 26, 34–5
Bahr el Ghazal, 1, 4, 18–21, 23, 34–5, 38, 46, 49
Baker, Sir Samuel W., 35
Bakié, Baram, 57
Bakota tribes, 16
Bambari, 6, 9–10, 65–6, 69, 123, 133
Bamboté (writer), 148
Bamingui, 5, 12, 19, 35–6
Banda groups, 11–13, 16–18, 22–31, 34–6, 38–40, 48, 55, 57, 69 76 172–3; exodus of, 20, 23–4; famine among, 59–60; important tribes, 24; traditions, 27–9
Bandia family, 21, 38

Bandio, J. A., 123, 127, 155, 161, 164, 168
Bangassou, 7, 9, 12, 46, 64, 69
Bangassou, King, 21, 25, 27, 35, 38, 46, 57
Bangui, 2–4, 6–7, 9–12, 18–19, 24, 31, 48–9, 52, 55, 61, 66–9, 76, 79, 83–4, 88, 110, 120, 127, 130, 149–54; airfield, 113, 142, 153, 163; Boganda stadium, 148; Bokassa orders buses for, 162; communications, 67, 95–6, 98, 142–3; funeral of Boganda, 106; international dealers flock to, 159, 171; joins Free France, 66–7; opposition to reform, 73–4; schools, 75, 107, 115; suggested as capital of United Africa, 148; trade and industry, 141
Bantu tribes, 11–13, 15–17, 22
Banza, Alexandre, 153, 155, 157, 159, 162, 164, 167–8; arrest and death, 170–1
Banza tribes, 22–3
Banziri tribe, 20, 30, 48, 93
Barberot, Colonel, 124
Bari, King, 35
Barth, Heinrich, 35–6, 41, 47
Bassamongou, Ferdinand, 149
Basse Kotto, 12, 63, 86
Batangafo, 9, 12, 67
Bateke (Tyo) tribe, 16, 42
Baya groups, 2, 3, 8, 11–14, 16–17, 21, 31, 47, 69, 172–3; migrations, 20, 22–6, 29, 42; new groups and names, 22; riot (1954), 89–90; 'war of the hoe-handle', 26, 63 war with Issa, 39–40
BDPA, 137, 145
Belgians, 20–1, 25, 40–1, 43–7, 51–2, 58, 61, 166, 173

199

Bella (parl. candidate), 82–3
Bello, war-chief, 40
Ben Bella, 150
Benoué, 14, 47–8
Beran-Djoko, Chief, 57
Berberati, 2, 7–10, 12, 69, 78, 106, 140, 146; riot, 89–91
Berlin, 4, 43, 47, 50
Bernard, Georges, 96
Birao, 2, 6, 10, 19, 37
BIRD, 166
Bir Hacheim, battle of, 67
Boali, 12, 85, 142
Bocaranga, 8, 12
Boda, 8, 12, 91, 106
Boganda, Barthélémy, 17, 28–9, 75–110, 115, 117, 120–1, 129–31, 133, 140, 154, 164, 169, 177–8, 182–3; elected Deputy, 75–6; founds MESAN, 79–80; intervenes in Berberati riot, 90; campaign against officials, 94–5; backs Guérillot's coffee scheme, 97; discouragement of, 98–9, 116; plans new 'United States', 101–3, 182; extensive reforms as first President, 104–5; death, 106
Boganda, Mrs, 78, 80, 82, 107
Bohndorff, Frederick, 37, 45
Boigny, Houphouet, 123, 150
Boissoudy, Guy de, 72
Bokanga village, 81–2
Bokassa, Jean-Bedel, 152; *coup d'état*, 153–4; as Head of State, 155–75; foreign relations 157–9, 164–6; economic and domestic policies, 159–64; quarrels with Chad, 169; received by de Gaulle 170, 175 fear of plots, 167–8
Bomboko, Justin, 169
Bongo, 2, 18–19
Bongou, R., 14, 18, 33
Bordier, Paul, 96, 122
Bornu empire, 22, 33, 48
Bororo shepherds, 8, 13
Bossangoa, 8–10, 12
Bossembele, 8, 65

Bouar, 3, 7, 9, 12, 14, 89, 168
Boubangui tribes, 3, 4, 16, 22, 32, 41–4
Boubangui village, 75, 154, 165
Bouca area, 12, 158
Bourges, Yvon, 122
Bouzims, Marcel, 105
Brazza, Pierre, 16, 41–5, 47–8, 52, 61, 69
Brazzaville, 2, 44, 49, 55, 57, 61, 69, 75, 83, 89, 109–10, 119, 127, 149, 154; putsch (1940), 66, 72; conference (1944), 68, 80; agreements signed at (1959), 109; meeting of Heads of State (1960), 122, 124; revolution (1963), 146; Treaty (1966), 151–2, 166; meeting of E.E.C. countries (1968), 169
Bria, 8, 9, 38, 66
British, 46–7, 49–50, 67, 148
Browne, W. G., 5, 19, 34
Bruel, Georges, 61
Brustier, discovers diamond, 65–6

Calonne-Beaufaict, A. de, 25
Cameroun, 1–3, 5, 9, 13, 15, 23, 47, 50, 55, 67, 102, 164; cotton industry, 126, 137, 142; new projects, 143, 145, 151, 182
Camerounian ethnic group, 11–12,
Cammas, General, 66–7
Carnot, President Sadi, 46
Carnot region, 3, 8, 12, 23, 66, 70
CEA, 161, 166, 169
CFDT, 137
OGTA, 96, 112
Cha, 25, 34–5
Chad, 1–6, 20–1, 23, 36, 47–8, 51, 53, 62, 72, 82, 102, 110, 151, 165–6, 169–70 cotton, 85–6, 142; insurrection, 172; military zone, 55–6; people of, 9, 13, 19; railways planned, 95, 142; refusal to join new republic 103
Chad, Lake, 5, 48
Chambellant, M., 89

Chari, R., 1, 3, 5, 17, 19, 22, 26, 32–3, 47–8, 50, 55
Chauvet, Paul, 83–4, 90
Chevalier, Auguste, 64
Chiang Kai-shek, 149
Chinese, 148–50, 154, 158
Chinko, R., 4, 17–18, 35–7, 39
Chouanga, Father, 179
Chou En-lai, 149
Chrétien-Marquet, Henri, 141
CIC, 144
Clémentel, Etienne, 58
Climate, 6–8
CMOO, 87
CND, 139
CODRO, 97
Coffee, 8, 31, 38, 63–5, 74, 87–8, 111, 115, 126; Guérillot's scheme, 96–7 Patassé's reforms, 160
Comité de l'Afrique Française, 50
Comité Français de Libération Nationale, 71
Compagnie Forestière, 58, 61, 75
Compagnie Ngoko-Sangha, 52
Compagnie des Produits de Lobaye, 51
Compagnie des Sultanats, 51, 58, 64
Concessionary companies, 50–3, 56–66, 178
Congo: Belgian, 4, 23, 64, 66, 69, 75, 102, 110, 118; Free State, 4, 46; French, 55–6, 61; kingdom of, 16, 32, 41
Congo, R., 1, 3–5, 13–14, 16, 41–4
Congo-Brazzaville, 2, 5, 15, 50, 143, 169; revolution, 146, 172
Congo-Kinshasa, 1, 13, 47, 149–51
Constitution (1959), 105–6, 182
Co-operatives, 77–9, 81, 160, 173
Coppens, Yves, 13
Cornevin, R., 14
Cotonou, congress at, 100
Cotton, 8–11, 30, 63–5, 74, 97–8, 111, 113, 115–16, 180; companies, 85–7; Dacko's reforms, 136–8, 142, 160; drop in output,

126, 146–7; under Bokassa, 160–1
Crampel, Paul, 46, 48
Crampel area, 8, 12, 53–4, 61
CTFTF, 144
Cucherousset, Archb. J. 179
Customs Union, 67, 109 (*see also* UDE *and* UDEAC)

Dacko, David, 9, 93, 103–4, 107–10, 116–63, 176–7; elected President, 107; replaces French administrators, 122, 125; visits Israel and France, 132–3; economic policy and industrial reforms, 135–46, 181; rash foreign policy, 148–50; imprisonment, 153–9, 162, 170, 172
Daigre, Father, 59
Dar Challa, 2–4, 19, 33, 36
Dar Fertit, 23, 33
Darfur, 1, 2, 4, 5, 19, 21, 23–5, 27, 37, 46, 49, 55; slave trade, 32–5
Dar Koulla, 6, 19, 34
Dar Kouti, 5, 23, 25, 36, 48, 51, 55, 57, 64; sultans of 11, 18–19, 27, 34–5, 39
Darlan, Antoine, 77, 80, 82, 89, 92, 108
Darlan, Georges, 78
DDI, 87, 127, 139, 159
de Gaulle, Charles, 66–7, 78, 80, 110, 140, 158–9; visits Bangui, 88, 99–100; receives Heads of State, 118, 132, 170, 175; recognises China, 148; death of, 173
Dejean, Maurice, 153
Delavignette, Robert, 182
Delcassé, Théophile, 46
Dem Zubeir, 39, 49
Diamond trade, 3, 31, 63, 66, 74, 87, 111, 126–8; Dacko's reforms, 138–9, 152; under Bokassa, 159–61, 171–3
Dja-Ngoko, R., 5
Djesser Pasha, 37
Djougoultoum, *see* Omar

Dolisie, Albert, 44
Dolisie, Michel, 42, 46
Douala, 2, 5, 50
Dumont, René, 8, 86, 126, 145, 182
Dybowski, 48, 64

Eboué, Felix, 13, 24, 64, 67–8
Education, 69, 75, 107, 114–16, 162, 176–9
EEC, 131–2, 136, 148, 165, 169, 183
Egypt, 15, 21, 25, 34–9, 49
El Fasher, 34, 47
El Tounsy, Mohammed, 33
Emin Pasha, 37–8, 46
Ethiopians, 49, 69
Ethnic groups, 11–13
Etienne, Eugène, 48
*Etincelle de l'*AEF, 78, 83

FAC, 113–14, 158
Fang tribe, 16, 22, 26
Fashoda, 46, 49
Fatrane, Edouard, 123, 130, 156
Fayama, 100, 107, 120
Ferry, Jules, 43, 176
FIDES, 112–13
Flandre, Paul, 77
Flegel, Eduard, 40
Floret, Paul Coste, 76
Fodio, Dan, 22, 39
Forestry, 7, 13, 15, 31, 58, 61, 88, 144, 161, 167
Fort Lamy, 18, 110
Foulbe tribes, 3, 23–6, 39–40, 48
Français, Jean, 157
France, *passim*; first stakes in Congo, 42–4; troops withdrawn from CAR, 148, 150; troops return, 167–8; technicians expelled, 172–3
Franck, Mme, 162
Free France, 66–7, 80, 88
French Equatorial Africa (AEF), 2, 5, 7, 55, 63, 66–9, 83, 90, 99, 107, 111; Colonial partition 50; organisation of, 56; political reforms demanded, 71*ff.*, revenue, 86; liquidation of 104, 109–10; independence granted, 118–21
Fresnel, Consul, 34
Friedrich, Eugène, 82
Fulani, 8, 12, 13, 22

Gabon, 50, 67, 69, 102–3, 110, 118, 151, 164, 171
Gallin-Douathé, Michel, 82, 120
Gamana-Leggos, Maurice, 155
Gazargamou, Chief, 22
Gentil, Emile, 48
Germany, 2, 5, 35, 45–7, 50, 52, 58, 144
Gessi Pasha, 21, 37–8
Gide, André, 62–3
'Godobe', 31
Gold, discovery of, 65–6
Gordon, Charles George, 37, 41
Gouandjia, Maurice, 163
Goujon, Alphonse, 23, 47–8
Goula tribes, 6, 19, 23, 34
Goumba, Abel, 19–20, 93, 97, 100, 104–8, 119, 121–4, 180; supports MEDAC, 108, 119; conflict with Dacko, 122; trial and sentence, 130
Goumba, Michel, 93
Gourou, Pierre, 53
Grandin, Bishop, 75
Grenfell, George, 4, 44–5
Gribingui, R., 5, 12, 23, 33, 36, 51–3
Grimald, Aimé, 83–4
Grimari, 75, 115
Guéret, Dominique, 155, 168
Guérillot, Roger, 89, 92–8, 104, 126

Hamani, Diori, 123
Hanssens, Capt., 20, 44
Hassen, Clement, 141
Haute Kotto, 10, 12, 18, 23–4, 55, 60
Haute-Sanga region, 2, 11, 14–16, 22–3, 40, 47, 56, 62, 82, 144; coffee, 65, 126; diamonds, 66
Haut Oubangui, 26–7, 36, 48–51, 54–5, 62, 105; creation of, 46, 55; sultans of, 21, 57

Health, 54–5, 114, 162–3, 179–80
Herly, Jean, 165
Hetman, Chief, 57
History and pre-history, 13–26
Hitler, Adolf, 50
Hofrat en Nahas, 18, 36
Hubler, Jean, 152
Hunting, 145
Husson, General, 66

ICAF, 127, 138
ICOT, 142–3
ILO, 89
Indo-China, 71, 74, 84
Institutions, new, 109
Ippy, 8, 66
Isreal, 132, 144–5
Issa, Chief, 39–40
Ivory Coast, 122–3, 145
Izamo, Chief of Police, 153–4

Jacquinot, Louis, 84
Jamot, Colonel, 55
Janot, Raymond, 106
JPN, 145, 155
Junker, Wilhelm, 37–8, 45

Kara clan of Birao, 19
Karinou, Chief, 63
Kazangba, Mt., 3
Kemo, R., 4, 11, 12, 24, 51
Kezza, Antoine, 155, 157, 164
Khartoum, 34, 36
Kheir Alla, 35
Kinshasa, 44, 61
Kirdi tribes, 33
Kisantu seminary, 75
Kji river, 57
Kober, Sultan, 25, 35, 39, 48
Kongo Ouarra war, 26, 63
Kordofan, 20, 34, 37
Korea, 149
Kotto, R., 4, 18, 21, 24–5, 35, 37–9, 46, 50–1, 57
Kouango, R., 4, 16, 17, 20
Kouch, kingdom of, 14, 15
Koudoukou, Lieut., 67
Kouka, 17, 34

Kounde, fortress of, 39, 47–8
Kousseri, battle of, 49
Kreich tribe, 17, 18, 25, 35, 38, 55

Labassou, Chief, 57
Lamblin, Auguste, 60, 63, 65
Lancrenon falls, 5
Language, 19, 20
Larminat, Col. de, 66
Lecourt, Robert, 106
Ledot, Jean Gautier, 162
Le Hérissé, Deputy, 54
Leon the African, 17, 25
Leopold II, King, 4, 21–2, 40–1, 43–6, 51–2, 104
Leroy-Beaulieu, Paul, 51
Leyder, J., 25
Lhuillier, Jean, 77
Libreville, 149
LICA, 89
Liotard, Governor, 48–9
Lobaye: co-op, 77, 81; region, 15, 23, 40, 50–2, 56–7, 62, 83, 88, 106–8, 144–5; river, 2, 4, 5, 11, 16, 22, 25
Logone, R., 5, 50, 55
Loi-cadre, 92–4, 98, 100, 114, 154
Londres, Albert, 62–3
Lopez, 32
Lupton, Frank, 21, 38, 57

Mabengue, Chief, 21
MacMichael, H. A., 25
Madagascar, 74, 118, 164, 169
Magalé, Andre, 155
Mahdists, 21, 38–9, 49, 57
Maistre, M., 48
Malbrant, René, 72–3, 78–9, 82–3, 87, 89, 175
Malendoma, Timothée, 155, 157, 159, 167
Maleombho, Pierre, 104, 107–8, 120, 123, 130, 164
Mali, 110, 118, 143, 151
Malraux, André, 119, 176
Mamadou, Joseph, 93, 104
Mandaba, Capt., 171

Mandjia tribes, 3, 11–13, 17, 22–3, 25–9, 48, 53, 55, 57, 70, 109, 120
Mangin, Charles, 52
Manville, Marcel, 130
Marchand, Capt., 48–9, 58
Martineau, Alfred, 56
Martin-Leboeuf mission, 54
Massenya, 34, 36
Maumon mission, 165
Mba, Léon, 26, 118, 149–50
Mbaiki, 9, 12, 69, 82–3, 91, 106, 154
Mbaka tribe, 11, 16, 93
Mbari, R., 4, 18, 21
Mbili, Chief Yango, 39
Mbomou, river and region, 1, 3–4, 7, 11, 15–22, 35–9, 46–7, 49, 70, 88
Mboum, 3, 12–13, 22–3, 26, 39
MEDAC, 108–9, 119–23, 130, 164; deputies censured, 123
Mehemet Ali, 34
Mela, Mt., 3, 19
MEOC, 70
Merlin, Martial, 56
Merwart, Emile, 55, 57
MESAN, 79, 89, 91, 93, 98, 100, 103, 105–9, 120, 129–30, 140, 146; organised by Dacko, 133–5; relations with Bokassa, 155–6, 162–3
Middle Congo, 56, 103, 107
Mieng Yeng, 150
Milz, Major, 46
Missionaries, 30, 32, 42, 69–70, 75, 154, 163, 178–9
Mitterand, Francois, 83
Mizon, Lieut, 47
Mobaye, 17, 19, 55
Mobutu, Genl., 19, 150, 164, 166, 169
Modat, Capt., 57
Mofio, kingdom of, 10, 35, 37
Mokako, Chief, 44
Monteil, L. P., 46–7
Mouka, 3, 66
Mounoumbaye, Jean-Baptiste, 156
Moutet, Marius, 72

Mpoko, R., 4, 12, 50, 56, 85
Mpoumbou (Stanley Pool), 15–16, 32, 42
MRP, 75
MSA, 129
Mulélé, Pierre, 169
Musy, Albert, 46, 48

Nachtigal, Gustav, 36, 41, 47
Naguemon, Kombot, 171, 173
Naud, René, 89, 92, 98, 123
Ndayer, Bishop J., 179
Ndélé district, 12, 19, 23, 25, 34, 57, 70
Ndorouma, King, 37
Ngakola, Chief, 27
Ngao group, 23–5, 35
Ngaoundéré, 8, 23–4, 39–40, 47–8
Ngaro, Dr. 163
Ngounio, Etienne, 104, 107–9, 120, 123
Ngoura, King, 21
Nicolet, Raymond, 130
Niger, 143, 171
Niger, R., 34, 47, 49
Nigeria, 123, 151, 167
Nile, R., 1, 4, 13, 20–1, 25–6, 28, 34, 40–1, 46–7, 49
Nkoundjia, 44–5
Nkrumah, Kwame, 148
Nola, 5–7
Noorouma, chief, 24
Nubians, 4, 16, 29, 32
Nzakara people, 11–13, 17–21, 24–6, 35, 38, 57

OAU, 148, 164
Obo, 2, 8, 10, 12, 70
OCAM, 157, 164, 166
Ogoué, R., 26, 63
Omar, Prince, 23, 34
Ombella-Mpoko, 4, 12, 85
OND, 159
Ondomat, Charles, 146
Opangault, Jacques, 103
ORD, 145
Ouadaï, 19, 23–6, 33, 46, 48–9

Ouaka, R., 4, 12, 14, 16–17, 23, 57
Ouaka-Kotto, 70, 74, 86
Ouam-Pende, 70, 82
Ouanda-Djallé, 12, 19, 57
Ouarra, 4, 21, 34–5, 39
Ouayo, Blaise, 171–2
'Oubanguians', 11–13, 20
Oubangui, R., 1–50 *passim*
Oubangui Chari, colony of, 32–70; slave trade, 32–43; European powers compete for, 43–50; foundation of, 55; insurrection and conquest, 56–8; rubber crisis, 59; coffee, cotton, gold and diamonds (*q.v.*), 63–6; in World War II, 63, 66–7, 71; Eboué's new policy, 67–9; Boganda's political initiative, 71ff.; first visit by a Minister of Overseas France, 83–4; bad conditions in cotton industry, 85–7; becomes semi-autonomous, 92; draft Constitution agreed to, 101; becomes Central African Republic, 103–4
Oubangui-Chari-Chad, 56
Ouham R., 5, 33, 50–1, 53
Overseas Labour Code, 91

Paoua district, 2, 8, 12
Patassé, Ange, 155, 157, 160
Payao, Albert, 137
Pende, R., 5, 12, 50
Pétain, Marshal Henri, 66
Pigafetta, 32
Pointe Noire, 2, 61, 86
Pombeiros, 16, 32
Population, 1, 9–13, 116
Porterage, 51, 53–5, 60
Potagos, Panoyotis, 36–7
Pour sauver un peuple, 80
PRA, 100
PRS, 89
Psichari, Ernest, 55
Pygmies, 13, 15, 35

Rabah Zobeir, Genl., 3, 18–19, 21, 23–5, 35, 37–9, 48–9

Rafai, Sultan, 21, 27, 37–9, 46, 57,
Railways, 61–2, 95–6, 98, 142–4, 151, 164, 173
RDA, 82–3, 129
Religion, 11, 29–30, 69–70, 178–9
Renard, Edouard, 69
Reste, François-Joseph, 65
Rivierez, Hector, 89, 93, 103, 130
Roads, 6, 10, 67, 112–13, 176
Rouanet, Gustave, 52
Roulet, Capt., 49
Rounga group, 12, 23, 34, 36
RPF, 78–80, 82, 89
Rubber gathering, 30, 38, 51–2, 59–60, 64, 75, 111, 180
Russian explorers, 37, 40

Sabanga, 17–18, 23, 37–8
Saccas, Athanase, 96
St Germain-en-Laye convention, 131
St Mart, Governor, 66
Sanga, R., 3–5, 14, 16, 25, 32–3, 43, 50 (*see also* Haut Sanga)
Sango tribe, 20, 29
Santandrea, Father, 19
Sara tribes, 5, 11–13, 17, 25, 27, 29, 34–6, 62, 172
Sasa, Sultan, 39
Sato, Albert, 104, 108, 123
SCADIA, 127
Schnitzer, Dr., 37
Schweinfurth, Georg, 15, 26, 36–7, 41
SEEE, 135–6
SEITA, 137
Senghor, Léopold, 72, 100
Senoussi, Sultan, 18–19, 23–4, 27, 48, 55, 57
SIAN, 144
Slave-trade, 5, 8, 15–19, 21, 23, 26, 32–43, 178; chief dispatching centres, 34; Léopold's war on, 40–1; suppression of 38
Sleeping sickness, 16, 20, 30, 54–5, 180
SNEA, 145

Central African Republic

Social structures, 26–30
Société des Batignolles, 62
Socoulolé, 77, 81
Somraï tribe, 36
Songomali, Jean-Baptiste, 92
Soustelle, Jacques, 78
Soviet Union, 148–50, 173
Stanley, Sir Henry, M. 40–2, 44
Stanley Pool, see Mpoumbou
Stanleyville, 149
Sudan, 2, 6, 13, 16, 17, 19, 34, 37–9, 45, 57, 151; Bahr el Ghazal granted to, 49; Bokassa's visit to, 164; refugees from, 168
Sudanese-Guinea zone, 7–8
Suleiman, Prince, 21, 35, 37–8

Taiwan, 149
Tanghe, Mgr B., 25
Tardieu, André, 52
Taxation, 9, 26, 30, 54, 60, 64–5, 86, 97, 126, 131, 135, 146–7, 160, 178
Teilhard de Chardin, R. P., 14
Terre Africaine, 148, 158, 164, 178
Tikima, King, 21, 35, 37
Tobacco, 111, 137, 145
Togbao, battle at, 49
Tombalbaye, President, 118, 150, 158, 165
Toqué, Georges, 54
Toumba, Lake, 13
Traditions and customs, 27–30, 70, 178–9

UCCA, 137, 145, 160
UDE, 131, 142, 165
UDEAC, 150–2, 157–8, 165–6, 169–70
UDSR, 83
UEAC, 166, 169
Uele, R., 3, 4, 15–16, 20–1, 25–6, 35–7, 45–6
UGTC, 146, 163–4
UNELCO, 135–6
Union Congolaise, 59
Union des Femmes Centrafricaines, 162
Union des Forces Vives . . . , 120

Union Française, 77
UNO, 144; admits CAR, 120
'United States of Latin Africa', 102–3, 109, 182
Upper Volta, 123
Uranium, 161, 169, 171–2
USA: market for diamonds, 87; Peace Corps, 158, 181

Vakaga, 10, 17, 19
Valabrègue, André, 140
Vangèle, Capt., 44–6
Viale, Jane, 77
Vidal, P., 14
Vidri tribe, 24, 57
Villages, present-day, 180–2
Violette, Maurice, 58
Vodo tribe, 17
Vogel, Eduard, 36

'Water-People', 19–20, 24
Wauters (king's geographer), 44
Wilheim II, Kaiser, 47, 50
Wilickond, Honoré, 93, 104
Willot Bros, 142–4

Ya, island of, 20
Yadé massif, 2–5
Yakoma, 4, 19–20, 30, 46
Yameoga, Maurice, 123
Yanguéré-Banda, 16, 23–5, 40, 47
Yetina, Louis-Martin, 88
Youlou, Abbé Fulbert, 103, 110, 118, 127, 146
Youlou, clan, 19, 57
Youth movements, 129–30, 140, 145, 155

Zande: conquest, 20–2, 24–7; kingdom, 10, 35; tribes, 11–13, 15, 17–18, 20–2, 36–9, 46, 57, 63, 70, 168
Zanzibar, 35, 149–50
Zemio, 7, 12, 22, 55, 70
Zemio, Sultan, 21, 27, 35, 37, 39, 46, 57–8
Zongo, founding of, 46
Zubeir, Prince, 18, 21, 23, 25, 27, 34–5, 37–8, 40, 47